The Christian Science Monitor
"10 Best Books of August" Pick

"Fans of women's history and adventure stories will cheer this engrossing account." —*Publishers Weekly*

"*Olive the Lionheart* has it all—secret chambers, lost love, and the dwelling place of a devil. Ricca mines emotions and real fears in this incredible true story." —Brad Meltzer, bestselling author of *The First Conspiracy: The Secret Plot to Kill George Washington*

"Brad Ricca's Olive MacLeod is my favorite sort of woman from history—bold and unconventional, utterly unsinkable—and her story is so full of adventure and acts of courage, it's hard to believe she actually lived. And yet she did! Brad Ricca has found a heroine for the ages and written her tale with a winning combination of accuracy and imagination." —Paula McLain, author of *Love and Ruin* and *The Paris Wife*

"Ricca makes the most of this engaging story." —*Booklist*

"[Ricca] successfully conveys the powerful, nearly hallucinatory state of grief that MacLeod must have endured over the course of her journey. A swift-moving re-creation of an intrepid, rare spirit of her age." —*Kirkus Reviews*

"This incredible true story of one woman's quest to find her missing fiancé is the perfect summer adventure book. In 1910, Scottish aristocrat Olive MacLeod received word that her fiancé, the famed naturalist Boyd Alexander, was missing in Africa. So, she went to find him. Though there are wild animals to fight and inhospitable forests to whack through, MacLeod's incredible journey becomes even stranger as she goes on." —*Town & Country*

ALSO BY BRAD RICCA

Mrs. Sherlock Holmes
Super Boys

OLIVE
THE
LIONHEART

*Lost Love, Imperial Spies, and One Woman's
Journey into the Heart of Africa*

Brad Ricca

ST. MARTIN'S GRIFFIN
NEW YORK

Published in the United States by
St. Martin's Griffin, an imprint of St. Martin's Publishing Group

OLIVE THE LIONHEART. Copyright © 2020 by Brad Ricca.
All rights reserved. Printed in the United States of America.
For information, address St. Martin's Publishing Group,
120 Broadway, New York, NY 10271.

www.stmartins.com

Map by Henry Sene Yee

Designed by Michelle McMillian

The Library of Congress has cataloged the hardcover edition as follows:

Names: Ricca, Brad, author.
Title: Olive the Lionheart : lost love, imperial spies, and one woman's journey to the heart of
   Africa / Brad Ricca.
Other titles: Lost love, imperial spies, and one woman's journey to the heart of Africa
Description: First edition. | New York : St. Martin's Press, 2020. | Includes bibliographical
   references and index.
Identifiers: LCCN 2020010731 | ISBN 9781250207012 (hardcover) | ISBN 9781250207029
   (ebook)
Subjects: LCSH: Africa—Description and travel. | Temple, O. (Olive), 1880–1936—
   Travel—Africa. | Temple, O. (Olive), 1880–1936—Correspondence. | Alexander, Boyd,
   1873–1910—Correspondence. | Women explorers—Africa—Biography. | Africa—Social
   life and customs—20th century. | Temple, O. (Olive), 1880–1936—Friends and associates. |
   Talbot, Percy Amaury, 1877–1945—Travel—Africa. | London (England)—Biography.
Classification: LCC DT12 .R48 2020 | DDC 916.04/312092 [B]—dc23
LC record available at https://lccn.loc.gov/2020010731

ISBN 978-1-250-79669-1 (trade paperback)

Our books may be purchased in bulk for promotional, educational,
or business use. Please contact your local bookseller or
the Macmillan Corporate and Premium Sales Department
at 1-800-221-7945, extension 5442, or by email at
MacmillanSpecialMarkets@macmillan.com.

First St. Martin's Griffin Edition: 2021

10 9 8 7 6 5 4 3 2 1

For the boy in the blue sweatshirt

Contents

As this Grammar is chiefly intended for the use of officers and civil servants beginning the study of the language, every endeavour has been made to render it as simple as possible, and a key has been attached to the exercises, so that the student who is without a teacher may be able to correct his own mistakes. For the same reason the first half of the Grammar has been printed in Roman characters, and the second half has been printed in Roman as well as in the Hausa characters. It is thus possible to read the whole without acquiring a knowledge of the written language, though this latter is strongly to be recommended to serious students of the language.

—CHARLES H. ROBINSON, *Hausa Dictionary* (1906)

For now she need not think of anybody. She could be herself, by herself. And that was what now she often felt the need of—to think; well not even to think. To be silent; to be alone. All the being and the doing, expansive, glittering, vocal, evaporated; and one shrunk, with a sense of solemnity, to being oneself, a wedge-shaped core of darkness, something invisible to others . . . and this self having shed its attachments was free for the strangest adventures.

—VIRGINIA WOOLF, *To the Lighthouse* (1927)

First begin between selves, set a definite time, at each at that time put down what the other is doing. Do this twenty days. You shall find you have the key to telepathy.

—EDGAR CAYCE, Reading no. 2533-7

CENTRAL AFRICA

— 1910 —

NIGERIA

KANO

MAIFONI

ZUNGERU

FIKA

YOLA

RIVER BENUE

LOKOJA

RIVER NIGER

FORCADOS

KAM

BIGHT *of* BIAFRA

LAKE CHAD

DAR FUR

ILARNE

ABECHIR

WADAI

HAJER-EL-HAMIS

KAUA BAGA

The SUDAN

FORT LAMY

KUSSERI

RIVER LOGONE

TCHENKA

CHAD

BONGOR

LERE

The DEVIL

GARUA

ERUN

N

MAP ILLUSTRATED BY HENRY SENE YE

Dear Reader

This is a true story. For nearly a hundred years, the diaries of Olive MacLeod lay hidden on a locked shelf in Dunvegan Castle on the Isle of Skye. There, off the coast of Scotland, they have sat as visitors made their way through the castle, marveling at its history and charm. They sat quiet through Royal visits, a fire, world wars, countless beautiful summer days, and an eternity of freezing black nights. And a lot of bagpipes. After working on Olive's story for a long time, I had the odd feeling in the back of my head that I had missed something. A day later, I found the mysterious record of her diaries in a cranky Scottish database. I couldn't believe my eyes. I pictured myself in a creaky boat floating up to Dunvegan with the mist rising around me, come to find the lost secrets within. But truth is never that fictional. My wife was pregnant and I am not that strong a swimmer, so I stayed home instead. I filled out a form and explained that I wanted to use the diaries for my book. I hoped for the best.

Several months later, with new baby Alex sleeping near me, Jeroen Roskam, a friendly Dutchlander and former cavalryman who lives in (and looks after) the castle, responded to my request and began sending me the diaries piece by piece. The story told by Olive's diaries spoke to something bigger than her, than us, and even Africa itself. Ever since I first encountered Olive's story in a strange newspaper article, I wondered if hers was a story I could even tell. Not because of where and when it took place, or what it was about, or who I was—but, frankly, *because* of all those things. But after reading the diaries, I realized then that the only way to tell this story truthfully was to let Olive tell it herself. I have endeavored to frame it from her perspective—during the times she lived, with the words and characterizations she was accustomed to. I didn't want to reach in from the future and fix things. I could see her story only when I began to disappear.

This is a true story. That is, it is a narrative based on factual sources: a book, diaries, journals, letters, photos and drawings, and other first-person accounts. But this story is not just about where Olive traveled or what she accomplished or even of colonial Africa. Because of her writing, we have the great privilege of being able to know Olive not as someone else's version of herself, or as some kind of historical construct, but as who she truly was.

Prologue

May 24, 1910: Olive Has a Vision

Olive was dreaming. Or at least it felt like it. She saw the native carriers in Africa standing before her. She saw about seven of them, one standing behind another. They were all staring at her. But each time Olive looked at their faces, their eyes moved to and fro in a very fast and disturbing manner. This was unnatural: the Evil Eye.

Olive began to feel very uncomfortable as a white woman. She looked around in the jungle for a mirror that she might turn against their stares and bamboozle them. She desperately wanted to see their full, uninterrupted gaze.

She woke with a physical pain in her heart.

THE FAIRY FLAG

1893: A Girl Tells a Magical Story to
Her Younger Sister

The fire crackled quietly inside the stone room. Olive, who was thirteen, had her knees pulled up under her chin. Her long red hair curled all the way down to the floor. She was shaking. Not because of the cold, but because she was certain that a fairy princess from another world, in all her bright and terrible glory, was going to appear before her. The walls flickered in the firelight.

Olive drew up a tartan wool blanket. Her older sister, Flora, was seated across from her in a rocking chair. Flora's young face, squared by brown shoulder-length hair, became nearly wicked in the smallness of the room, filled with trembling shadows. Flora began to tell her sister, in quiet tones, a story that happened a long time ago.

This was the story of the MacLeod family of Scotland, said Flora, more or less. One summer's day, the clan chieftain, a wise and handsome warrior, walked onto his green lands on the lonely Isle of Skye. After getting just slightly lost, he came upon a small stone bridge with an arch cut through the middle. Though he did not completely know how, the good and lost chief felt that the bridge had a strange feeling about it, like the air before a storm. Overcome by curiosity, he put his hand on his sword and walked across the little bridge. Olive listened as her sister, who was fifteen, took her time to enunciate the next part very carefully. By crossing the bridge, the chief disappeared from the world and entered another. He had found the way to the magical realm of the *Sith Sidhe*: the Still Folk, the Other Ones.

The Faerie world.

The chief was brave, so he did not fear this glittering, beautiful place. At least that's what he told himself. In truth, the chief could never fully recall the time he spent there. Except for one detail. During his time in the magical kingdom, the handsome young chieftain did the unthinkable: He fell in love. She was a fairy princess, a *Bean Sith*. She was beautiful, with long red hair and a shimmering green dress that shone like an emerald. Flowers that never wilted were neatly set into her hair. But her father, the grim and powerful Fairy King, forbade them to be married. When she begged him to reconsider, the king proposed a "hand-fasting," a trial marriage, on the promise that it would last only for one year and a day. When their time was up, his daughter would have to return to the fairy kingdom—alone, and never to leave it again. The couple agreed, and their almost-wedding was held on the chief's birthday. Their hands entwined, they passed back over the bridge to the proper world. There, on the Isle of Skye, they enjoyed a full year of married life in the family castle of Dunvegan. The couple were happy beyond all other measures of worth.

Near the end of the year, the princess gave birth to a healthy—and exceedingly loud—male heir to the MacLeod line. But their time had expired, and the princess had to leave her bonny boy behind to return to her magical homeland. She and her husband made secret plans to escape, but in the end they knew that the magic of the Fairy King was too powerful. He would find them wherever they went. So, on that last day, that painful one day after a year of perfect happiness, the princess walked tearfully across the bridge. But just before she passed into the bright world, she begged that her baby son never be left alone, for the sound of his crying would be too much to bear. The princess, who was now a mother, knew that no matter which world she lay in, she would always be able to hear her son. Her husband agreed and watched her go.

That night, the chief's beard was wet with tears. To lift his mood, the clan threw a birthday feast in his honor with rich food, dancing, and music. The baby was kept in his room in the castle tower as a nursemaid watched over him. But the night was long, and the boy's nurse could listen to the sounds of revelry for only so long before she sneaked away to join the festivities, leaving the baby alone in the cold tower room.

When the baby started to cry, no one heard him over the skirling bagpipes below. As the party went on, the chief sat at his head table, his head heavy with drink. But when he looked out over the room and saw his son's nurse dancing up a storm, his wits returned to him. He sprang from his chair and ran upstairs to the tower.

With each step of the stone stairs, his yellow-and-black kilt whirling behind him, the chief began to hear the words of a strange, haunting song:

SLEEP, MY LITTLE CHILD, HERO GENTLE BRED,
DREAM, MY LITTLE CHILD, HERO BATTLE BRED.

When the chief reached the room, he slowly creaked open the door. The song was louder now, sung by a voice like spun silver:

SKIN LIKE FALLING SNOW, GREEN THY MAILCOAT,
LIVE THY STEEDS, DAUNTLESS THY FOLLOWING.

He knew that voice.

The chief, his heart beating like a great drum, stepped in. He saw his baby son in his cradle, lit by the dancing fire. Sitting in a rocking chair was the chief's fairy wife, more beautiful than ever. She was singing her son to sleep. The chief saw her for a moment—an instant—before she vanished into thin air. His mouth was parted; he had just started to say her name.

Dumbfounded, the chief stepped closer to find his child fast asleep. The boy was wrapped in a bright silken blanket left behind by his mother. The chief knew then that she would never return.

Years later, when the child had grown into a man and the chief's beard was streaked through with silver, the son told his father that he had a dream about the white shawl he had been given as a child. He said it was more than a scrap of cloth; it was a mighty fairy gift. It wasn't a blanket, the son said, but a flag. The son said that if the clansmen ever found themselves in peril, they need only wave the flag three times and the fairies would come to their rescue. But, said the boy—for that is how his father always thought of him—the flag could only be used three times until it would disappear from the world forever, taking the bearer with it. The chief's eyes narrowed thinking of this possibility. All these years this little blanket could have been the means to reunite with his beloved, whom he still greatly missed. He could wave it three times right now and be with her again.

But the chief, in his age and wisdom, had become a man who did things rather than only pretended them. He thought of his once-skinny self making his way across that bridge. He made his way up the old stone stairs of the tower, perhaps a bit slower, but as thundering as ever. His son followed him. In the old nursery he cast aside boxes until he located the fairy blanket. He looked at it very closely. He shut his eyes for a moment. He felt the embroidered stars between his thumbs. He could, he thought, hear the whispers of that old song again. How did it go?

He opened his eyes. He pushed the back of his hand over his face before anyone could see. He then ordered the flag to be locked away in an iron box until such time as the clan might need it. They called it the *Bratach Sith,* or the Fairy Flag. He lived the rest of his days alone.

Hundreds of years later, the ruthless MacDonalds, the mortal enemies of the MacLeods, raided Dunvegan Castle and set the church on fire. The surprised MacLeods were all but routed. The last of their forces, bloodied by sword and cudgel, met on the beach with the last of the clan's treasure and remembered the old story that had been handed down from fathers to sons. They found and unfurled the flag and waved it over the cold sand. When they were done, their forces seemed to have increased magically, perhaps by tenfold. They marched on the MacDonalds, who were filled with fear and fled. The flag was put away again.

Many years passed, and a plague swept over the Isle of Skye, felling the Highland cattle and the sheep that provided soft wool. Famine came swiftly and without mercy. The starving MacLeods waved the flag in the wind once again. The fairy host appeared, glinting and without number, and rode out onto the meadows, touching each dying animal with their magic swords. The cattle stirred and the sheep bleated as the animals stood up again: The clan was saved.

There was only one more wave left of the Fairy Flag, said Flora eerily, from the rocking chair in front of the fire.

Where was it now? asked Olive quietly, though she already knew.

It was lost for a long time, Flora continued. Then, two hundred years ago, a witch named the Brahan Seer spoke a terrible prophecy. This witch was just a boy on the Isle of Lewis when he found a strange blue-and-black stone with a hole in it. When he picked it up and peered through, he was blinded in one eye, but was given the power of second sight. His prophecy was very specific—as witch's prophecies sometimes are—and said that a day would come when three things would happen to the MacLeods: the clan heir would die; the MacLeod Maidens, that set of landmark rocks on the coast, would become the property of a rival family; and a single red fox would have her litter in the castle tower. On that day the MacLeods would fall from Dunvegan. The flag would not save them.

Worried at the strange nature of the prophecy, some of the men of the clan—the loud and substantial ones—roughly searched the old tower and found a steel chest. They were certain it contained the flag, which had not been seen for centuries. The men forced it open, but it was empty. Then, one of the men's small sons spied a lump in the chest's red lining. Hidden inside was a little key. It opened a second chamber in the bottom of the chest. When it clicked open, there was a strong scent of wood. The boy carefully lifted out a white square of fine silk, with crosses made of pure golden thread. There were tiny elf-spots—the marks of magic—stitched in red with great care. They had found the Fairy Flag.

At that same moment the MacLeod heir, a fine young man, died in an accident at sea. The rival Campbells assumed ownership of the Maiden Rocks, and a fox was seen pacing nervously in the west turret.

Olive drew her knees closer.

But luckily, though the flag itself had triggered the curse, it was not actually waved that day. Its presence alone was strong enough for the MacLeods to hold Dunvegan Castle. They hold it still today.

Flora nodded, satisfied with her telling of the tale. It always changed, as it had to.

As she went to sleep that night, Olive told herself not to be scared. It was a ridiculous tale.

Olive looked around her. In addition to the fireplace, with its orange fire, there was her blanket, colored poppy gold with thin lines of red and black. There was a high table, a piano, and the door. A crest was also visible, picturing a bull's head over sable. On the other side of the fireplace a cold stone staircase wound its way up.

It was a truly ridiculous story, thought Olive, and no doubt Pooh-oh (her nickname for her sister) had added parts to make it even scarier.

But for all that Olive tried to convince herself of the fictitious nature of the story on that cold, drafty night, it would have been much easier if she and her sister weren't in the Fairy Room itself in Dunvegan Castle on the Isle of Skye. It would have been easier if their last name were not MacLeod. Olive looked at the wooden door, imagining the long hall behind it.

Olive would sleep much better if the Fairy Flag itself weren't downstairs in the drawing room, in a glass case next to an old cup and horn. The white flag was there, as Flora had described it, and just as Olive had stared at it every day since they had arrived.

Sleep might come easier if the story weren't real.

2

THE PARTY GIRL AND
THE NATURALIST

*April 1908: Olive MacLeod Visits the Regent's
Park Zoo, Attends a Boisterous Dinner Party,
and Later Meets a Man of Science*

The snow fell gently upon the hippopotamus. The animal did not seem to mind, not in particular, but it was hard to know for sure. It was a cold, gray April day at the London Zoological Gardens, and though some of the animals shunned the snow (the lions) or even tasted it (the monkeys), for the most part it was viewed by visitors as an unavoidable natural phenomenon. Everything was outlined in a thin, cold layer of white.

A young woman walked briskly down the path from the Gazelle House. She was wrapped in a coat and wool scarves and wore fashionable black boots. As she turned her head, she pushed a long strand of red hair back until it disappeared somewhere on the other side of her ear, and behind her large hat. She looked anxious, as if someone were chasing her. She began to walk faster.

From behind her came a dull kind of stamping, followed by a roar.

Emerging in a loud swell of noise was a pack of boys, mostly school-aged and in far fewer layers of winter clothing. The lads bolted toward the caged hippopotamus, nearly knocking the redheaded woman down in the process. As her lock of hair escaped back to a less-than-agreeable position directly in front of her right eye, she lost sight of the children for a moment. She sighed. Of course these were *her* boys, the ones she was in charge of. As such, she imagined the worst sort of circumstances: fisticuffs, chomping, and the inevitable destruction of property. With a huff, she pushed the strand of hair back and, her vision restored, tried to focus on her charges. She counted quickly: ten . . . eleven . . . twelve . . . all were accounted for. The hair bounced back in front of her face, but she didn't seem to mind. As the boys pointed and laughed at the hippos, Olive MacLeod felt satisfied that her little animals, the boys of the Children's Happy Evening's Association, were safe at least for the moment.

As they walked through the zoo, Olive followed the boys. They kept their distance from the bears, tried to get the parrots to say rude words, and argued whether what looked to be a clump of rope was really the tufted end of a lion's tail, hiding away from the snow. The boys, in their thin flannel and caps, seemed utterly oblivious to the cold. But Olive could feel it. As always, the popular boys clumped together in laughing clusters of activity. The lonelier boys stood off alone and watched. She could see their faces. They saw apes, a pair of moose, and a finicky ostrich. They watched the sea lions sit on pedestals and bark. As they pushed their way across the paths, Olive even saw a stork, standing quietly in the background. The children did not have the time to see every animal, but they certainly tried. Olive liked the zoo well enough, but it was not her favorite thing. At least the snow had taken the edge off the zoo's distinctive odor. Olive had a dinner party that night and didn't want to have to make too many changes to her wardrobe.

At the end of their walk they met up with the other groups from the association at the zoo entrance. Olive's group, well known for its misbehavior, arrived last. Olive noticed that all the other children were very excited. She saw that they were waving around small picture postcards of the animals. Olive's heart sank. The other chaperones had bought these cards from the penny machines as souvenirs for their children.

Olive quickly turned to her group. They watched as the other boys traded photos of yawning lions for lumbering elephants. Olive panicked. Why had the others not told her of this? She quickly eyed the machines and thrust her hands into her pockets. She had only folds of notes—not a penny among them. Olive looked around and grabbed the hand of one of her charges.

"Go," she said, stuffing some pound notes into his hand, "Get some coppers for the penny in the slot!" But the boy just stood there, staring down at the significant amount of money that she had just put into his hand.

"Go!" she said. The boy sped off to the ticket gate.

Olive turned back to her group. They had seen the money. They were all staring up at her.

"Please, Miss MacLeod, we don't want the cards," said one boy with shiny black hair. "They are only bits of paper." Olive smiled at his genuine sentiment, but she wanted them to have those postcards. The other boys who had them were beginning to brag.

There was another in her group who had worn the same wool cap all winter long. He came up to her and begged her to reconsider. This lad was younger and smaller, but the other boys liked him very much. He was also the son of a gentleman who had come down in the world to the level of the poor. As the boy urged his fellows to agree, Olive saw a hole in his darned trousers that revealed bare white skin. It was still snowing.

THE CRUMBS HAD HARDLY BEEN brushed off the white tablecloth when Olive watched her father, Sir Reginald MacLeod, leave the table with great, wobbling purpose, and make his way to the sitting room. He had a broad smile on his red face. He was the registrar general for Scotland and held a knighthood, but he certainly wasn't acting like it. Olive laughed, knowing full well what was coming next. Her father's tradition after their many dinner parties together at their country home in Vinters Park was well known. Everyone watched as he seemed to sway over the hearth rug as if it were some teetering boat, put his hand to his chest, took a deep breath, possibly burped, and made his familiar proclamation, in a very loud manner:

"And now," he said, "let us be merry!" rolling both *r*s to their fullest, most slippery potential.

Across the table, Violet Asquith, the daughter of the prime minister, with her curly dark hair and wearing a black dress, rolled her eyes almost imperceptibly. "Old Waxworks" was their nickname for Sir Reginald because of his pinkish complexion and cotton-white side-whiskers. Once again he had been too eager. The dinner table was still filled with scraps of food, not to mention seated people of sophistication and intellect, talking to one another about politics and religion. They weren't ready for games *yet*. Violet turned back to her conversation with a handsome man who was not her Archie. Not that it mattered.

From the head of the table, Olive stared at Violet's choice of confidant. Violet tried to change position to avoid Olive's glance, but it was impossible. She had a basilisk eye, that one, thought Violet. Some of the guests stood up, ready to give in and retire to the games. Olive rose herself, satisfied that Violet had noticed her attention. As she stood, people turned to look at Olive, as they always did. Olive was pale and lithe with sharp blue eyes, and though she was not very tall, her pulled-up red hair—wild and fiery—made it seem otherwise.

In the sitting room Olive became hostess, leading the party in games of epigrams, abstract conceits, and so forth. Theirs was always a bookish crowd, making the games a bit more competitive than the usual London party. Casual visitors who enjoyed dinner and conversation often vowed never to return after the singular experience of the games at Vinters. But for those who enjoyed the thrill of the clash, this portion of the party always went long into the night.

The party had moved to a game of aphorisms, where each player was supposed to describe another member of the group in the wittiest way imaginable. Someone described Sir Reginald as "a sunny peach on a garden wall," at which he bowed so deeply that they feared he might have died. One of their friends called Violet "a blooming cornfield," at which she laughed so infectiously she had to hold her hand to her mouth. Sir Reginald, having recovered from his bow, then pointed out a particularly colorless cousin who was sitting in the back of the room. He called her, in very polite tones, "a glass of water fit for a lady," and the party roared. Olive laughed, her hands on her knees.

Suddenly one of the young men of the party crawled before Olive, his hand over his heart.

"Marry me," he said.

Olive laughed again, which doubled as her response.

As the man walked off, defeated yet still smiling, he said with great style: "Her beauty was the embodiment of repose."

This party had been going on for years.

As a girl growing up, Olive's only friend was her sister, Flora. But she had been gone for a long time, having married a very serious man named Hubert Walter. When Flora accepted his proposal, Olive remembered Flora sitting and staring at her engagement ring as if it were locked to some invisible chain. Flora had most recently been in Belgium with her husband, who was helping to negotiate the government's takeover of the Congo after atrocities had been reported there. Olive had recently attended a lecture on the subject, which was quite boring despite the horrors described.

Olive's friends were a more eclectic group. First among them was Violet, the daughter of the newly elected prime minister, H. H. Asquith. There was also Blanche "Baffy" Dugdale, the gentile Zionist intellectual who lived in London and wrote letters to *everybody*. The men they socialized with were of similar pedigree and wealth if not entirely their equal. They included Archie Hamilton-Gordon, Violet's beau, and Maurice "Bongie" Bonham-Carter, who worked for the P.M. and was a batsman for the Oxford Cricket Club. Olive's trustworthy old friend Mr. Hardy was always there. But at the dinner parties Olive was always accompanied by her father. Everyone knew that Olive's mother Agnes was ill, but she wasn't seen very much about Vinters. She was rumored to be off with a relative or friend.

As the summer wore on, Olive and her friends congregated at dinner parties, teas, and on excursions to the Continent. They had a party on the *Sunbury Belle,* a boat on the Thames covered in cherries, grapes, and bananas. They drank iced coffee on the white deck. There were suitors, of course, but Olive treated them like meals at a table. She and Violet were often engaged to dance partners ten feet deep on any given night. Olive would creep up next to Violet at a party and say, "So-and-so is a dangerous character and you mustn't dance with him." Violet would just laugh in her face and declare it "the *greatest* rot." They danced and laughed with all manner of men until, as Violet often put it, "the birds came out." They would then retire to their core group and motorcar until dawn, their minds a blank as the sun rose to shed light on the ruins of their evenings.

Life, in fact, was rich and brilliant. Sometimes Olive looked around like she barely recognized it.

So when a friend asked her to come meet an explorer of some renown, it sounded somewhat boorish, but it held at least the promise of perhaps being interesting—which was her favorite thing—so she agreed, after only minimal persuasion.

THE MEADOWS WERE FLUSH with oxeye daisies when Olive and a friend drove south to Cranbrook on a late-summer day in 1908. They were traveling to Swifts Place, a country estate where Jane Austen had once lived, located near the quaint town of Cranbrook in Kent. As they drove, Olive took a deep breath, inhaling the smell of hay and the motor. The man they were going to meet was some sort of taxidermist who had built his own museum. The fact that he stuffed birds was hilarious to Olive. He was probably yet another Rifle Brigadier. No wonder her friend wanted company: She would need the protection. At least the ride had been worth it.

When they chugged along the main drive, Olive's eyes widened at the sight of Swifts Place, a towering manor with three brick chimneys. Surrounded by green grass bursting with richly colored flowers, the house was grand and palatial. Olive guessed it must have at least twenty rooms. The explorer who was born there, was now living in Wilsley House, located on the back of the estate. As they passed Swifts Place onto a bumpier road, Olive saw another car quickly turn from the other side of the home and speed off in the other direction. The man who was driving was laughing.

They made their way for a bit until they saw the back of another house. As they pulled up to Wilsley House, a charming brick-and-tile house with steep gables, Olive saw that their host was waiting for them. He was trim and wore a light suit with a dark tie. His chestnut brown hair was parted on his left and close-shaven on the sides. His mustache was long, tapered at the ends, and full above his upper lip. As he welcomed them, his smile lay in his cheeks and in the outside corners of his dark eyes. Olive shook hands with him. He looked and felt military.

"Lieutenant Boyd Alexander," the man said.

"Olive MacLeod," she replied.

They sat down inside to a white tablecloth set with bone china. Olive was only half there, tired from the previous night's festivities and the long drive. They were joined by a few other family and friends. The interior of the home was lain with oak panels. Olive saw various types of scientific equipment. She also spied books, mostly about Africa, but also works of Oscar Wilde, H. Rider Haggard's Allan Quatermain adventures, and a slim volume titled *Leaves of Grass*. In one room, the walls were covered with dark murals. Along the bottom were painted a series of lean, white dogs that were hunting a terrified hare who occupied the furthest left panel. The upper panels were something else entirely. Olive saw that they depicted, in older, even darker hues, scenes from the Bible. She saw Sodom burning in fire. Someone must have seen the surprise on her face because they told her that the room had previously been used as a chapel.

As they lunched on soup and roast chicken someone remarked that Mr. Alexander had recently returned from Africa himself. In fact he had just been awarded the Founder's Medal by the Royal Geographical Society. Olive perked up at this impressive news. She knew little of Africa other than it was beastly hot.

After some coaxing, Mr. Alexander told the table that his latest expedition had begun in Nigeria before going on to map the mysterious Lake Chad; the journey had taken three years. He said he eventually made his way to the Nile itself—an astonishing feat. Olive studied Mr. Alexander's face as he pushed his spoon through his soup. As he spoke, in a thin voice, he seemed a thousand miles away.

Olive didn't know how it came up, but Mr. Alexander—or someone else, she couldn't remember—brought up that two of the expedition's number had unfortunately died on the journey, a hunter named Gosling and a man named Claud. Olive found this to be terribly sad.

"Claud was my brother," said Mr. Alexander.

There was another man named Talbot, but he departed the expedition before its close. Mr. Alexander had a trusty servant named José Lopez who remained, but he also left before the final journey. When Mr. Alexander reached the Nile, in rags and parched for water, he was the final member left of the original party.

Now Olive regarded this Mr. Alexander with something close to pity.

Lunch was finished on milder topics. As the others dispersed, Mr. Alexander beckoned his two guests: It was time to see his museum.

AS THEY LEFT THE DINING ROOM, Olive imagined a great, two-story gallery filled with stuffed leopards, apes, and perhaps even a lion skin. Majestic birds of near-prehistoric size would be suspended from wires above the rich wooden display cases. She shivered, wondering if Mr. Alexander's great collection might include some shrunken heads.

Olive was surprised when they walked outside the grand house and back into the sun. Olive blinked and looked around—she spotted a carriage house down the lane. But when they walked right by the carriage house and into a small yard, Olive grew even more confused.

"Here it is," said Mr. Alexander.

They were standing in front of an outhouse.

The small structure was built of horizontal slats of wood. The roof was slanted, and there was a rectangular door on hinges. Olive could not believe it; she was already rehearsing what she would tell Violet.

"There is only room for two," he said.

When he opened the door and beckoned Olive inside, she caught her breath, but only because she could not believe what she saw.

Inside this wooden outhouse, covering every interior inch, was a sprawling miniature jungle. Olive's gaze got lost in the series of branches and leaves twisting and flowering from the ground up to the gables of the roof. But the real wonder of the scene was that covering the branches were countless birds of the most colorful shades and shapes. Olive soon realized the precariousness of their position. She instinctively went to shut the door so that none of the birds would escape the little sanctuary. But then she realized that wouldn't be necessary. All the birds were cold and stuffed, frozen and still in their dead Eden.

There were tiny birds with yellow beaks, larger ones with orange tufts on their heads, and red birds with feet of the brightest white. This secret, surprising jungle was one of the strangest and most spectacular tableaus Olive had ever seen.

Boyd Alexander seemed to come alive in that tiny, sacred place. He rattled off the names of the birds with great skill, especially when it was in another language. He told her stories about where he had found this bird and that. They all had stories, though their names were being said so fast that Olive could hardly remember them.

"The red thrush is more lovely in voice than the nightingale," said Mr. Alexander, "though shyer than she." He told Olive how he had waited for hours "to catch sight of the maker of such pure music—but never to see more than a flash of red in the interval of silence." This Mr. Boyd Alexander, who was standing very close to Miss Olive MacLeod, had a way with words. As he talked, Olive spied his signet ring, which showed a crescent, an elephant, and a fleur-de-lis in silver-white and black.

After Olive left the little museum, it was time to make their good-byes. Mr. Alexander smiled under his mustache, and his dark eyes softened when he came to Olive. As they drove home, Olive was glad she had come. Mr. Alexander had proved to be a most interesting host, though she had to admit she found him lonely and lost.

She was surprised when she got a letter from him.

He wanted to see her again.

WHEN OLIVE SUSAN MIRANDA MACLEOD was born, in St. George's Hanover Square in London, on February 17, 1880, her two-year-old sister Flora was anxiously awaiting her. From that moment forward, as the family moved around London, to Scotland, then to Kent, the sisters were inseparable. Flora was very sensible and practical: Olive was always the more rebellious one. When their mother tried to separate their bedtimes, Olive simply refused. In fact, their mother soon found that it was pointless to try to punish Olive for anything. If Olive was sent to bed early, she would sleep late the next morning. If she was told she couldn't have a treat, she would loudly claim that she no longer liked it. This is why Olive chose to invite Mr. Alexander to Vinters, where Flora could function as her conscience at the ready. Flora had recently come home with her husband and young children, and though she had been somewhat removed from Olive's life since her marriage, her opinion still very much mattered to her.

Olive also wanted Flora to meet Mr. Alexander because her sister was a first-rate investigator. Almost as soon as he arrived and sat himself down to dinner, Flora began asking him about his personal losses in the jungle.

"How helpless you must have felt," said Flora, "seeing them die." She was relentless in her interrogation and unafraid to ask questions of men.

"It made me more determined to succeed," answered Mr. Alexander. "The expedition had cost us so dear; I could not afford to fail."

"Isn't that splendid grit?" said Flora, glancing down the table at anyone who was listening.

Mr. Alexander told them another story of how he and his companion, José Lopez, tracked down an okapi, a rare and most curious animal that most had considered a myth.

Once again Olive noticed that Mr. Alexander became excited when talking about Africa.

"The sublime creature is short," he said, his hands moving to help in the imagining, "with horizontal, zebra-like stripes on its two legs. Its body is covered with a soft brown fur, making it difficult to spot. Its head is deer-like, with some white and grey." His eyes drifted far away during the minutely detailed description. Mr. Alexander explained that they finally found and shot one, bringing its striped skin back home with them as proof of their deed.

As the table congratulated him, Mr. Alexander was sure to paint the victory as a shared one between himself and José. When asked how they met, Mr. Alexander said that he had rescued José as a boy from a small fishing village on the island of St. Nicolas during an expedition in Cape Verde. Since then, they had been on numerous adventures together, some of them quite dangerous. Mr. Alexander paused, his eyes on the children, then announced that he supposed he could tell them another story from Africa.

It was early evening when he found himself wandering down a path in the jungle, sick with fever. Mr. Alexander stopped when he noticed two lions, a male and a female, calmly sitting on the path ahead. Mr. Alexander backed off, went the long way around, and sent word to José, who was following behind, to do the same. But his friend did not get the message and later saw the male lion at a pool, where he took a shot that felled him. But after a few moments, the lion rose up again, with only some broken teeth to show for it. José went to find Mr. Alexander. They were in trouble.

Knowing they had a wounded lion in the area, Mr. Alexander and

José got their long guns. But Mr. Alexander was still sweating with fever, so as José left to scout, he looked quietly around the camp. It was then that Mr. Alexander described seeing a "large mass of live yellow, crouching under the screen of branches of an overhanging bush." The lion roared and leaped at the shivering Mr. Alexander. He was done for. But just then, José appeared from the trees and fired a shot that made the lion bound away in fear. His friend had saved his life.

When someone asked what happened next, Mr. Alexander took a sip of his drink and said that they hunted the beast down, and he shot him in the head.

At the conclusion of the interview masquerading as a meal, Mr. Alexander went to the next room to play with Flora's children, who seemed to adore him. In addition to his practical jokes, he won them over with tales of the arched and scaly pangolin. He then only slightly terrorized them with stories of huge vampire bats with teeth like sharks. Flora smiled. She had been the recipient of near-infinite advice about men from Olive over the years, almost all of it critical. But Flora now beckoned her sister's ear. Her only criticism was that Mr. Alexander seemed a little tolerant of the Congo government, but Olive thought she felt that way about everyone. Boyd believed that native rulers should be worked with closely to help eliminate the slave trade. His eyes burned with a fire of hatred when he talked about slavery. Olive could not imagine the horrors he had seen firsthand. Flora was quite pleased.

"I have never seen anybody," said Flora, "so simple nor so generous, nor one who thought so slowly—the combination is charming."

Flora, the safe and good storyteller, had made her pronouncement. Olive had much to consider.

BY THE TIME THE SUMMER HAD RIPENED into September, Mr. Alexander had no doubts about his feelings for Olive MacLeod. Even though he had never been in love before, he told his brother Herbert, a well-regarded watercolorist who entertained thoughts of visiting the South

Pole. Though he was initially wary of this new woman, when Herbert met Olive he understood his brother's position completely. Of all Boyd's living siblings—including Marion and Robin, his identical twin—it was Herbert who was closest. Herbert had helped Boyd write his last book, *From the Niger to the Nile*. When they were done, they set off fireworks into the night sky over Swifts Place in celebration.

To her friends Olive seemed to be a little worried. She found Boyd Alexander interesting. She couldn't put her finger on it, but there was something about him that greatly intrigued her. But it was all so sudden. There were other things to consider. Yet, he interested her. When he sent her a bit of heather from the Weald, the wild fields around Wilsley, she put it in the locket around her neck.

But there was something on the horizon that threatened everything. Before he met Olive, Mr. Alexander had been planning a return trip to Africa. He was going to leave at the end of the year, along with José Lopez, to map a new route through the forbidden deserts, all the way up to Egypt. And, of course, to collect more birds. Though he had been a soldier, Boyd was first and foremost a birder. Even as his column marched across Africa to the battle of Kumassi in 1900, José still followed as part of the relief crew, collecting the birds that Boyd felled along the way. Boyd was once reprimanded by his superior officer for running off to a forest to look for birds with José even though the area was still crawling with enemy soldiers.

The trip they were planning would be filled with danger on a grander scale. Wadai and Dar Fur, the vast, unmarked regions east of Lake Chad and southwest of the great city of Khartoum, were places of unrest. Muhammad Ahmad, the Mahdi who was prophesied to bring about the end of all evil, had defeated the British at Khartoum just over twenty years ago. The Mahdi hung the head of his adversary, Maj. Gen. Charles George Gordon, in the branches of a tree.

Followers flocked to the Mahdi, believing he was created from the sacred light of the Prophet's heart. When he died of typhus the following year, his regime fell apart, and the British—with the Egyptians—retook

Khartoum. But the death of one leader begat the rise of another. A young Arab fighter named Ali Dinar assassinated and replaced the sultan of Dar Fur. A mysterious ruler who shunned any kind of visitation, he was the one the British were worried about.

This was the inferno that Mr. Alexander was set to travel through. It was going to be quite an adventure.

But then came Olive.

Since their second meeting Olive had decided to read Mr. Alexander's book *From the Niger to the Nile*. One passage seemed to explain why he had to leave: "Every explorer looks upon the map of that part of the world which particularly calls him," he wrote, "and endeavors to find a spot that still affords opportunity for the special powers he may possess for finding out the secrets that it hides."

Boyd knew that his mother, Mary, did not want him to go, but he suspected she would be eager to be rid of José for a while. She frequently complained, in her own cultivated way, that one kitchen maid or another was giving far too much attention to José, who was presenting the girl with brooches and compliments. Boyd couldn't help but laugh in agreement. José's dark eyes had earned him a reputation among the servants at Swifts Place. There was also the issue of money and resources that had already been committed to the trip. It was simply too late to cancel. Mr. Alexander had to return to Africa.

"Well, it's got to be done now, everyone expects it of me," said Mr. Alexander to Herbert. His trip to the Nile had won him medals, awards, and scientific acclaim. He felt he could not do anything less. "You see," he said, "when once one is a marked man one is not allowed to stop." He then added with a laugh, "I don't suppose I shall get any rest till I leave my bones in Africa."

Olive had told no one about Boyd except for her sister. Their friendship felt like a secret, but not the kind that hurt to keep. They met and walked among the lime trees of Swifts Place, where they sat on a bench and had a deep conversation. That is why it was not a surprise when, soon after, Boyd Alexander asked Olive MacLeod to marry him in the church near his family home. Not long after, he shipped off to Africa from Liverpool on December 12, 1908.

Boyd promised Olive he would see her again in one short year.

He said he had something to do.

AFRICAN EXPLORER
MURDERED.

———

FATE OF LIEUT.
BOYD ALEXANDER

———

VICTIM OF NATIVE
FANATICISM

The Foreign Office Has Been Informed By The French
Government, Through The British Ambassador At
Paris, That News Has Been Received From Nyeri, In
Wadai, That Lieut. Boyd Alexander, The Well-Known
Explorer, Has Been Murdered. No Details Of The Trag-
edy Are Yet To Hand.

3

LEVIATHAN

Olive didn't cry until she was on the train. By then, chugging across the bumpy tracks, she felt more invisible. She wept in the car, hiding in the corner of her seat. She already missed her father. Her farewell with him had been necessarily formal, as it had to be. He awkwardly gifted her a small quantity of Shakespeare's plays. And that was that. They both knew they could afford no visible breakage. She knew he did not want her to go. Her good-bye with her mother had been different. Confined to bed, her mother had seemed downright cheerful. Olive composed herself and faced forward.

When the train pulled into Liverpool's Riverside station, Olive stepped onto the cavernous platform. The warm light above was crossed by thin trellis shadows. As a motorcar conveyed her to the North-Western Hotel, Olive saw crowds of people in dark clothes standing around near the flat tracks leading to the train sheds. She knew from the papers that there was a massive transport strike going on, brought about by workers who felt misused by their spendthrift employers. The strike was growing larger by the day.

That afternoon Olive stepped outside to go to a store she had seen on her way in. After a short walk along the brick streets, Olive stared up at a sign that read "Foto-graphy." When Olive walked in, she was surrounded by dozens of cameras poised on wall shelves, their single, green-black lenses almost stretching toward her. The shopkeeper greeted her, then asked what she needed. Olive showed the man her new Kodak, only a few weeks old.

The shopkeeper nodded and went about getting her film. There, in that moment of silence that happens in all shops at the moment of transaction, Olive couldn't help but say it:

"I'm going to Africa," she said.

The shopkeeper looked up, and like the quiet cameras around him, seemed to see her from different angles at once. Olive, pretty and short, in a long dress, with her red hair billowing out from its pins, was obviously not the usual epitome of an African explorer. The shopkeeper had seen scores of them readying for their trips to the Dark Continent. He had seen many leave. He had developed their photographic plates of forests, elephants, and lions when they returned. Some he never saw again. He dropped her purchases into a bag. Olive paid him, thanked him, then turned to leave.

"Turn back," said the shopkeeper.

Olive stopped in the door. The shopkeeper thought she might be offended, but she was not. Olive thought it some required sentiment, some eleventh-hour lament about the deadly dangers of Africa from a protective old man.

"If you go," the man said carefully, "you should almost certainly lose your life."

Olive MacLeod smiled thinly, or at least tried to, and walked out the door, leaving the bell's ring stinging in the air.

DURING THE PAST WEEK OLIVE had planned, packed, unpacked, and repacked multiple times per day. At the same time, she had to give her sister constant assurances that she would be safe in the hands of her escorts in Africa, Mr. and Mrs. Talbot. She had met them only a few weeks ago, but they had already proved their helpfulness. Percy Amaury Talbot was a seasoned African explorer who had traveled with Boyd. He knew how to arrange their passage, procure provisions, and secure their all-important credentials. Given the status of colonial Africa, carved up like a cake by the great European powers, these papers would be necessary to get them across the various territories and borders. His wife, too, had experience in the bush that would be invaluable. Their plans were to land near the mouth of the Niger, take boats up, and then switch to the march all the way to Fort Lamy, where Boyd had last been seen before heading east. Then they would visit Maifoni and elsewhere, if all went according to plan. Though her father did not want Olive to go, he knew he could not dissuade her, so he bankrolled the trip and peopled it with the very best he could find, starting with the Talbots. There was nothing he wouldn't do for Olive.

Now, after a fortnight of chaos, Olive and her bulging trunks were at last ready to board the steamship. Olive was convinced that the Talbots, upon seeing her baggage, would judge her packing—and her—in an unfavorable light. When it was time, Olive held her breath as Mrs. Talbot went through her shoes, her outfits, and even her underclothes. The purge was quick and merciless. Olive was relieved that she had (mostly) passed muster. She was forced to leave behind a few dresses and some extra boots, but that was the extent of it. Surely she wouldn't miss them.

To make matters worse, last-minute packages were still arriving. Violet had sent along a beautiful little volume of the *Imitation of Christ*. Another new pair of boots also arrived. Olive put them on with a little difficulty but found them to be quite comfortable. There was a slight twinge along the edge of one foot, but it would be fine. The Talbots were still missing some items that had not arrived, including their own boots and several outfits for Mrs. Talbot. Olive couldn't believe how little it bothered them.

The next day Olive approached the SS *Dakar*, the long black steamship that made the run from Liverpool to the western coast of Africa. She said good-bye to Herbert Alexander, who had made the trip to wish her luck. He had become a good friend. She turned to leave. There were crowds of strikers along the docks, but Olive had a clear path toward the smokestacks of the ship above them in the gray sky. As Olive felt the noise and smog of England already at her back, the shopkeeper's words echoed in her mind.

She stepped onto the walkway of the ship.

OLIVE SAT ON THE EDGE OF HER SMALL, rigid bunk and tried to negotiate silently with the contents of her stomach. She was determined to remain composed, though both moving properties—the bed and her stomach—were urging her otherwise.

Olive MacLeod was no stranger to the sea. She had been on rowboats, fishing boats, and party boats. The *Dakar* was no dinghy, but Olive could feel the waves roll and push the boat to and fro, back and forth. At that moment the very idea of an engineered vessel being put straight down in the middle of such fury seemed incredibly ill-advised. Even when she could start to feel a rhythm to it all, the waves would start again. When she finally purged her stomach, involuntarily, it brought only a few moments' respite.

There was a knock at the door. It was Mr. Talbot.

The man walked in, his head tilted to the side. Clean black boots rose up past his ankles, his pants tucked tightly inside. He wore a white-collared shirt and a short, open field jacket. He was thin and young, with a square, clean face framed by hair that exercised a slight curl at the top and the sides. When Olive made her wishes known to travel to Africa after the news came, it was Mr. Talbot who had agreed to take her. She knew she could rely on him absolutely. After all, not only was he a district commissioner in southern Nigeria, but in 1904 he had been part of the famous Alexander-Gosling expedition that cost Boyd's brother Claud his life. He had already been there.

Mr. Talbot was holding a small red book in his hand. He had made a habit of this, coming to visit Olive after supper, in order to further her lessons. He was determined, in the short time they had on their sea voyage, to at least introduce Olive to some of the barest constructions of Hausa, the language of West Africa that was spoken across the region. As Mr. Talbot sat across from Olive and worked through the exercises, the waves seemed to recede into the background. They began to run through the basic rules of corresponding pronunciation:

The English letters used in transliterating Hausa in this Grammar are pronounced as follows:—

a as the *a* in *father.*

b as in English.

ch a soft *ch* as in *church* or *cherry.*

d as in English . . . in the pronunciation of which the point of the tongue touches the edge of the upper teeth, a sort of *dt*, which somewhat resembles the French or German.

e as the *a* in *fate.*

f represents usually the English / but in certain words, e.g. *fushi,* anger, the *f* represents a sort of bilabial sound.

g a hard *g* as in *gale,* never a soft *g* as in *genius.*

Olive recited the lesson, but all she could think about was that this man in front of her had been with Boyd in Africa. She searched his eyes, as he read, for some reflection of those times. Olive knew that Mr. Talbot had great love for Boyd. She wanted him to talk about it. He focused on the lesson instead:

h as in English: always pronounced when inserted.

i as the *i* in *ravine* or as *ee* in *feet*.

j as in English.

k as in English. The Hausa term for it is *k mairua*, i.e. the watery *k: kh*, a rough form of the Scotch *ch* in *loch*. It resembles the sound made in trying to raise something in the throat.

1 as in English. There is heard also an *l* where perfect contact is not made of the blade of the tongue with the palate intermediate between *r*, thus we may write *jariri* or *jarili*, an infant.

The little book claimed that Hausa was spoken over a region of a half million square miles, encompassing about fifteen million people. Hausa-speakers formed 1 percent of the whole population of the world. For Olive, it was beginning to sink in that they weren't going somewhere far: They were going somewhere gargantuan.

Hausa was very similar to Arabic, largely due to its being modified by the rise of Mohammedanism in Africa over the last century. The Hausa people believed their ancestors came from far east, even beyond Mecca.

r as in English.

sh as in English.

t as in English.

u as in *flute*, or *oo* as in *tool*.

w as in *win*.

y as in *yard*. It is never used except as a consonant.

z as in English.

1. There is no article in Hausa. Thus, *mutum* means man,
a man, or the man.

Mr. Talbot remained just as mysterious to Olive as the strange African words. Feeling bold, Olive asked him a question.

"If you don't mind my asking, Mr. Talbot," Olive said, "what do you believe in?"

Mr. Talbot closed his eyes, almost as if he had known the question was coming. He shut his book and replied something about Christianity and Buddhism, which he found particularly fascinating.

"Do you believe in telepathy?" asked Olive, "or other existences?"

Mr. Talbot thought about it and said he believed in a future reunion with those lost in life. He thought there might first be a period of rest and assimilation, but then there would be a perfect future life. Olive nodded. She wasn't sure if he was just humoring her or truly believed it.

After Mr. Talbot left, Olive pulled out her paper and a fine gold pencil from a small strongbox she opened with a key. She lay in her bottom bunk, feeling the dark sea creak somewhere far beneath her. She took out and wrote in her diary. When the Talbots came back, she swiftly hid it away.

In a few days Olive's stomach settled down so that she could finally leave her cabin. For all its stature, the *Dakar* was a vessel whose primary purpose was the mail. The African Steam Ship Company operated several such ships due to the high demand of connecting England with the colonial African outposts. The symbol of the company was affixed to everything on the ship. One night at dinner Olive looked at her plate to see, stamped on the bottom, Lady Britannia drawing back a curtain to reveal an African coastline ripe with palm trees. On the sandbank was a kneeling African woman, who offered up elephant tusks and colorful fruits. The curtain revealed the company motto, *SPERO MELIORA*, "I hope for better things."

The flag of the company whipped above the ship itself: white with a red cross and a yellow crown, imperial and sharp in its colors. Olive found life on the top deck to be delicious, though the heat was positively dripping. After just a day, her face was the color of a tomato. At night, the moon and stars were lovely and deep. Olive enjoyed it very much. She had her meals with the Talbots, and another man, a Mr. Coe, along with his wife. Olive found Mr. Coe most entertaining. He was enormous and overwhelming, a sharp contrast to his tiny wife. They were from the United States and were going to the city of Bauchi in northern Nigeria to live an isolated life that Mr. Coe was convinced would be good for business. His wife seemed game though she didn't say much.

Olive began to be conscious that people were talking about her. She could hear the tail ends of whispers and could see eyes being averted when she turned around. It was the newspapers. Before she left, the press had been filled with stories of the grieving young fiancée who was taking a trip to Africa to visit her beloved's grave. The Reuters story claimed that she was the first woman to attempt such a journey to Africa. One of the papers even said that Olive was making the dangerous trip because Boyd's spirit had visited her in a dream. When people did speak to her of it, they were usually sympathetic. Olive appreciated that. Other times, they just whispered. She would drop her head and keep walking, letting the dull sound of the sea take the foremost spot in her mind.

One night at dinner Mr. Talbot's wife told them a story about Africa. Dorothy Talbot—though Olive didn't call her that—was a slight bit older than Olive, and of a seemingly quiet disposition. She had a narrow face and pulled her dark hair up in a willowy bun. Olive found her to be very helpful at times, but her long-winded stories always seemed to emphasize the *ands*—and were beginning to get on Olive's nerves. Olive looked around—people were once again complaining about the food or the ship or some combination of the two. She didn't know if people were truly griping about these things or simply had nothing else to say to one another. As Mrs. Talbot went on about some sort of jungle plant, Olive's mind got very woolly. Mr. Coe got Olive's attention and showed her, under the table, a tiny pistol, very neat and light, rested against his thigh.

The ship's captain joined them and tried to guess Olive's age. He said

"Twenty-five . . . and I would not go beyond a full twenty-five!" Olive, who was thirty, could only smile weakly. After the captain left, Mrs. Talbot told them all how she had a dream that her husband was about to be married to a disagreeable girl. Mrs. Talbot found this very annoying, mostly because she said her dreams while on water always came true. She told them that she was sometimes able to see the surroundings of her previous existences. Olive knew that her husband must have been talking to her. She wondered if this was all a play because the Talbots felt so bored on this timeless ship. Olive very much wanted Mrs. Talbot to like her, but she seemed cold. At sunset the captain gathered them on deck where he threw a marine light overboard. They watched it float away until it was at least three miles off, barely a wet flicker in the darkness.

"Just now everything seems unreal to me," Olive wrote that night in her diary.

ON THE NIGHT OF AUGUST 24 OLIVE HEARD a shout from the upper deck. She ran up the wooden stairs. The ocean's roar was deafening. The massive darkness only heightened the wildness being held back by the dizzying motion of the swinging deck lanterns. Olive saw people pointing off the side of the boat. She edged closer to the outer rail. The water below looked like a swirling mixture of dark paint.

"Look!" someone shouted.

Olive stood at the port side of the ship, on the very edge of the maelstrom, and tried to see what was happening. Out in the water, very close to the boat, a large mass, black and shining, slowly pushed itself out of the deep. Water sprayed as the shape seemed to move. The people shouted and pointed again, much of it indecipherable over the crashing of the waves. White-capped water splashed in the raging storm. There was wind in the air, but that was all; it was as if the sky had reversed itself and they were watching some terrible storm taking place where the earth should be.

The water again began to mimic life, moving of its own volition. Olive wondered what terrible thing had been revealed—had someone jumped overboard? The water settled for a moment; there was nothing there. Had they stumbled upon a shipwreck? Her heart quickened. Or was it the sorcery of the sea itself, flaunting its own obvious threats?

"There!"

The black part of the waves surfaced again, faster now, as something emerged from the ocean. It moved slower as it pushed into the air, this time at a greater height above the waves. But this wasn't just a heave of foamy water; this was something else.

Olive strained her eyes until she saw the gigantic black gloss of the sperm whale slide and roll through the surf. She spied a single eye.

Olive was so astounded that she barely noticed how soaked she was getting. A whale! Then, as the beast slowly moved into the deep waters again, Olive saw something even more impossible unfold before her.

Olive watched in horror as two, then three, giant red ropes slowly extended themselves just above the surface of the water. They stopped ominously above the whale's back, swaying like strange trees in the wind.

Olive first thought it might be a cuttlefish, but someone corrected her. It was far too big. It was a kraken!

The thrashing tentacles wrapped around the whale and were attempting to squeeze out its great breath. Olive looked down into the waters and thought of the shopkeeper's words in that small store in Liverpool—*"You will lose your life."* She stood there, soaked and surrounded and significant only in her ability to witness. Olive watched the creatures struggle as long as she could, her eyes squinting in the spray, until the ship had passed far beyond the battle, or they had drifted deeper into the sea. Olive felt uncertain of the victor, or even if there was any loss to mourn.

Olive had not yet arrived at her destination. Yet already she had seen monsters.

4

THE ARRIVAL

*August 28, 1910: The SS Dakar Makes Its Way across the
Atlantic and Down the Western Coast of Africa,
Finally Landing in Nigeria at the Port City of Forcados*

O live woke up, pulled on her skirts, and ran up to the deck of the
ship. It took a moment for her eyes to adjust. She could see a long,
brown coast, slick with the ocean. On it lay a city with a seawall, a white
windmill, and a long wharf, all set below a gigantic blue sky. This was
Forcados, and it was their last stop. Olive saw a cawing cluster of seabirds
making their way to the coast, gliding on their outspread wings.

When the *Dakar* finally slowed, then stopped, Olive put on her new
pith helmet to make things official. But instead of jungles or elephants,
there were only boats and people, busy at their work. As Olive sat with
her luggage, Mrs. Talbot came to join her as her husband went to secure
their next passage. Olive tried to examine her face. Mrs. Talbot was still
an enigma. Their mutual awkwardness was disrupted when men came
onto the boat and started moving the bags. They also moved a large, heavy
wooden box that Olive had brought from home. Olive's heart fluttered
when she watched them handle it.

"Careful," she said to herself.

Olive heard some words in Hausa and craned her head, but she had no idea what they were saying. All she knew was that Africa was, as she had expected, beastly hot indeed.

By the time Mr. Talbot returned with a sheaf of papers in his hand, the heat had already reached a suffocating eighty-five degrees. Mr. Talbot had obtained the official documents from the governor's office that would grant them passage all the way to Maifoni. Olive looked at these papers, rolled up and white. As Mr. Talbot made his way up the gangway, Olive was grateful for her friend.

Mr. Talbot had not returned alone. He was followed by a meandering line of native men and boys, all wearing different lengths of loose, white clothing. Mr. Talbot directed them to the luggage. Olive knew that they would have to hire many more natives to complete their final expedition. Olive watched them pick up her heavy boxes onto their backs. Mr. Talbot referred to them only as "the boys."

Mr. Talbot led them off the ship to a different dock. The boys transferred their things to the *Sultan,* a smaller mailboat that would take them into Nigeria to the village of Lokoja. The paddle steamer was painted white in spots, made of wood, and had two thick stacks that chugged and puffed gray smoke into the sky. Mr. Talbot had a word with the rough-looking captain, showed him the documents, then slid them back into his inside pocket. Their passage on the *Sultan* had been arranged by no less than the acting governor of Nigeria, Mr. Charles Temple. Olive walked aboard, feeling quite important herself.

Below deck Olive squeezed through the narrow hallways to get to her room. She couldn't believe it when she opened the door and looked upon an actual bed. She had not been gone from home for very long, not really, but the sight of a genuine mattress looked heavenly to her. There was no other furniture in the room, and they would have to cook their own food, but Olive didn't mind. She unfastened her hair, removed her boots, and lay on the bed as it gave out a squeak. When the boat began to chug—in smooth river water—Olive fell quickly asleep.

. . .

THE DECK OF THE *SULTAN* HAD a small sitting area covered by a striped canopy. The air was a little cold, but Olive and Mrs. Talbot could watch the shoreline go by like an endless painting scrolling out before them. Unfortunately, what landscape they could see was little more than an uninterrupted stripe of brown mud. This was not the emerald interior that Olive had dreamed of. They heard the paddles slap the filthy water beneath them.

"Look," said Mrs. Talbot.

The river narrowed, and they began to see a colorful transformation as everything changed from brownish sludge to vibrant flowers; from pale bronze to bright green. There were matted tangles of creepers that dipped into the water and exquisite orchids on the ends of thin green arms, curling out of the leaves. Olive saw a tall, bare tree that was almost completely white. She had to look harder to see that it was blanketed with egrets, which turned to look as the boat moved by.

From under her hat, Olive found this version of Africa to be much more like the gardens she had left behind in Vinters. Flower blossoms surprised them from every angle. There were some plants she had not even the words for. As they passed, Mrs. Talbot would point them out with an expert's tongue: *"amaryllis," "yams," "cassavas," "bananas."* Variety colored everything.

Again Olive secretly inspected Mrs. Talbot, who now looked more at home on the damp boat, pointing out flowers and vines, than anywhere else Olive had seen her. At times Olive felt that Mr. and Mrs. Talbot must be perfect for each other, united by a romantic passion for natural biology and travel. But Mr. Talbot was always fiddling with his charts and instruments and was currently nowhere to be found. Mrs. Talbot pointed to the coast again.

The blur of green before them was interrupted by one, then two, and then whole clumps of thatched houses with palm-leaf roofs.

Natives.

Olive caught glimpses of her first native village—she didn't know of which tribe—washing their things by the river or moving in and out of their huts. Some of them looked up and stared, though most did not. Olive noticed that some of the houses had a carved statue or piece of cloth outside them.

"A juju house," said Mrs. Talbot, sensing her curiosity. These were the places they worshipped their gods.

As they continued on the river, Olive saw children swimming near the docks by some of the larger villages. Laughing, they swam in complete, naked indifference. Olive thought it was picturesque to see them in such a primitive state. As she watched, Olive spotted a black-and-green pebbled rock float up from the water near the swimmers. It was moving swiftly.

"Crocodile!" she gasped. The animal was headed right toward the children. Olive took a breath to scream, but the children had already spotted the creature and swam away without the slightest fear or care. The children seemed as at home in the water as they did on the ground.

Sometimes the jungle would flatten, and they would see a plantation, the trees cut and beaten down to the barest dirt. At several of these places, the *Sultan* stopped to unload mail, and Mr. Talbot would leave to get supplies, disappearing down the thin path that vanished into the green jungle.

As they traveled farther up the river, their deck time became limited due to the weather, which was now downright miserable. Olive looked up to the gray sky and felt the raindrops starting again. She pulled her coat on. They headed below deck to eat. Mr. Talbot had laid in a whole stock of steamer foods. Olive greatly disliked the foul, assorted native vegetables that seemed intent to choke her, but at least they had a salted ham. Olive was not overly fond of pork, but when combined with swizzled butter at a very high temperature, it was quite delicious. Afterward she stuck her head outside to find it raining wholeheartedly. The smell of their meal still filled the air.

"It rains here," Olive said with a laugh, "in a determined Britannic fashion."

When Olive was little, the family had traveled to Sweden to the famous eye clinic of Dr. Pagenstecher because her mother's eyesight was failing. Olive remembered the place as cold and quiet. One of the rules was that patients, nearly all of whom were blind, could not talk of their afflictions there. Nonetheless Olive's mother tried to make conversation with some of the other patients. One day lightning began to flash through the windows as a hard rain began to pour down outside. Mrs. MacLeod commented on the obvious thunderstorm, but she mistakenly used the word *Donnersturm* instead of *Gewitter*. Bellows of laughter from the other patients filled the room, which must have been especially painful to someone who could only hear them. Neither could she see Olive's face turn bright red. The doctor was able to stave off her mother's blindness, at least for a while, but her illness was spreading and soon after, she would begin to show signs of paralysis. But for now, as a celebration, the MacLeods traveled to Lucerne, where the girls loved riding the cable cars. They rode them up and down, as they creaked against the backdrop of white mountains. But when they went to check out of their hotel, their father didn't have enough money to cover the bill. So he paid for his and his wife's share and went home, leaving Olive, Flora, and their nanny at the hotel. Reginald sent a check back to release them.

WHEN OLIVE AND MRS. TALBOT finally got to leave the boat, the skies had cleared and the sun was blazing. Olive stepped slowly onto the ground, excited as they walked behind Mr. Talbot and some of the boys. When the trail opened into a native village, Olive saw men and women sitting on the ground, some on the bare dirt itself. Laid out before them were foods of all kinds: peppers and chilies, groundnuts, and tiny tomatoes, among other things. Olive saw colors and textures she could almost taste, and others she had no desire to.

Among the Hausa being spoken (it still fell past her ear like smooth stones), Olive also heard a constant clinking sound. She finally realized that most of the natives wore brass anklets attached to large round shields. The anklets were so big that when the wearers stood up, they had to keep their feet wide apart. Olive noticed Mrs. Talbot looking at these unusual ornaments with ravenous intensity. She knew the British Museum would be eager to have them. Mrs. Talbot tried to buy some of the anklets, but their owners refused to part with them. Though disappointed, Mrs. Talbot and Olive bought some food and trinkets and headed back to the boat. They were the last two people to leave.

Olive watched Mrs. Talbot walk ahead of her, back down the path to the river, her fingers swiftly plucking flowers beneath her. Olive began looking herself, longing to find success in the discovery of a bone or the hidden track of a rare beast. But all she saw was grass, which brought her to the sad realization that the commonest growth in Africa was the same as in England.

Mrs. Talbot continued to examine the landscape with dogged purpose. Olive watched as she sidestepped a particularly sharp rock. Olive's breath caught as a black snake wound its way from under the rock and between Mrs. Talbot's feet before it curled back into the undergrowth. Olive pointed.

Mrs. Talbot looked in time to see the end of the serpent disappear.

"A black mamba," said Mrs. Talbot. It was deadly poisonous. Mrs. Talbot looked at Olive's ankles and said that perhaps they should adopt the precaution of wearing higher boots.

Olive laughed, though not without anxiety. As they walked along, Mrs. Talbot turned to Olive and said to her in a direct manner that perhaps it would be best if they collected grasses instead.

WHEN DINNER WAS SERVED that night, Olive was overjoyed to see soup, fish, and chicken set out before her, their treasures of the market. As good as a week of salty pork had been, Olive enjoyed her supper with great pleasure. Afterward, during their Hausa lessons, Mr. Talbot surprised Olive by telling her she might call him by his first name, which pleased her though she tried very hard not to show it. They were off to the British fort of Lokoja. Mr. Talbot informed them that there was a chance that José Lopez, Boyd's right-hand man, might meet them there.

That night, with Mrs. Talbot snoring lightly, Olive took out the small strongbox once more. She inserted the little key and opened it, pulling out her diary. The notebook itself was small and brown, just a simple thing. The light was out, making writing very difficult, but Olive persevered; she had to. She wrote about her adventures on the ship and the black snake. When she was done, Olive closed her entry with two words:

Help me.

·5·

THE PROTECTORATE

September 3, 1910, Nigeria: Olive and the Talbots
Visit Lokoja, Their First British Fort, Encountering Some
Resistance in the Form of a Stubborn Man;
Olive Climbs a Mountain

As the waters of the Benue opened out into the wide Niger River, the *Sultan* came into view of Lokoja, the British-held town that was the next circle on their map. As the ship slid up to the dock, Olive saw dozens of natives, men and women, waiting at the shore. When Olive and the Talbots disembarked, the boys lifted their trunks and bags, leading the way up a narrow path that split through the deep grass.

Olive walked through the beautiful grasses and took photographs. She saw colors of brown, green, and sometimes purple that she wished she could capture, the low hills on the horizon only adding to the scene. They had reached Lokoja earlier than anticipated, and when the resident finally arrived, Bertram D. Byfield greeted them, especially Olive, in a grave manner that she supposed she would have to get used to. After passing under the gates, they walked up a cleared road to a large white house that stood on a hill, overlooking the rest of the camp. Along the way, Mr. Byfield made notes to himself of at least a half dozen things he saw that needed to be done. As the appointed administrator of the area, he had many responsibilities. He was also clearly one of those Englishmen, thought Olive, who was constantly on duty.

"This is the Governor's House," Mr. Byfield said, with a wave of his hand, obviously proud. "Acting Governor Temple has put it at your disposal." Mr. Byfield then introduced them to three other British officials: Mr. Elliot of the Marine Department, Mr. Stone, a British police commissioner, and Major Rose of the army. Olive felt as if she were back in London, shaking hands with men she didn't know, who nodded and muttered. The gentlemen, though smartly dressed, couldn't hide that they too were at the mercy of the pooling Nigerian heat. When she was done shaking their damp hands, Olive looked around but there was no immediate sign of José Lopez, whom she very much wanted to see.

They entered the large house and walked through its clean, well-swept rooms. The resident's home was finely appointed, with comfortable wooden furniture and dour official portraits. As Olive made her way through the large central living room, flanked by two large bedrooms, she saw vases of freshly cut flowers in water. Olive, who was used to gliding through rooms just like these at parties to make conversation, now found herself overwhelmed by such civility in Africa. Through the back doors Olive observed a roomy veranda that wrapped around the house, overlooking a sandy road. As Mr. Talbot talked with the men about affairs of state, Olive drifted outside in the hopes of a breeze.

Olive shielded her eyes to look down at the white bungalows below. She could see British soldiers, moving over the fields of deep green grass around the buildings. Olive looked harder. These were not wild fields, but a polo ground, a grass tennis court, and even a golf course. She could barely see the native village that lay past the bungalows at the base of Mount Patti, the small but striking mountain overlooking Lokoja.

The next day Mr. Talbot brought news that they were going to have an exceptional guest at dinner. Olive immediately thought of José Lopez, but Mr. Talbot shook his head. The acting governor himself was going to join them. Though he was normally based about two hundred miles to the north at Zungeru, he happened to be nearby and had adjusted his schedule to meet the travelers from England. Olive wasn't sure what to make of this. Mr. Talbot had written to him during the planning of their trip to ask for passage, but Temple had stalled, ordering them to postpone their expedition due to the rainy season. Olive had never heard of this man then, but—fearing the trip might have to be canceled—she was furious with him. But Mr. Talbot kept pressing the issue, and he had finally consented, though Olive feared it was reluctantly. Still, he had arranged their passage on the *Sultan*, which had been a great help. Perhaps he deserved a second chance.

When the acting governor, Mr. Charles Temple, walked into the residence, Olive was surprised that he was limping and used a dark cane. Mustached and slight, he did not seem a bully at all. As they ate, the talk at the table ranged from local politics to the warm weather, until it finally wound back to their trip. Mr. Temple asked if they had any plans other than visiting Maifoni. Before Mr. Talbot could respond, Mr. Temple said that any such action would be beyond the purview of their visit. This was more than advice; this felt like a threat. Olive had definite plans to visit Lake Chad and possibly even farther east. Mr. Talbot only nodded in the affirmative. "Good," said Mr. Temple. He looked up at Mrs. Talbot, bypassing Olive, and said that if it were up to him, wives should not be allowed to accompany their husbands to Africa.

"With all due respect," he added, returning to his soup.

Olive felt the blood rise in her cheeks. She was sure he noticed it, but she did not care. He probably said that because he had no wife to accompany him.

After dinner Olive stalked off alone to the adjoining room. She was sitting in a comfortable chair when the governor came and asked if he could sit down next to her. She nodded.

"I feel I must be straight with you," he said, "and explain my reasons for disapproving of wives coming out to Africa."

Olive was a bit surprised. He had seen her reaction. She shifted in her seat. Mr. Temple did not.

"Well," he said. "For one, they must be sent to big stations on account of the difficulty of their husbands either taking or leaving them to an unsettled part of the district. The problem with that is that appropriating them to these better stations comes down very hard on the unmarried men, you see." He paused. Olive could see the point, though she had no intentions of conceding it.

"In addition," he said, "any marriage short of complete success could be shown up at once under these climate conditions, when at home it might have jogged on comfortably enough. But here it's just too difficult."

Olive stared at him. She knew that he knew her story, his office had approved their visit, meaning that he was either totally without feeling, or simply cruel by nature. She felt her face flame again.

"Excuse me," she said, and left the room. Someone else swooped in behind her, to try to get his attention on another matter.

As Olive stood out on the porch in the breeze, she felt her face cool off. But she was still angry. It was then that she heard a sharp sound come down off the mountain. The noise was like a dog's bark, but with more of a rough echo to it. The noise seemed to crack off the very edges of the valley.

"Baboon," said Mr. Stone, who was framed in the door behind her.

He walked up next to Olive and looked up at the green and mysterious Mount Patti. He pointed to the low, flat peak. "They live," he said, "in such numbers in those hills and are so daring that they often hold the road, and a single man, though armed, dare not press past, for they are very fierce, and should he wound one of their number the whole pack would fall upon him."

It seemed that Mr. Stone was trying to scare her or impress her—or some odd combination of both. Either way, Olive was not scared by a man bragging about the prowess of a single ape. In fact, after the ghastly events of the evening, she felt an intense longing to climb that hill and see those beasts, every one of them in turn, no matter their snarling teeth. The howl of hyenas, the haunting cry of the chromatic bird—each fresh sound and sight added to her desire.

"I want to see them," she said defiantly. "The baboons."

"I'll arrange it," said Mr. Stone.

After the governor left, Olive again rejoined the party and walked up to Major Rose, commander of the British battalion at Lokoja, and asked if he might teach her to shoot a rifle. He very kindly agreed.

THE NEXT MORNING, just after dawn, Olive woke early and met Major Rose on the gun range. The major showed Olive a Lee-Enfield .303 rifle. He explained that its model designation was "MLE," at which she nodded.

"We call it Emily," he said.

Major Rose snapped the bolt open with his palm, then reloaded it with one of the shiny bullets that looked like long, golden teeth. Then he flipped his hand over in a continuous motion to force the bolt shut again, with a strong push with the heel of his hand. The major raised the rifle to his shoulder and held it tight to his cheek.

"The men call it Smelly," he said.

KRAK!

The major hit the target of the bull's-eye but was not close to the center circle. He showed Olive how the box magazine could hold ten cartridges. He loaded it up and pulled open the bolt again before snapping it shut and holding the rifle out to Olive.

The gun, made of black steel and walnut, was about four feet long and lighter than she had guessed. Olive pulled it up to her cheek just as the major had and stared through the rigid iron sight. She fired. Again. The trigger was difficult, but she continued shooting until there were no bullets left.

Olive lowered the rifle and peered down the range. Out of ten shots she had hit the target twice.

One was a bull's-eye.

The major pushed his hat up. "Beginner's luck," he muttered. By now, there were other soldiers at the range who were itching to try their luck against the lady. As they shot away, their results were far less precise than Olive's.

"After a while," explained the major, looking at his own missed targets, "the climate affects the eye, you know."

AFTER THEIR RETURN FROM THE MARKET, Olive and the Talbots had lunch outside with Mr. Stone and his wife at their home. They were talking of their upcoming trip to Mount Patti when a loud crash from the servants' quarters startled them.

Mr. Talbot jumped from his chair and ran up the porch, Mr. Stone and Olive close behind him. In the living room they saw two native boys, seemingly floating in the air. One of them was balancing on a log, another on a dresser. Shrieking in terror, they both pointed to the door to the kitchen.

"*Gamsheka!*" they shouted. For some reason, this Hausa word had stuck with Olive from the very beginning.

Cobra.

Mr. Talbot grabbed a polo mallet from the corner and made his way into the kitchen. Olive followed him, looking over his shoulder. She held back as Mr. Talbot poked under cabinets and around corners, but he couldn't find anything. The snake had made its escape through a corner somewhere out into the outside world.

After the house was deemed safe and the boys felt confident enough to touch solid ground again, Mr. Talbot stared coldly at Olive.

"You should not have joined in this search," he said.

The cobra was a deadly adversary. But now Olive feared that Mr. Talbot would feel the same way once they got out into the bush. She did not want to be left out of any adventures because of her sex. She vowed to visit the practice range again tomorrow.

That afternoon Major Rose took them on a tour of the prison, a small but sturdy building in the back end of the fort. As they walked in past the gates and guards, Mr. Stone told them they had fifty wardens on duty for the hundred or more prisoners, which allowed the inmates to be very comfortably treated. But as Olive looked across the large open halls, she saw something different. She saw natives, thin and withdrawn, huddled together in a place with no beds, but despite feeling great sympathy for these men she said nothing.

On the walk back, they did some looking for grasses and even signs of baboons, which Olive still hoped to glimpse. As they neared the residence, Olive noticed a little gray squirrel in the garden. It had a fuzzy white stripe running along its side. Entranced by the little fellow, Olive pointed him out to the Talbots. Mr. Talbot swiftly took his rifle off his back and shot the squirrel dead. Olive hardened her heart; she did not want to show emotion or weakness. But when Mr. Talbot walked over to skin the poor animal where he lay, Olive had to look away.

Early the next morning, with pink clouds still lingering in the high air, they set out to climb Mount Patti. Mr. Stone told them that Sir Frederick Lugard, the British colonial official who was one of the earliest visitors to the area, had a small bungalow at the summit that he used as a weekend residence. Olive looked forward to picnicking there, on the rooftop of Nigeria.

Of more immediate concern was what to bring. Olive was once again flustered about what to carry on this, her first field excursion. She eventually decided to bring water and some books. She imagined spending a lazy hour or two in the bungalow, indulging her reading in the quiet sun, while leisurely having lunch. She brought a chair in case there were hungry ants. Mr. Talbot watched Olive pack but said nothing she could hear.

As they walked up the rising path—it wasn't so steep as to be an actual hand-over-foot climb—the green jungle seemed to loom higher the farther up they went. Mr. Stone pointed out various features of the landscape, mentioning that lightning was very dangerous on the mountain because of the ironstone rock. At various points they made hard, hairpin turns on the path, as the mountain seemed to tilt on its axis. They saw no baboons, which made Olive sad, though they could smell their overpowering odor.

When they finally reached the top, Olive and Mrs. Talbot were mopping their brows with towels that no one had offered them, which Olive found unsurprising. Stopping at last on even ground, they stamped the dust off their feet and looked around.

Though there were no baboons, yet again, it was a magnificent sight.

The top of the mountain was almost perfectly flat, dotted by grass and brush. Stretched out in the middle was the guesthouse, a one-level structure made of a patchwork of irregular local stones. A great baobab tree stood to the left of the building, twisting even as it was still. The flat roof had a slight downward slant; the wooden door had brown shutters.

Olive walked inside the bungalow. At the far end of the large room stood two curved chairs, separated by a small table. Two photographs hung on the wall. One was a serious-looking, balding white man with a bushy walrus mustache, wearing a dark English uniform weighed down with a fruit salad of medals. The other picture was of a beautiful woman with short, curly white hair. She wore a dark dress, and her hands were folded around flowers. These pictures were of Sir Lugard and his wife, Flora Shaw. She had been a journalist when she was assigned to cover the British endeavor in that part of Africa. When Lugard first took her to the roof of Mount Patti, she looked out on the river below and proclaimed it "Niger-area," which she immediately shortened to "Nigeria." An Englishwoman had named the country they trod on.

Mr. Stone told them that Lugard had built the place in 1900, only a few years before the country became an official British protectorate. But the bungalow had a dual purpose. The site gave him an ideal place to see everything from boats to coming invaders. Olive looked out onto the plain herself, watching as the Benue swirled into the Niger, the sun mixing it all into gold.

As they made their way down the mountain, Olive experienced even more rips and tears to her stifling outfit. There were no baboons in sight, though at one point Olive was almost certain that she could hear one laughing at her.

"One thing we have learned," said Mrs. Talbot, as they stepped off the mountain, delicately wiping her shining brow, "is that neither of us brought suitable hunting costumes."

THE NEXT DAY OLIVE AND MRS. TALBOT went to the fort's supply store. Mrs. Talbot pulled out some spindles of military khaki and purchased them on the spot. She also arranged for a tailor. Later that afternoon, a man in a dirty frock coat arrived at the residence. Mrs. Talbot looked at the tailor disapprovingly but gave him the fabric anyway, together with a patterned white skirt and shirt that she wanted him to duplicate. When the man eventually returned, all their clothing was filthy with grime. In addition, the new items he had made were wholly original constructions. After he left, Mrs. Talbot held up one of the skirts and turned it back and forth.

"A barbaric job, Mrs. Talbot," said Olive, "completely devoid of symmetry."

Mrs. Talbot laughed. "Call me Dorry," she said.

"Well," said Olive, very pleased at this turn of events, "at least we have some variety. What part to make front, back, or side will be a matter for daily choice."

Later that day Mr. Byfield took Olive and the Talbots down the camp road to the native village outside the fort. At the market the vendors squatted in their rows of low stalls, shielded from the yellow sun. Native sellers hung their wares from ramshackle roofs or laid them out on the dirt. They sold mostly colorful fruits and vegetables, though they tried their best to sell Olive scent bottles—something she wasn't sure how to take.

The village marketplace at Lokoja was different from the others they had seen. Lugard had rearranged the lines of the market according to the plans of Sir Hesketh Bell, the governor on leave. The little market was, in fact, the perfect model English town, set in a plan of straight-lined streets and perfect right angles. As they looked at the wares, Mrs. Talbot tapped Olive's hand.

She looked up to see that a small crowd of natives from the market had assembled in front of them.

Olive reached for her camera.

A group of twenty had stopped to regard them. There were children wrapped in long, heavy blankets, woven with thick zigzag patterns and ragged at the edges. One girl wore her blanket just above her waist, her left hand perched crookedly on her hip. A necklace, bracelet, and head wrap were her only other accoutrements. Other girls wore thin scarves wrapped around their heads, their torsos completely bare. Some of the girls held tins with washing. The boys had their hair shaved except for a puffy mound down the center of their heads. They almost smiled. One wore his blanket all the way to his armpits, looking as if it had been hastily tucked in by his exasperated mother.

One little boy, somewhere around five or six, Olive guessed, had a tall tuft of hair rising from the center of his clean head. He stared at Olive with both hands on his hips. He was completely naked, and his tiny belly-button stuck out like a thumb. He had dark, daring eyes. The adults wore lighter robes and were tall. Most were bare armed; some had white head coverings.

Olive made the picture, trying to put the little boy in the center. She could not tell, for all the superior observation of the camera, whether he was barely smiling at her or being defiant. The photograph complete, Olive nodded and her subjects began to disperse. They seemed to have sat for a camera before, but she couldn't be wholly sure.

As Olive followed the Talbots through the market's various enchantments, she watched how her friends bargained for everything. Olive had some success, but wasn't nearly as proficient as Mrs. Talbot, who cut down prices like weeds. After some scent bottles were purchased, the sellers became sure that homemade calico was the next item they needed most. The material wasn't horrible, thought Olive, as she looked it over. Mrs. Talbot took it, turned it over again, and pointed to the words printed in red ink directly on the fabric: "Niger Company." This wasn't superbly crafted native cloth, it was from the official trade company of the British Empire.

When they were done at the market, Mr. Byfield arranged for them to meet the ruler of the tribe, Chief Abbiga, who resided nearby. Olive was excited; she had never met an African chief before. She couldn't wait to see his palace.

Mr. Byfield walked toward a small hut. There was an old man sitting outside, whom Olive thought was about seventy. She guessed he was a trusted adviser to the chief.

"I am Chief Abbiga," the man said.

The man had a small but full white beard that almost reached the top of his chest. Olive asked to take his photograph. He stood up straight, pushed his broad shoulders back, and hung his right hand on his walking stick, which was angled into the dirt.

The chief wore a cloth with white stripes, tied at the waist, leaving him an open, natural pocket for his left hand. His head was wrapped in a white cloth. He looked as if he had never worn shoes in his life. There were no shrunken heads or juju beads on his person, at least that Olive could see. He carried no weapons. She didn't know whether to bow or curtsy so she did an odd combination of both. The chief looked at her and sat down again.

Chief Abbiga sat in the dirt and held court. When he spoke, his English was perfect. He told them how he had traveled with the great explorer Heinrich Barth and had been with Adolf Overweg when he died. Olive had read of Barth, a German explorer whom some tribes called the Rain King. Overweg had been the first European to completely circle Lake Chad on a boat that he and his companions had carried on their backs across the Sahara. He died somewhere near Lake Chad after swimming in its cold waters. Abbiga had been Overweg's guide.

"Buried him deep-deep," the chief said, pointing downward, meaning far away from the claws and teeth of wild beasts.

Chief Abbiga then told them he had once toured Europe and met Queen Victoria. Olive was astounded at this. The chief said that at an official reception, the queen gave him the sum of forty pounds. After this generous act, each lady he shook hands with that night slipped two shillings, sixpence, or five shillings into his hand. The chief chuckled as he told the story. He also once dined with Kaiser Wilhelm II at his palace in Berlin with a party of two hundred guests. When they met, the kaiser thumped Chief Abbiga on the chest and said he was "a piece of black mahogany."

The chief remembered all the places he had been. He said he judged the places he visited by their wealth of produce. Olive was amazed at this man, chief of his tribe, who had traveled the globe and met royalty. He was clearly a great man, yet Abbiga's hut was small and his means seemed thin. Olive wondered if this was by choice, bad luck, or the orders of the British governor. Olive opened her mouth to thank the chief, but Mr. Talbot spoke first. The chief listened intently, with half-open eyes, to news of Mr. Talbot's projects. This went on for quite some time until Olive realized that she and Mrs. Talbot counted for exactly nothing at all.

AT HER NEXT RIFLE LESSON Major Rose had invited Lokoja's crack marksman, a thin, sour-looking fellow, to join them. But when Olive once again raised her rifle, shot her rounds, and again posted excellent scores, they tested her rifle and found its sighting false.

Olive thought she had never seen men brighten with such relief.

In the days that followed, as Olive got sharper and more confident on the range, Major Rose lent her the rifle to take on an expedition. Olive initially resisted, but the major explained that it was safer to have one. He placed it in her arms.

"Should emergencies arise," he said.

Mr. Talbot also gave Olive a small revolver. "Use the rifle for lion, the revolver for baboon," he told her. He then gave her a small tin of peppermints. He clicked it open. But instead of candies, the box was filled with familiar gold cartridges. "Bullets," said Major Rose. Olive put the weapon on her belt and the tin in her bag. She felt heavier.

Olive and the Talbots ate supper at the soldiers' mess hall. Olive expected a spartan affair, but it turned into quite a celebration. The band played Scottish tunes in her honor, and late in the evening Olive even tried to play the piano. Just as at Vinters, the red-haired Scottish girl was the center of the party. Olive feared her playing was quite dreadful but was relieved when Major Rose complimented her. As they laughed, she made him promise that if he ran into José somewhere in the interior, he might interview him for her. The major knew what she was talking about. Olive nodded many times and was very serious about this. He agreed.

Olive retired quietly to the residence. She wondered, as she often did, if people were being nice to her because they liked her or because of Boyd. Maybe it was the whiskey, but it all felt familiar in some strange, opposite way. After the news of Boyd Alexander's death first reached England, Olive dressed in black widow's weeds and became secluded. She mourned publicly at Vinters and at Swifts Place as a guest of his family. The newspapers wrote that Boyd's death was particularly heartbreaking because of its effect on Olive MacLeod, his new fiancée.

But what no one knew is that after Boyd proposed to Olive, she wrote him a letter. He received it just before he left for Africa.

November 4, 1908
6 Eaton Place

Dear Mr. Alexander
  It must be no.
  I cannot persevere in inflicting what amounts to the ruin of my greatest friend's life; and I think you are strong enough and noble enough to feel this for me—I had wanted to write and tell you so last week. . . . I tell you this so that no shadow of dishonesty may be between us.

I know that I am deliberately cutting myself off from all right to ask you anything, but will you please bear in mind that your life is a very valuable one and that you must not escape it without great object—I shall watch your career, though from afar with more than interest,

Good-bye.

Olive MacLeod:

6

A CORRESPONDENCE, PART 1

November 10, 1908, Eaton Place, London:
After Telling Boyd She Will Not Marry Him Because of
an Unknown Suitor, Olive Writes Him Again

Olive sat at her desk and debated breaking the rules. It had only been a week since she had written to Mr. Alexander and told him "It must be no" in regards to his marriage proposal. Olive knew that she must *not* contact him again, much less write to him about the same delicate matters. It was simply not done. But in the end, the need to explain herself outweighed decorum and she wrote him anyway, as she always knew she would, in a strong hand on manila paper.

November 10, 1908

Dear Mr. Alexander
  My other note has been misunderstood.
  I am not engaged to GGH and cannot be unless he succeeds in rous-ing love in me—I think I owe you this explanation though perhaps you never made this assumption.—I don't know you enough to tell whether

you would like to see me again before you start or not, but if you do, I shall be at 6 Eaton.

Olive Macleod:

When Olive posted the letter, she felt a mixture of fear and relief. It was true that when Mr. Alexander asked her to marry him, Olive was under another obligation. Her friend of many years, Mr. Hardy, had only recently declared his intentions toward her. He was a good, kind man. She had not yet told Mr. Alexander about it because it was complicated. She had planned to, but then he proposed.

Days passed and Olive waited for a reply to her letter. When it did not come, she wrote him again. Olive knew that Mr. Alexander was going to Africa soon and could not bear the thought of going unheard. Or perhaps he *had* heard her and now wanted nothing to do with her. She hoped that wasn't the case, though she assuredly deserved it. She had to explain herself. So she took up her pen and decided to write the truth.

November 23, 1908

Dear Mr. Alexander

You will be surprised to receive another letter from me and I feel very doubtful whether I am acting wisely and rightly by you in sending it, but I can't bear that you should go away in ignorance. . . . I had thought that I should see you but I see now that it is better we should not meet just yet.

You have roused in me a feeling I did not know I was capable of and though I should have wished to see more of you to test it I can now have little doubt what that result would be—only I feel it my duty to sacrifice you and perhaps myself to my great friend. You see he has cared for more than three years and though I only guessed it a few months ago I did allow the intimacy to continue—thinking that friendship was the best I had to give.

*His people . . . told me he was on the verge of madness and that any-
way his life would be wrecked—even assuming that he got over it in two
or three years (which they don't admit) he would be incapable of work
now, just at the time when his career at the bar hangs in the balance, I
felt it impossible to do otherwise than save him by saying 'no' to you. Now
that that fear is over, I am haunted. . . . Again I must ask for forgiveness.*

*I have thought so much that I have no more confidence in my
judgment,*

Olive MacLeod:

*For fairness sake I reiterate that my first letter to you stands absolutely,
and that I am free to yield to G now or later—as free as you are never
to think of me again; only I am very unhappy.*

Olive did not say "yes" to Mr. Hardy, though many thought she probably should have—she was almost thirty and he was well-positioned
as a barrister. But she did not rightly say "no" either. For though she
did, the endless roll of parties and nightly conversations kept them
together so that total separation was impossible. Olive did not want
to hurt her old friend. Perhaps she *could* say "yes" . . . someday? She
second-guessed what she was doing almost every waking moment.
But she knew that amid all of these tentacles, she had to turn down
Mr. Alexander.

Olive wanted to let Mr. Hardy off, but his people—his parents,
his brother Alfred, and others—would not hear of it. They told her
that Mr. Hardy would go mad. Olive thought this was probably true
given his disposition and it broke her heart. She agreed to the trial
period of staying at Eaton Place until March to see if Mr. Hardy could
be someone she could love. When Olive told the Hardys about Mr.
Alexander, they said it was fine to write him about other matters, but
nothing else.

She had made a promise, they said.

. . .

AS DECEMBER CAME AND BEGAN TO CHILL the streets of London, Olive had still not heard from Mr. Alexander. She knew he was leaving any day now. Or, she feared, he might have already gone, having never read her words. This thought made her very sad, though she wondered if it wasn't for the best.

Then she received a letter.

December 9, 1908

Dear Miss MacLeod

I know the kindness of your heart and that you will not resent my sending you these few words to say Goodbye. It gives me pleasure and makes me forget for a little while that my heart is bleeding. As I am going away, I feel I have a privilege to speak, I implore you by that sacred feeling which exists between us, not to sacrifice your happiness. You will bring woe upon yourself and perhaps upon your children.

I know that in your heart you have some spark of feeling for me. Let me breathe upon that gently that I may start it into a flame. You asking me not to forget you is beyond my power.

I leave for Liverpool on Friday and the next morning for Africa. Would it be too much to ask you to send a message? It would help me so much upon my journey.

Goodbye and may there be for you bright days in store.

Boyd Alexander

Olive read his words many times. His heart was *bleeding*. She had meant everything she said—she could not promise him anything. She could not. She had to be steadfast.

She wrote him back the very next day.

December 10, 1908

Dear Mr. Alexander

I am glad you wrote to say good-bye—and I should have written anyway to wish your expedition great success and big results, and yourself happiness throughout it. Please enjoy it and carry out all that you wish it to do without thought of me—neither prolonging nor shortening it on my account. I don't pretend that I shall not be anxious, but I am resolved not to worry—and shall try to believe, as you do, in Destiny.

If you like to do so will you write me news of your expedition from time to time, but I only ask this in the trust that you will not do so if you think it better not—do not propose a correspondence as it would not be fair either to you or GGH, til I regain my freedom of action towards him in March, so I will not write myself—you know my position so I need not repeat it, but I will remember your advice and will try to act for the best—as long as you care so much it is not only myself to sacrifice and that makes a difference. He cares very much, and I had not thought your feeling could have had enough foundation to outlive my conduct towards you. Please forgive it. I do so want your expedition to be untroubled.

Olive McLeod:

Olive sent off her letter, expecting that it would be the last she would hear from Boyd Alexander for some time.

The night before he left for Africa, Boyd was at his club in London, making last-minute preparations for his trip when he realized that he had left certain papers back at the British Museum. He gathered up his coat and scarf and plunged back into the snowy cold. He walked up the street, only half-aware of the wintry surroundings, when he looked up and saw her.

It was Olive, bundled up, in boots, walking up toward him.

December 18, 1908

Dear Miss MacLeod

You have healed my wound and I shall go forward strong again to carry out my work. I know that you have been troubled—but be only yourself and you will see how things will shape themselves of their own accord for your happiness. Your expression of sympathy for my work and success has touched me deeply. It is rare to find sympathy applied in this way. It is, to my mind, the highest form—for is it not easier to sympathize with a friend's trouble than with his welfare? We are always more prone, I think, to take this course. It is in fact the most primitive form of sympathy and one we possess in common with the life of animals.

Since I feel that you are behind me, giving me energy and hope to carry out this expedition, which may I say not only belongs to me but to you also? I will tell you all its details from start to finish . . . I feel hopeful that I shall make some good discoveries.

Let me venture to hope that the dark clouds have parted and that sunlight is beyond. I long to hear something of your movements and can only hope that when March comes around, you will be able to write me a letter.

It was a curious thing meeting you the other day in London. To go to the Museum at that hour is a thing I have never done before—Then who should I see coming towards me alone on the pavement but you! That surely could not have been mere accident! Our lives, I feel, have met, and no power but one can break the bonds between us.

Boyd Alexander

Throughout the holidays, Olive felt her connection with Mr. Alexander to be a source of secret warmth, even though she knew it must stay hidden. The Hardys were still holding her to her promise and she had every intention of giving Mr. Hardy a chance. But she very much liked writing to Mr. Alexander, even though she had no idea where he was, or even if her letters would reach him. She wrote anyway.

January 1, 1909

Dear Mr. Alexander

You will be surprised to get a letter from me, after my telling you that I could not write till March; but as you want to hear I thought it better to insist—and I have told the Hardys I am going to write—which I shall do every fortnight. They won't let me off my promise and, as it is difficult to write with constraints you must forgive dull letters.

It was a great pleasure getting your letter and hearing that you were happy and looking forward to your work . . . are you doing survey as well as ornithological work? You see I am so hopelessly ignorant . . . how interested I shall be in any news you have to send me—and to plead that you will tell me the bad as well as the good, though I trust there may be none of the former. It is worrying if one thinks there is anything kept from one.

Olive MacLeod:

His next letter came soon after.

December 23, 1908

Dear Miss MacLeod

There are a few lines to remind you that you are always in my thoughts. May I hope that sometimes you think of me!

This is the first place we touch—on the African coast, making the eighth time for me. The sight of black faces again almost gives me a thrill of pleasure and I somehow feel that I have never left them . . . the last time I saw it was with my brother—and the sight of it now makes me sad. Now once more, another life whom I love has entered into mine. Do not forsake me, while I am away.

Boyd Alexander

By the time Olive received this last letter, things had changed. She sat down and hurriedly wrote her response. It was imperative that she post it so that he could read it as soon as possible.

January 16, 1909

Dear Mr. Alexander

    I had been thinking of you and how deeply you would feel your brother's absence . . . but one would not be without a single recollection in spite of the pain & longing they bring with them, and your associations with him must be very precious. I wish I could have known your brother.

    I think that when you come back my answer may be different. It would not be fair to either of us to promise that it should, for we may find on closer acquaintance that we are mistaken in each other; though I cannot think that is very likely.—Anyway let us try and see—unless indeed you still want a definite answer at once. Are you amazed at these continuous changes or are you more than ever convinced that vacillation is the keynote of my character?

    Yesterday I got a letter from GGH releasing me from my promise, which was to give him every chance of rousing my love till March, when we return to Vinters. I don't know how much of the situation was explained to you, for I wanted to write you everything, but did not think it fair to do so. Now I will tell you, but only briefly as it hurts so much and I am longing to be happy.

    I did not know he cared for three years. Therefore I felt guilty towards him, and I was so ignorant as to think you and I could both stifle our feelings without long pain—so I yielded to my fear for him and told him that though I loved you, I would try and crush it out of existence.

    But that of course I could not marry him until that was done. Then I gradually learnt that I was attempting the impossible. The Hardys told me it was natural and what they had reckoned on and that after you had gone I should return to my old frame of mind: so they would not let me off. Don't think me selfish about it, for they were genuinely concerned it was for my happiness as well as for G's—Now he has written me a delightful letter, saying he will not write to nor see me "for a long time," but that whatever I say or do he will not give up hope. It was a perfect letter, in strength, dignity, and love—and it makes me very sad to cause him so much misery, but I cannot help rejoicing at being free once more to say what I will to you. I am afraid I behaved very badly towards you and I can only ask you to forgive me; but I truly thought you would get over it soon.

It has been hell, but now we need only think of what is hopeful and nice—When you know please give me some idea as to the probable date of your returns so that I may have that to look forward to.

I wrote to ask your father for your address—I am trying to pluck up courage now to ask him about your plans—whether you have gone on your own or for the Geographical Society or who—?

I stayed in London till the 7th, to see Flora and then went North to a clan meeting with father . . . People told one another their intimate interests, sad and happy, quite simply just because they were sure of sympathy and felt one ought to know. The only person I found it hard to be cordial to was the clan historian, for he recited a crushing ballad. I will quote you two lines

LIKE CUNNING WOLVES WITH RUDDY MAWS
ALL RAVENING FOR THEIR PREY.

Aren't they awful?

We motored into this function on the most superb night, Clear, cold, with a full moon and brilliant stars—and in the distance the mysterious lap of the sea. It was wonderful. We were staying with the Asquiths, who are amongst my greatest friends . . . I look forward to their becoming yours too—perhaps.

Olive MacLeod:

7

ON THE HUNT

*September 1910: The Party Makes Its Way Across
Nigeria into German-Held Territory; the Company Is
Hired; Olive Goes on Her First Hunt;
Whispers of Evil in the East*

Olive adjusted her shirt, but it was not cooperating. She tucked in the folds and pulled on the sleeves, which seemed to only make things worse. She desperately wished for a full-length mirror. After so many parties and government officials, Olive was ready to get on with it. After a last trip on the *Sultan*, they had made their way to Yola and were soon to embark on the long road to Maifoni. From now on most of their journey would be on horseback, canoe, and foot. Since they were taking to the march, Olive thought it was time she looked the part. She put on the khaki suit that was made for her by the odd tailor in Lokoja. Olive wasn't sure how it looked, but her options were few. So she put on her hat, took a breath, and walked outside into the sweltering heat.

When Olive emerged, Mrs. Talbot looked up. The material of Olive's outfit was fine, but for some reason there seemed to be three sides to her skirt rather than the usual four. The shirt was so uneven that the neck had to remain unfastened for it even to sit on her shoulders. Olive looked up hopefully, but as soon as she saw Mrs. Talbot's face, she knew. Olive sat down in defeat as Mrs. Talbot stifled a smile combined with a look of pity. Mr. Talbot looked at Olive, but his countenance didn't reveal much, though it seemed, for an instant, that he might start to laugh. But he coughed instead, saving all involved.

Yola was a fascinating city. Situated on a deep plain, its market was bursting with fruits and vegetables. Along the way Olive stared at a tattooed woman and watched as one man shaved the head of another. All the natives wore loose-flowing white robes. Olive saw a baobab tree, gnarled, twisted, and winding, that was said to be ten thousand years old. She took photographs and bought cloth of a very high quality.

They dined that evening with Mr. Holst, who worked for the Niger Company. As Mr. Talbot related their plans to journey to Maifoni, Mr. Holst warned that two black merchants had recently been found murdered on the road. "It is very dangerous," he said, as there was silence in the room. Mr. Talbot looked at Olive and then told Mr. Holst about Boyd Alexander and why they were going there. Mr. Holst looked up in surprise. He put his napkin down, placed his head in his hands, and wept bitterly, right there at the dinner table. He had known Boyd well and always found him to be a good and honest man.

In Yola, Mr. Talbot had been at work hiring the remainder of the company. After a few days Mr. Talbot had engaged a full complement of specialists and carriers. Olive wanted to take a picture before they left, so she lined them up, side by side, on the edge of the road. Cooku was to be their cook. He was young and wore dark high pants and a khaki shirt with a white belt. His hair was soft and grown out. Cooku was not his real name, but that was the one he kept giving them. Momo was the interpreter, who was ironically very quiet. Situ was hired as their wilderness butler, who would attend to everything that they required. Tall and sharply thin, he wore white shorts, a white shirt, and a perfectly tied belt. He wore a small pith helmet to indicate his high role in the company. He was accompanied by a very likable boy who served as his adjunct, who was almost swimming in his white shirt and high pants. When Mr. Talbot asked him for his name so that he could add it to the official retinue, the lad answered that he knew himself only as "Small Boy" and became troubled when Mr. Talbot pressed him for another name. Standing next to him was Mandara, who was slightly older with a clean shaven head. Moussa, even taller, stood next to him. They all wore white.

Mastaba was a grown man who was bald, of strong build and medium height. He wore a flowing white outfit with sleeves, shirt, and long pants. His real name was Mustafa. He had Anglicized it for the party's benefit, but the end result was hard to perceive. Mastaba knew many languages and would function as the party's diplomat—their headman—when they reached the outer villages. Olive knew they would be relying on him a great deal while on the march, and she could see that Mr. Talbot was already talking to him often about official party business.

Kukaua was an ex-soldier whom Mr. Talbot had hired back in Forcados, though Olive did not know which side he had fought for—or even in which war. He was lean and his head was clean-shaven. He wore darker clothes, greens and tan, in accordance with his job: He was going to be the gun boy. His orbit was Mr. Talbot alone, and his job was to clean, load, and supply him with his rifle when needed. Olive imagined that it had taken Mr. Talbot quite a long time to select this man for this role.

A cook's mate and a washerman completed the party, along with Moussa, Olive's horse boy. Washerman, for that's what they knew him as, was young, and wore a collared, long-sleeved brown shirt with ankle-length pants. His wife was beautiful; she wore a narrow dress with a scarf and a decorative head covering. She played with her hands in her lap. Olive found her cheerful and kind; she had already contributed greatly to all the boys' comfort.

Everyone in their service was paid varying wages according to their job. Olive knew that their interpreter earned thirty-three shillings a month, a significant amount. At fifty shillings a month, Cooku received by far the biggest wages of the party, which Olive hoped would be worth it. The rest of their equipment, food, supplies, and everything else—including the large wooden crate they had brought from England—would be carried by the sixty or so other locals they had hired as carriers. These boys would form the long string of humanity that would be following them into the jungle—a group that would change and grow as they burrowed farther into Africa and hired new carriers for each new region they would cross.

As she liberated her feet from her stiff boots, Olive breathed a sigh of relief. She prepared to sleep in a tent again for only the third time in her life. The mosquitoes were already massing: She could hear their hum go in and out of her ears. Olive was glad she had taken her five grains of quinine, though that didn't stop the tiny legions from biting, sometimes even despite the net. As she settled into bed, Olive felt a sticky, bulbous mass against the small of her back. She jumped up and turned to find a great fat frog blinking up at her. She touched the slimy beast, recoiled, shouted, then picked up the frog and threw it outside the netting.

She felt bad at first, but then, once she spotted it safe, took great delight in watching it jump around just outside the net. Its friends soon joined, before he disappeared into their swell of identical forms and sounds. Soon they all began to try to jump over the part of the lamp that was about five inches tall, which they attempted again and again. Like tiddlywinks, Olive thought. As she watched, she realized that they were jumping over the lamp in hopes of gobbling up the insects attracted by the light. Olive's clothes, folded nearby, were covered in them. It became less fun after that.

Olive watched until she heard a hyena laugh, far across the plain. She heard a baboon grunt too, quite a bit closer, though enveloped by the darkness. Apparently she would only *hear* a baboon in Africa. Olive then did something she had avoided until now: She took her revolver, loaded it, and placed it under her pillow. It gave her some discomfort at first, but she fell asleep soon after.

The next day, as they began their preparations to march, Mr. Talbot received a telegram. Since they were soon going to leave the primary Nigerian mail route, this delivery was probably going to be their last for some time. After signing for the telegram, Mr. Talbot read it and put a hand to his head. He called over Olive, his wife, and Mastaba. He gave his wife the telegram, which was from Governor Temple.

The governor had wired Mr. Talbot to forbid him to map the area past Yola. This was problematic because that job was the party's official reason for being there. Even worse, the governor forbade the ladies to go anywhere that a military escort was required. When Olive asked where that might be, Mr. Talbot answered that the main road to Maifoni was one of those very places. Mr. Talbot looked out to the east. The governor had effectively barred them from going to Maifoni. Olive thought of the frail Mr. Charles Temple and felt great fury toward him. To make matters worse, he intimated that the expedition was to bear all its own expenses while in the area.

They spent the entire rest of the day trying to make other plans. That night Olive removed her unwieldy, disproportionate dress. She felt it was funny how the government was expecting them to do at once everything on their own and yet nothing at all. It was absurd. Olive thought about it some more and let her better self win; she regretted the ill feeling that was obviously behind Governor Temple's decision, though she surely could not understand it.

They could not take the road to Maifoni, that much was clear. But the governor had not said anything about the place itself.

They just had to find another way to get there.

BY THE NEXT DAY THEY HAD FOUND a boat willing to take them up to Garua, a German fort from which they would attempt the march to Maifoni on a different path. Most of the carriers would walk and meet them there. Governor Temple had said that the ladies couldn't march on the road; he hadn't said anything about their carriers. The country was more unsettled, and the way more difficult, but it was still a way. No doubt the governor would catch up with them eventually, for he had many eyes in the country, but for now at least the party would start on its own. Olive found it exhilarating, though she was still somewhat fearful of the way they had been loosed into Africa, both officially and financially.

"When you get home, you ought to write a book," Mr. Talbot said to Olive, as the sun finally set, "if only for the sake of hard cash."

Olive scoffed at the thought: "Think of the humiliation if someone read it!"

The boat voyage to Garua was uneventful. When they disembarked, Mr. Talbot noted that they were now in the Kamerun, the peak-shaped spike in the map that was held by the Germans. But as courteous as the Germans were, the party wasn't going to stay. Mr. Talbot found out there were three patients in their hospital with blackwater fever, a very severe form of malaria. The German doctor, Herr von Rankin, showed them his laboratory, a dark place that smelled like wet leaves. "We are working on a means to defeat the insect tribes," the doctor said. There was a long table filled with fat African toads, croaking and pulsing. He released a clear jar full of mosquitoes, and the toads proceeded to use their tongues to eat them, provided they didn't have to move.

The company was finally ready to set off on its first march when they realized Kukaua was missing. Hearing a strange, animal-like sound, Mr. Talbot found him hiding behind a tent. There was a woman next to him. The noise got louder. Was a lion cub nearby? Mr. Talbot shifted his eyes. There, in the arms of the woman, was a small infant—a *piccan*—crying and making faces. It was a baby girl.

Kukaua stepped forward. He explained that the *piccan* was his. He had smuggled the girl and his wife on board the *Sultan* to take them back home to Maifoni. That was his home—and where they were going.

Mr. Talbot shook his head. It would be unconscionable to subject such a small child to the long marches they were going to attempt. Mr. Talbot shook his head again, even more emphatically this time. It was out of the question.

Olive regarded the brown-haired baby, who seemed, in her own way, very philosophical about what was happening to her.

The mighty soldier Kukaua clasped his hands, dropped to his knees, and pleaded with his employer. Olive looked at Mr. Talbot. He narrowed his eyes.

Finally he agreed, but only if Kukaua would engage a man—on his own coin—to carry the baby while they were marching. Olive understood. Kukaua was being paid twenty-five shillings a month, so he could afford it. Perhaps Mr. Talbot had just decided that he could not go forward without his gun boy.

Kukaua was grateful. Olive and Mrs. Talbot spent some more time with the baby. Not long after they returned to their preparations, however, Mastaba came stomping up to Mr. Talbot with a furious look on his face, pointing behind him. Apparently Kukaua had given the baby to Mastaba with the command that Mr. Talbot wanted him to carry her. Mastaba was not pleased, but Mr. Talbot quickly fixed things.

Olive got onto her horse, her *dohki*. He seemed like a gentle-enough creature. She was pleased to start riding because her boots had begun to hurt a little. They would probably loosen up. Olive was helped up and the horse trotted forward, but then took off at a terrific speed. Olive lost her hat, and her red hair began to fly dangerously away from its loosening bun. Olive stiffened but stayed on her horse, which everyone found to be quite impressive. When the horse stopped, it seemed the worst of it was over. Olive sighed, trying to fix her hair.

They hadn't even started yet.

OLIVE HELD HER RIFLE STEADY and trained her eye along the long barrel, just as she had done at the fort in Lokoja. But there was no thin paper bull's-eye ahead of her. There was only grass swaying in the wind, and the fear and threat of what might be sneaking up behind it.

Olive scanned the grass ahead of her with the rigid aiming sight at the end of her rifle. She settled herself, became quiet, and very gently nudged the gun an inch or two closer through the air. Olive felt her finger along the trigger, curved out like an elephant ear.

They had been on the march for a few days. They were sleeping in tents and eating chop, usually *garri,* a powdery, sour dish that differed from day to day. Olive had finally found a way to make her dress work but it was getting dirtier by the hour. It was all incredibly tiring and Olive was sore in every muscle, but they were finally moving.

When the sun broke that morning, slowly flooding over the bleached grass, Mr. Talbot and some of the boys decided to go hunting. Olive invited herself along. Mr. Talbot gave her a look that meant she should stay in the back with his wife. Olive thought of the cobra incident. She bowed under her hat and followed with her new rifle. The boys took the lead.

The sky was bright blue and made the spare trees more solid somehow. Olive followed along the narrow path that disappeared into the hall of dry grass. Olive looked for tracks in the earth but saw only clumpy dirt. This was a language—the hunt—whose vocabulary she didn't know yet.

The boys however, were much more fluent. They easily picked out the tracks of a Senegal hartebeest, a gazelle-like creature with smooth striped skin. Olive watched as the boys split off the path into the thick undergrowth in search of it. The grass was now five or six feet in height, so thick at times that Olive couldn't see over it.

The party, separated into a forking pattern, still moved at the same pace. They walked forward, slowly and with purpose, their heads turning as they searched for movement, for eyes, for muscle. Then they heard it. They all heard it: a low, rising sound that seemed to start at their feet and fill the open air with an almost electrical charge. Olive had never heard the sound before, but she knew exactly what it was.

This was the sound she had heard in the back of her head ever since this whole enterprise began. She had, of course seen them lying lazily in the zoo and had read of them in stories. But hearing the roar here, in the open, in the world, was an entirely different experience. The sound she heard, loud and echoing, wasn't a response: It was a volley. They were trespassing on the lion. In an instant all thoughts of dinners and social engagements and polo grounds were gone.

Everyone became still. Olive crouched, her skirts in the dirt and her eyes trying to see through any breaks in the grass. She couldn't see Mr. Talbot or the boys—were they still ahead of her? Where had the roar come from—from which side? She almost wished it would sound again. Olive held her .303 up against her chest and lined it up to her eye again. It smelled of oil and smoke; her hard hat kept the sun from her eyes.

Ahead of her, Mrs. Talbot dropped to her knees. She searched her belt until a look of surprise and horror seized her face.

She had forgotten her pistol.

Mrs. Talbot motioned for Olive to give her a revolver. Mrs. Talbot's wrists weren't strong enough for the rifle. Olive paused for a second, her eyes on the grass in front of her, then slowly lowered her rifle to the ground. She unholstered her revolver, grabbed the small tin of ammunition, and slid it to Mrs. Talbot in the dust, the gun flashing in the sun.

Olive watched as Mrs. Talbot placed the revolver on the ground, then tried to open the tin. Her hands were shaking. Meanwhile Olive had raised her rifle to aim at the grass directly in front of her friend. Mrs. Talbot finally opened the tin and let out a loud gasp. She showed it to Olive.

The tin was filled with peppermints.

The grass in front of them began to move. Mrs. Talbot clutched Olive's hand.

A dark shape passed through the curtain of dry grass. It was Mr. Talbot. He gave them a harsh look, one equal with any lion's, and bade them forward with a gesture of his hand. There was no lion here, at least not close by.

Mrs. Talbot showed the tin to her husband. He protested complete innocence; It must have been a mistake. Or an unfunny trick of the boys. Mr. Talbot was very credible, but Olive still couldn't be sure that he was trying to keep her away from the more dangerous aspects of their expedition. Perhaps he had another motive, or perhaps he just feared her having a gun.

They continued to march. The ground soon began to give more, as it become soft and marshlike. There were some peaked limestone hills nearby as the hunting party made its slow way up to look down on the prairie below. They saw an even more desolate landscape—small hamlets nestled in tiny clearings in the foliage. Though very low, the hills seemed very sharp.

They never saw their lion. Olive and Mrs. Talbot swore up and down that he had been hidden in the grass just ahead of them. Mrs. Talbot remarked that they had been lucky. She had obviously not expected a lion on their first hunt; neither had Olive.

AS SHADOWS BEGAN TO FALL, Mr. Talbot did not waste the opportunity and succeeded in felling a great many birds from the air. When he spotted one flying above, he would stop, still as stone. His long rifle would angle upward, sweep through the air, and—*KRAK!*—a dark-colored shape would fall fast from the sky.

Immediately the boys ran off into the brush grass to find the murdered birds. Olive watched all this carnage and saw only two birds escape Mr. Talbot's gaze. His hunting was precise and exacting, but it was also methodical and time-consuming. The invisible lion had been more exciting.

When they finally returned to camp, Olive was struck by how professional their little enterprise had become. There were tents, a fire, and provisions and supplies stacked everywhere in their bustling kingdom. As they settled back into camp, Mr. Talbot asked for a volunteer to clean and dress the birds he had just shot. Apparently, when he was last in Nigeria, his sister-in-law had done the grisly task and he now needed a replacement. Mr. Talbot was only the executioner, it seemed.

Olive had made a determined promise to herself that she would not be squeamish about anything on the expedition. She wanted to try new things, to be unafraid.

"Me," said Olive.

The boys and Mrs. Talbot turned to stare at her. Mr. Talbot nodded, and Olive made her way to the butcher's table set up near the central fire.

His shirtsleeves rolled up, Mr. Talbot began a demonstration. He reached toward his belt and took his knife, a foot-long razor-sharp blade, and pulled a large, hideous gray bird over to him. He turned it over and blew on the soft feathers to expose the pale skin beneath. He cut swiftly into its breast. Olive watched as his blade slid, with some resistance, down the length of the bird. Mr. Talbot then reached in and pulled out a tangled clot of viscera while Olive observed, determined not to be affected by the blood and gore. Mr. Talbot removed something from the neck before setting the red knife down. He pushed the next bird in front of Olive as if it were some grisly meal.

Olive took up the knife and used it to push into the black-feathered flesh. The blood came out in a spurt, not the rivulet it had with Mr. Talbot.

"Too deep," said Mr. Talbot immediately, grabbing her hand. His tone was instructive. He slid the knife out of her hand in one swift motion.

"Trust more to your nails than to the knife," he said, as they both stood over the still bird.

He showed her the technique again, which did not give Olive any sort of impetus to continue.

Olive took the knife again. Mr. Talbot helped Olive in certain tricky spots, but by the time they were done, it was obvious to all who watched—which was most of the party by now—that the prospect of Olive becoming any good at this task was a remote one. Blood and feathers were everywhere. Olive suggested she practice on the fowls they were to eat for dinner, but Mr. Talbot seemed to think that far too risky. Mr. Talbot thought for a moment, then called over Mastaba, who thus became the new official bird dresser. As she stepped away, Olive thought Mastaba might have cast her a glance. She wondered if he knew that even as Mr. Talbot was instructing her, she had disobeyed as much as she dared under the scrutiny of his gaze. Mastaba seemed to understand, just as Olive now did, that Mr. Talbot, for all his expertise, would sometimes have to be ignored.

OVER THE NEXT DAYS the group traveled through territories that had recently been redrawn as a result of negotiations in Morocco, among the great European powers. The Kamerun protectorate, held by the Germans, extended to the east. With the new concessions, some of the invisible lines that separated these areas would shift, though the country itself would remain the same.

Just as important as the land were the African waterways. Traveling by river opened swifter commercial possibilities for the colonists. The French had recently begun using the route Olive and the Talbots were now traveling—up the Niger and Benue to Léré. This trip took less than two months as opposed to a lengthy and dangerous land march that could sometimes take up to six months. The river route was controlled at different spots by the British and Germans, but treaties had opened the route for commercial use. Unfortunately, the river was only passable for a mere few weeks every year after the rainy season.

Mr. Talbot led them, followed by Aji, his horse boy. Kukaua was close behind, as always, along with Momo, the interpreter. Mrs. Talbot was next, with her horse boy, Jimba-Giri, pushing her horse from the rear. Next came Olive, followed by Moussa. He was the youngest but was very vain. At every new village he adopted the local fashion of beads or necklaces. Jimba-Giri was not always helpful, and always demanded some small reward for a job done. But he picked flowers for Mrs. Talbot, which went a long way toward assuaging her frustration with him.

Olive found herself riding next to Mr. Talbot and decided to take the opportunity to ask about Ali Dinar.

Mr. Talbot paused a moment, then began to talk, his eyes facing forward. He told Olive that Dinar was on good-enough terms with the

British. He paid them a yearly tribute of cattle, but he communicated only in letters and no British official ever entered Dar Fur. The new worry was what Dinar might do now that the French had taken Abechir in Wadai, which was adjacent to Dar Fur. This act would be seen, almost certainly, as one of encroachment. Dar Fur contained several million people. British intelligence reports estimated that Ali Dinar had an army of at least twenty-five thousand men, with at least ten thousand guns.

In the uncertain days after the fall of the Mahdi, Dinar had been ruthlessly proactive. He assassinated a sultan, then took his place. A Mohammadan, his army was made up almost entirely of slaves. There were rumors that he had a magic sword with a hilt made of walrus ivory. It was said that a magic square was inscribed on the gleaming sword itself, along with several engraved couplets that praised the blade's skill in battle.

There were also miracles ascribed to him. One day, while Dinar and his party were hunting, a crazed man approached them with a spear. Proclaiming himself the newest incarnation of the Mahdi, the man claimed he would bring justice to all the world. When he tried to attack them, Ali Dinar used his powers to make the man's spear arm wither and become useless. Dinar questioned him; was he the Mahdi?

"I am undoubtedly the Mahdi," the man replied, "who am to appear at the end of time."

Dinar ordered his men to beat him with clubs until his flesh resembled *kufta*, a type of meat pounded in a mortar. Mr. Talbot became quiet. There were other miracles and sorceries ascribed to the sultan, but they were too obscene and immoral to repeat.

Mr. Talbot remained silent. Olive could sense that he was done, or that he wanted to be, so she thanked him and slowed down, her mind full of fear.

THE PARTY WAS MARCHING ALONG the Bulo River when they noticed it was starting to rise. The boys all moved behind the horses and began lifting their tails. Olive thought this was to keep the poor animals dry, but when she watched one of the boys accidentally fall backward into the water, she directed Moussa to leave her horse alone. He bowed, then moved to the front of her horse to lead it by the bridle. As soon as they began to move forward, Olive felt something fly up against her back. She turned around, in annoyed curiosity. The tail of her horse had swished back and forth to cover her shirt and skirt with thick stripes of liquid mud. She understood what Moussa had been doing.

Olive preferred walking anyway.

"My horse has many of the characteristics of a mule," Olive muttered, her anger turning to melancholy as she marched alongside her muddy steed. Their relationship had been strained since nearly the beginning. Olive felt that her horse was always sidling into every prickly acacia just to spite her, and that she had to remount the beast every time there was a tiny bit of marshy ground.

They changed course at the Mao Lui River, which was technically the boundary of the French and German territories. The heat was tyrannical. They were met there by a Senegalese French sergeant, who stood waiting for them like a tree. Though quiet, he produced a charming letter of welcome from Monsieur Bertaut, the French military resident at Léré, their next major destination. He whispered to Mr. Talbot. They marched on, but when the heat became unendurable, they stopped to rest at the picturesque Mundonng village of Bipare, which was wonderfully composed of small huts and high-domed granaries. When they got into the village, their carriers, who were Mundonng natives Mr. Talbot had hired, rushed to the common house and a porch on the chief's hut—both were covered and offered luxuriously cool shade. As Olive and the Talbots stood in the dust, the Senegalese sergeant sprang to life and ran their carriers all out of the cool darkness. Olive and the Talbots crawled under the low *zana* matting, a type of plaited straw. The cooling effect was instantaneous.

After a brief, guilty respite, Olive ventured outside again. Out in the yard she saw women squatting upon tiny stools, laughing and talking as they busied themselves with domestic tasks. Olive was able to deduce that each wife had her own apartment. When Olive explored one of these apartments, she found three rooms. There were living quarters, most of which contained a corn grinder and a wicker bedstead. There were water pots in the closets. Small children ran in and out with as much freedom as the goats and fowl that similarly wandered the rooms.

Olive heard a noise out in the yard. When she investigated, she found a tiny strange bird terrorizing some of the goats. It looked like a plump circle stuck with brown feathers covered with white dots. Its head was white and black with a flash of red that must have been the source of its courage. Olive found this bird, the African chicken, to be both comical and altogether impressive, for it was obvious it scraped together a mea- ger existence on what it could find, as no one troubled to feed it. Olive observed that this chicken seemed to be tolerated only for its eggs, which were small and looked rather questionable. Olive watched as a native woman ran her chicken down, grabbed it by its two spindly legs, and car- ried it away by the feet. Olive even saw a few chickens tied by their feet to a stick, like some unfortunate missionaries. Olive was much relieved when the woman dropped her chicken, which scurried back to the goats, having suffered extraordinarily little from the treatment.

When the Talbots finally emerged from the shade, the chief of Bipare gave them a gift. Olive was beginning to understand that this practice of giving a present—or "dash," as it is was called in pidgin English—was not only a gesture of friendship but also a hint for a gift in return. The chief gave Mr. Talbot a kid and some honey. The latter was bittersweet; not only was honey always very runny in Africa, but it almost always contained actual bees. The last part of the gift was, of course, eggs, which Olive looked at with both sympathy and gratitude.

When Olive woke the next day, she looked out of sorts. Mrs. Tal- bot asked if she was sick, and Olive stared at her before replying no in a smallish voice. They soon left Bipare and began their march toward Léré. The land was easier and seemed more cultivated. The trees were fairy-size at best, small and dainty. There were few flowers, but those that did appear were bright and conspicuous, especially the petunia that Olive thought trailed over the ground like a rug.

"Colored convolvulus," said Mrs. Talbot, pointing at its varied pinks.

As the day wore on, the trees seemed to grow bigger, until soon they were in front of a thick forest of palm trees. The fruit on the trees looked unripe but was reputed to taste like gingerbread. When Olive tried one, she was filled with great hope, though it went grossly unrewarded. They kept walking. Through the stiff, straight trunks, Olive was surprised to see not only the sky but a moving, diamond-like glint. As she moved through the forest, Olive realized that just beyond the trees was not the blue of the sky, but the water of Lake Léré itself, which sparkled and shone like some brilliant sapphire.

8

THE GREAT LAMIDO

October 1910: The Party Passes into French-Occupied
Chad, Where They Encounter Strange Men on
Horseback, Are Taken to a Great Chief, and
Olive Becomes a Spy

Olive was now convinced that her horse was trying to murder her. She was exhausted from being scraped against every bush and burr. To top it off, she was sore from the waist down, though she supposed that wasn't fully the horse's fault. Olive dismounted to turn the tables and lead the horse herself. After a period of this marching—which Olive hoped was instructional—she turned to get back on her horse and try again. She persuaded Mr. Talbot to let her exchange Moussa for his horse boy, Aji, to see if that would help. But Aji acted so miserable that Mr. Talbot was forced to switch them back. Once she saw him back with Mr. Talbot, Olive realized that to serve as a horse boy was bad enough, but to serve as one for a woman was apparently degrading. When Moussa, now back on his old job, helped lift Olive back into the saddle, she squinted up at the brow of the slight hill that stood ahead of them. A sound was coming toward them that was not from some beast.

Rising over the blurry ridge was a score of native men, growing higher as their horses elevated them into view. The mysterious riders flashed in the sun. As they rode closer, Olive saw that their horses had armor, and their saddlecloths shone with silver-and-gold stitching. The men wore rich robes of every hue, including red, blue, purple, green, and yellow. Olive was stunned by such a display. Some of the men in the back were playing an *aligata*, a guitar-like instrument that made a mournful sound.

At the crest of this wave of tribesmen, another shape came into view, though he kept a little distance. This man was tall. He wore dark robes and a short, wrapped headscarf like a French hat. The boys talked quickly to Momo, who translated to Mr. Talbot.

Mr. Talbot explained that this was the great chief, the Lamido himself. He was the chief of all the Mundonng people in the area, which was a significant kingdom. Mr. Talbot was pleased that he had come to greet them.

Mrs. Talbot kept her eyes on the oncoming horsemen. They were not slowing down.

As the horses came closer, they began to feel them as thunder in the ground. Olive and Mrs. Talbot stood with great resolution, despite the galloping force. The line of horses was getting nearer, the strains of the *aligata* players accompanying them increasing in volume. As they finally bore down upon the party, the riders turned and wheeled around at the last possible moment in a magnificent display of horsemanship. Olive realized that this was all a performance—of salutation or to incite fear, she was not sure—but its skillful execution was quite impressive. She hoped that her own horse felt so inspired.

As the riders stopped and hailed them, they made it clear that they wished to escort them on the final leg into Léré. The Lamido sat still on his horse. Mr. Talbot could not refuse. Olive noted that they were dealing directly with Mr. Talbot and seemed to treat her like some sort of appendage. Her horse also apparently learned nothing from their expert display, for it whinnied and lagged more than ever—so much so that within a few minutes, the Lamido and his men seemed uninclined to wait and rode out ahead of them. When Olive and the rest finally arrived on the outskirts of Léré, they were, in her eyes, humiliatingly late and wrung out by the heat. They were greeted by a short man in a blue French uniform astride a white horse. The man smiled at them through his long mustache.

"*Bonjour,*" he said. It was Monsieur Bertaut, the military resident, who spoke with a strong French accent that almost seemed to buzz. He bowed to them before bringing his horse around to take the lead. They followed and shortly reached the crowded central square of the village. The flat plain was thronged with a line of people waiting to honor the chief.

The Lamido, who had gotten off his horse, began walking down from the head of the greeting line in a regal manner. Olive and her friends immediately dismounted and took their place in line. Olive peered down the row of robes, arms, and spears. Mr. Talbot gave her a disapproving look, returning to a stiffer position, more appropriate to his role as the only official representative of England at the event.

Olive stared at the Great Lamido as he moved slowly down the line. She could see him much more clearly now. He was very different from Chief Abbiga. The Lamido was a big, dark-skinned man, with a full black beard and a wide smile. His head was covered and he wore a dark robe with pleats at the chest. When he met a small boy in the line, he gently placed his hand on his head, completely covering it. Olive was beginning to realize that seeing a chief in a British compound near the coast was not the same as seeing one out here, on the frontier.

From the edge of her vision, Olive saw a contingent of women arrive. Mrs. Talbot told her that these were the wives of Senegalese soldiers. Heavy beads were pinned to one side of their nostrils, and metal rings encircled their earlobes. Some of the women who didn't have metal used loops of string or nothing at all, though the areas were still pierced accordingly. Mrs. Talbot felt sympathy for these women, so she gave them a necklace that they unstrung and used to fill in the gaps of their wardrobe.

When the Lamido finally reached them, he shook hands with Mr. Talbot first. The chief moved on to Mrs. Talbot, who simply nodded to him. Olive—nervous and shifting her feet—was next. The Lamido walked to Olive, then paused, his hands at his sides. He looked her up and down.

Olive was dressed in much finer clothes than the rest of the women in the square and was less dirty (if not by much). And she had very red hair.

The Lamido's hands remained at his sides.

Olive, daughter of Sir Reginald, head of the great Clan MacLeod and herself a kind of royalty, smiled and put forth her hand.

The Lamido stared down at her hand; murmurs grew in the crowd. Olive wondered if she had made a grave error.

But the Lamido, whom his people called Great, looked Olive in the eyes and returned her smile before finally taking her hand in his. A hush of breathless excitement ensued, broken by the jingling sound of feminine applause.

When the chief finally left their presence and continued down the line, Mr. Talbot whispered in Olive's ear that this was a very significant event, for neither the Great Lamido nor his forebears had ever before shown a woman public recognition in the history of their tribe.

THAT NIGHT THE COMPANY DINED outdoors as M. Bertaut's guests. They were tabled just outside the official residence, an attractive house upon a natural hill that left them open to a comfortable breeze. They were joined by M. Bouhaben, who was there on a road survey, and M. Loyer, who had come to relieve the resident, whose term would shortly be up. The bright moon shone on them as their host's merry laughter echoed across the trees below. He had been drinking wine.

"You know," said M. Bertaut, with a pause, "it has been two years since I've seen a woman!" He stared at Olive a moment more before laughing heartily. Mrs. Talbot didn't count, it seemed.

"The presence of these new women from England has caused quite a stir in Léré," he continued, possibly realizing his mistake. Mr. Talbot turned the conversation around by asking M. Bertaut about Léré. The resident explained that they had been in operation since 1905, though their resources were lately strained.

"We are allowed sixteen carriers to bring stores that have to last two years," said M. Bertaut with a shrug. Olive was realizing how important it was to carry things in and out—it was the only way to survive in Africa. "I have to make the house and the furniture," he said, "but food is easily obtained and service is cheap. The two small boys, for instance, who waited on us at table receive a maximum wage of five francs a month."

Olive looked for their wee African waiters, but they had already disappeared into the house under clanking plates and glasses. She righted herself; she had been drinking whiskey.

"In the whole military territory of Chad," said M. Bertaut, "where there are twenty-three posts, there are only three doctors. They are government servants and may receive no fees for attendance on either white men or black."

"They are not bound to attend natives," he said matter-of-factly. "Though they are recommended to do so. Medicines are provided free of charge in all cases." He took another swig of drink, his mouth already full. "I hear every case of justice that the natives bring. The majority are complaints brought by women against their husbands and are usually prompted by a desire to marry someone else, for in no single case has any cruelty been proved against the man."

How different the French and British were, thought Olive, as if that notion surprised her.

"The Lamido himself is too great to acknowledge publicly the existence of women," said Bertaut, between mouthfuls. "They hold a higher position in the social scale than is the case amongst most tribes. The Mundonng address me as their father and mother, which denotes an inclusion of the female sex.

"I have spent much time explaining to the Lamido the . . . uh . . . white man's point of view about women," added M. Bertaut. He raised his glass toward Olive: "I am enchanted at the result, which had far exceeded my utmost expectations."

As they drank and spoke, Olive thought how different a dinner party they made compared with those at Vinters. This contrast was made sharper when a tiny visitor walked up to their table: a tame kob, a small deerlike creature common to West Africa. The animal made little crescendoing sounds, talking to them as a dog might. Its hair was short and soft as Olive ran it through her fingers. She fed it with her hands.

Afterward M. Bertaut took them to a small compound of straw huts where they would stay. A wall of *zana* matting was their only barrier against the natural world. In her bed Olive studied her Hausa late into the night, partly because she was going to meet with the Lamido at closer quarters the next day.

When she was done, Olive wrote in her journal:

> *It is sad how one fails to realize the great occasions of life. We knew only that we had condescended to shake hands with a black man and were in complete ignorance that we had participated in a revolutionary act, which was to stir every man, woman, and child throughout the Mundonng Kingdom. It was, no doubt, flattering to be the object of so much attention, but before the ten hours of our inspection was over, we longed for a few moments of rest.*

THE NEXT MORNING OLIVE WOKE to glaring heat and light. She staggered up and began to tend to the Medusa-like state of her hair when, in the corner of her small mirror, she saw a single white eye staring at her through a hole in the ceiling.

Olive screamed and threw her tea coat over her shoulders. Mrs. Talbot sprang up.

The eye blinked, then disappeared. Olive heard heavy scrambling on the roof as bits of grass crumbled onto the floor. She watched as a shadow darkened the ceiling and moved quickly to the edge of the hut.

Olive stuck her head out the door and looked up to see a young tribesman leaping from her roof, his feet stuck out behind him as he jumped to the adjoining hut. He ran off, hurling himself onto another roof. He had been watching her.

"Get out!" shouted Mrs. Talbot, brandishing her shoe. They heard more footsteps across the huts around them.

After dressing—with Mrs. Talbot standing guard—Olive walked outside again. Mrs. Talbot had figured out that each hut had palm-trunk ladders leading to the roof. There were also footholds cut into the roofs so that people could easily travel from one to another. This was not just a vulgar opportunity but a means of transportation. Olive was aghast.

After things settled down, Olive and the Talbots made their way to the palace of the Great Lamido, a large compound located just off the edge of the square. They passed under three golden bells. The Lamido stood at the threshold of a circular building, beckoning them inside. They walked through a short corridor to a larger hall. The curved walls were hung with weaponry, including long spears and bows. The wide, tall roof was supported by two massive pillars that had been blackened by some natural dye. The room was large and mostly empty; the only furniture was a hard divan in the center with a few items next to it. A garish red rug lay under the chair, stamped with the image of a snarling yellow tiger.

The Lamido slowly walked to the chair and sat. His retainers followed, squatting beside him on the floor. He chatted with his men while Mr. Talbot and the others walked in slow circles around him, almost in a kind of orbit. Mr. Talbot made notes and figures in his notebook. Olive knew he was making a sketch of the building, probably for his own records.

Olive was trying not to stare at the Lamido, but she had to look twice when she saw a tattered copy of *The Sketch* tossed cavalierly to the side of his chair. She wondered how—and why—an African chief was reading a London magazine.

Then, without announcement, a beautiful young woman entered the room from a curtained door behind the throne. Her hair was of medium length, and her skin shone softly. She wore only a thin loincloth. Olive knew she must have been a servant because of her demeanor. The woman bent her head, never looking directly at the Lamido, and sank to her knees before him. She raised a hollowed-out green gourd—a calabash—of water to her chieftain's lips.

The Lamido casually rinsed his mouth—and then solemnly spat onto the rug. He did this three times in succession.

The servant girl then brought out a long wooden pipe, which she held in both hands as the chief leisurely smoked from it. The odor was overpowering, causing Olive to stifle a cough. Attached to the pipe by a tiny chain was a small blade that the girl used to tend to the leaves in the bowl. When the Lamido was done, the girl brought more water, and he again rinsed his mouth three times, his attention seemingly elsewhere.

Through the curtain in the back of the room, Olive saw something move. Another servant, come to kneel at the Lamido's feet? But it was short and seemed to have four legs. Olive was surprised to see a large black-and-brown snout push its way through the fabric.

Into the royal room walked a full-grown ram. It made its way slowly around the back of the Lamido, who paid it no mind. There the ram stopped. The animal turned its head until an unblinking eye stared at Olive. Small children then spilled into the room through the curtain. They tried to lead the ram back by a scrambling force of numbers. When they all left through the same curtain, smiling and pushing, Olive saw a long corridor behind it. Mastaba whispered and Mr. Talbot spoke to Olive, apparently without fear of being understood.

"Back there are the apartments for his wives. His children and the patriarchal ram are permitted to wander between the two."

As the chief reposed in his chair, Olive came up closer to Mr. Talbot, and this time whispered in his ear:

"How many?"

Mr. Talbot looked at her.

"How many wives?"

Mr. Talbot huffed and stared at her again, but there was no putting her off. He asked Mastaba, who nodded, then spoke to the chief. The

Lamido listened intently. He answered with precision, his eyes far away. Mr. Talbot understood him immediately.

"Two . . . ," said Mr. Talbot.

Olive felt a little . . .

". . . hundred and fifty," he continued.

Olive tried to maintain her composure Two hundred and fifty! She couldn't fathom how such a thing was even possible. She flashed a look at Mrs. Talbot.

Perhaps anticipating that Olive's next question would be *Can we meet some of them?* the Lamido paused, then told Mastaba that he was short a score or so, and the rest were quite busy. None were ready to receive a formal call. He said this, nodded as Mastaba repeated it in English, and then resumed staring into space. Olive's face fell.

Though the Lamido had forbidden them a formal interview with any of his wives, Olive was determined to turn spy. As the men spoke, Olive took Mastaba and wandered around the back of the palace precinct. The compound was a curling maze of side-by-side huts centered around the chief's quarters, barricaded by an outer wall from the rest of the village. Each hut was identical, with a great, slanted door that flipped open. There were around two hundred structures, and Olive wondered if each was home to a wife of the Lamido. As they walked the narrow streets, she was able to see several of these women engaged in work, cooking food and boiling bark to make their dark dyes. They seemed to be endlessly on their hindquarters, either pounding grain or stirring soup. In their loincloths and dirty beads, they looked little like royalty.

Through Mastaba, Olive talked to some of the wives. Olive discovered that the Lamido had only twenty children: ten sons and ten daughters. Of this number, only two sons were in line to rule, though Olive did not understand the mechanism of succession. As she heard the word for "wife"—*matarsa*—Olive remembered Hausa's general rule that all words denoting the female sex, and in addition all words ending in *a*, were feminine.

When they finally left the grounds, Olive noticed a group of native performers playing music just outside of the gateway. Olive heard a strange, faraway wail that was familiar to her. The tune was long and trailed off into the sky.

It sounded like bagpipes.

She felt herself almost swelling to each sound, filled with an immense pride that was hers alone. The sound trilled and moved, punctuated and broken before healing itself again. But the tone itself was impure, not exactly like bagpipes, but close enough at times to remind her of home. Not just Scotland, but the island and castle where she had spent holidays and summers—the part of her heritage that her father desperately wished her to embrace.

As they made their way back to their huts, the notes still trailing above her, Olive wondered if, with 250 wives, there could be such a thing as love.

THAT NIGHT THE MOON SHONE high and clear. Olive found the atmosphere made her restless. She got up and woke Mrs. Talbot. Together they wandered silently into the city. In the white light and deep shadows, it seemed like some kind of fairy kingdom. Silence lay deep over all and mystery overcame everything.

The buildings were empty of people. Outside a few still forms were stretched in sleep, though sometimes a figure, crouching over the glowing embers of a wood fire, would rise to add a log that crackled and blazed as the flames started back to life.

They climbed a gentle hill just away from the town and found themselves free of houses, in a clear space of unshaded moonlight, where fields of maize rustled in answer to the breeze. The Mao Kabi River gleamed as it wound in great silver loops through the distant valley, now visible, now invisible, on and on, casting a spell of mystical enchantment, till the bright line merged into the magic waters of Lake Léré. There were little lamps that had been put along the path. When Olive asked, Mastaba said they were for ghosts.

Olive stood and stared into the darkness that was not dark, under a light that was not day. There was something there, behind it all, waiting and seeing; and though she could not see it, she was sure it was calling her. As they walked by starlight, Olive saw a small fiery star—like a comet streak across the black sky.

9

DEVIL IN THE FOREST

October 25, 1910: Near Lake Léré in Chad,
Olive Decides to Investigate Rumors of an
Angry Devil Who Lives in the Jungle

Olive and Mrs. Talbot enjoyed a few days on Lake Léré, using native canoes to explore the lake and its tiny islands. The water was cool and smooth, beautiful and still. Sometimes the water turned to dazzling sheets as the wind gave rise to endless ripples of light. Olive tried her best to remember to write these images down.

As they moved silently through the water, they saw low domes of villages nestled in the southern hills. On the northern shore, the land was flat, with only the shadow of palms in the distance. There they found numerous shells and deep narrow lines that suggested the presence of some great water lizard. Olive walked off on her own toward the hundreds of tiny footprints of birds who came there to bathe. Mrs. Talbot let her go.

The three islands on the lake were all uninhabited, save for hippos, which they saw only in the large broken stalks of reeds they left behind. Even the black rocks of mica on the shores were colorful with bursting amaryllids. Olive was examining these flowers when she saw a large worm as long and round as a sausage, with the consistency of an unshiny, dry slug. She saw more such creatures in heaps, lying so thickly on the ground that it was hard to avoid treading on them. When these beasts inevitably began to move, on countless feather-legs, Olive realized they were millipedes. Kukaua howled out in pain, but it was only from stepping on a bramble. They ran back to the safety of the water, pulling off their shoes and stockings to remove any stray worms. They walked out to a depth that made them refreshingly wet, but the usual penalty for good things had to be paid when they climbed back onto the burning-hot canoe.

As Olive floated in the delicious water, she looked up to the high terrain at the far end of the lake. There, somewhere far out of sight, were the Tuburi Lakes. She remembered hearing that if Lake Léré could be connected to them, there would be an unbroken waterway from the Atlantic to Lake Chad. She had heard M. Bertaut talk about some ambitious canal project that seemed doomed. Others thought that the Mao Kabi River, which joined with the lake, could be more easily diverted into an adjoining stream. The problem was that the terrain was not only difficult but highly mysterious. There had to be a place where the waters of the Tuburi Lakes somehow connected with Léré, but no one had seen it. There were stories of a secret waterfall, but many of the efforts that had been mounted to find it had never returned. Part of the reason was that no native guides wished to help in the search.

They feared a devil who lived there. They feared the Djinn of the Falls.

THE NEXT DAY OLIVE AND THE TALBOTS met M. Bertaut for lunch. Olive asked him about the mysterious falls.

"I sought the falls myself," he said, through a mouthful of food. "But an impenetrable tangle of bush and creeper divided me." He told them that M. Bouhaben had undergone the same experience. He didn't find the falls, having gotten distracted by hunting a giraffe he had come acrosss.

"No black man has seen these falls," declared M. Bertaut with authority, "for the tradition is that a Devil makes them his dwelling-place. Native guides are useless—they will not get close. . . . Nothing can induce them to go near a spot so haunted."

He took a moment of silence, thinking.

"Now that the time of my leave is fast approaching," he said, "I am resolved to attempt the exploration once again." Olive, who desperately wanted to see these falls first, felt hope rise within her.

"I am," M. Bertaut declared, "confident of success. Will you join me, Mr. Talbot?"

Olive's heart sank. It would be dreadful, she thought, to be excluded from such a thrilling expedition. Olive looked over to Mr. Talbot, trying her best to be calm and unselfish. M. Bertaut then turned to Olive.

"I regret that the expedition is too hopelessly fatiguing," he said. M. Bertaut further explained that the region was thick with tsetse fly, meaning that they would have to explore on foot since no horse could survive. Olive was furious; it had been her idea!

"Camping arrangements would only be of the roughest possible kind," he said.

This was not a tone Olive responded well to. She felt a tremble within herself, not of fear, but of contention.

"A woman," replied Olive, "is always capable of doing what she wanted to do."

M. Bertaut looked at her, replying that he indeed hoped that she and Mrs. Talbot wanted to come, but that he had not wanted to suggest it at first, as the conditions of the journey would be so trying. Olive then saw what he was trying to do.

"It is an area thick with game," said M. Bertaut, turning toward Mr. Talbot with a twinkle in his eye.

Despite his foibles, Olive had great affection for their French friend, especially in that moment. Mr. Talbot would not be interested in such a frivolous, dangerous quest as finding that secret waterfall, but the promise of a fine hunt might be too much for him to resist. Mr. Talbot nodded in affirmation.

"All is settled," said M. Bertaut with a smile.

TWO DAYS LATER OLIVE, the Talbots, M. Bertaut, and a small retinue made their way onto the Mao Kabi River in two rough-hewn canoes. The waters were clean but abundant with crocodile. There were rumors of hippos there that were bold enough to have attacked boats. The previous year two European traders had been upended by these beasts and were never seen again. Olive eyed the smooth shelf of water before them. M. Bertaut steered them toward courage by words he would repeat often: *"N'ayez pas peur!"* In an African context, his words took on a different flavor: Do not live in fear.

Their journey across the lake was without incident, until they made shore and the back of the main canoe unexpectedly tipped back into the water. Mr. Talbot began shouting. He pulled the canoe up and began rummaging wildly through the back end. He sighed in relief when he pulled up his own large strongbox that held his papers, bills, and accounts. Olive had never seen him so relieved. They watched some chairs and cushions float out to the middle of the lake. Olive's own little strongbox was safe.

They marched for eleven miles without seeing a single living person. The noon air was hot, so they sought a village to take refuge in. When one was spotted, they found every house empty. They kept going, wondering what had caused such desolation. There were fields of guinea corn that looked tended, and crops of pumpkins were strewn about the ground. The next village was similarly deserted. M. Bertaut had been silent, his eyes often darting to the ground. When the party came upon a particularly foul-smelling stable, he put a handkerchief to his nose and went inside. When he returned, he removed his hand and solved the riddle.

"Tsetse fly," he said grimly.

He explained that these people had lost their cattle, then their goats, and even their dogs. They had all been blighted by the fly. Wild beasts had also ravaged the neighborhood.

"From this village," said M. Bertaut, "seven women and ten children have been carried off." He had seen the tracks on the ground.

The group walked very quietly for a long time. They agreed not to visit any more villages.

AS THEY GOT CLOSER TO WHERE M. Bertaut thought the falls might be, the landscape became nearly impenetrable. He went first but showed great courtesy, for he frequently paused so that the group might be together if the falls were discovered. Olive found this to be very generous, especially considering that he was French. Other times it was Olive who took the lead, pushing her way through the high grass and trying to avoid the hidden spikes of granite that lay below. There were scattered yellow mimosa trees—"the lazy tree," a name that Olive, hot and sore, could appreciate.

Olive heard something and stopped.

Water.

They pushed through some particularly towering grass. But instead of finding the falls, they saw the river, where two tributaries had pushed together to form a wild rapids. They followed the churning water as if it were a map. When the river took a sudden sharp bend, they found themselves at a promontory and watched as yet another tributary added its volume to the swell.

The roar got even louder. They gained a little more height, with Mrs. Talbot slipping a little on the way. Olive looked down onto the intersection of the streams and saw a sign: the familiar X-shape of the *saltire*, like the white Saint Andrew's cross of the Scottish flag. It was, thought Olive, a good augury. After all that had transpired, finding these invisible falls had grown in her mind into something tangible and important— something she had to do.

They explored farther but found only obstacles. They camped nearby, not having found the falls or any real evidence of them. They worried that this could all be a series of interlocking rapids that could never be tamed or diverted. Olive fell quiet, still buoyed by the signs she had seen.

OLIVE AROSE THE NEXT MORNING with renewed strength for the search. Unfortunately Mrs. Talbot had indeed strained a leg and had to stay in camp. With a long face, M. Bertaut also announced that he was obliged to return to Léré for official business. As he walked back with some of the boys, Olive felt sorry for him. But now, if they could find the falls, the discovery would be theirs alone.

Only Olive, Mr. Talbot, Kukaua, and Aji were left. Their plan was to find and follow a more distant tributary to discover where it joined the Mao Kabi. They planned to then follow it back to the Saint Andrew's cross, to finally surmise how the water was reaching Lake Léré. As they walked away, Mrs. Talbot sat, her hurt leg stretched out before her. Olive waved before she walked away.

Several minutes later, they heard the barking of baboons. Olive crouched in the bush in time to see one of the apes barrel past her on all fours, almost rolling in its terrific speed. She couldn't believe her eyes. Mr. Talbot grabbed his gun and took off after it. Olive sat in the dust, abandoned, but secretly ecstatic at having seen her baboon. She listened for a skirmish that didn't come and wondered what temptation the Djinn of the Falls had prepared for a woman who didn't shoot her gun.

Mr. Talbot returned empty-handed and guiltily rejoined Olive. They made their way down to a dry riverbed filled with star-shaped blue-and-pink flowers. There were deep pools of water leftover from the rain that provided perfect mirror reflections. Olive noticed tiny footprints that crept up to their edges.

At the end of the riverbed, they looked down to see four massive sheets of rock, one almost forty feet high, looking like a set of tumbled steps for a giant. Despite the size, they got down rather easily, which surprised Olive. Luck seemed to be on their side. At the bottom of the stones they found a swampy area. There was stillness all around them. No bird moved, nor any beast, for the sun was already high and still. All living things seemed hidden in shadow.

Olive saw a small brae a few hundred feet away and suggested they use it as a vantage point. But from the hill they saw only a further impediment. Directly ahead of them was a sharp ascent of at least two hundred feet. Olive felt completely disoriented. Each new geographical obstacle seemed almost impossible in its design. When they reached the rocks, they found that their sheer surface captured the sun's heat like giant furnaces. As they climbed, their feet and hands swelled. Olive's throat was so parched that she could barely swallow. She called down to Aji, who was below her, for a drink of water. When the canteen was passed up, Olive tipped it over only to find that not a drop remained: It had sprung a leak on the way up.

She kept climbing.

Finally nearing the top of their climb, Olive saw green tendrils flailing out in front of her. As Olive's ill-fitted boot caught and slipped on yet another loose stone, she tried to grab one of the vines. Mr. Talbot, who had been making his way closer to her, grabbed her hand.

"Poisonous cactus," he said, slicing the vine in two with his knife. He kept moving upward.

The world began to spin for Olive. Whether it was poison or lack of water she couldn't say, because she wasn't really thinking at all.

"Wait," said Mr. Talbot, who had paused above her.

He started frantically searching through his jacket until he came up with a silver tin. He took his knife and turned the can open as it flashed in the sun. Olive saw orange. They were apricots, and they looked utterly delicious.

Mr. Talbot put the tin to her mouth, and she drank the sweet, satisfying juice. Olive implored him to take a sip as well. He gave a halfhearted tip of the container, and then handed back the tin. Olive pleaded that they share, but he insisted.

"I am not very heroic," said Olive, gulping down the remaining contents. She eyed the chasm below her.

Renewed, they pressed on until they finally reached the brow of the hill. Over the edge, lying some four hundred feet below their current spot, they saw the river, flowing with water. Mr. Talbot sent one of the boys at once, but the cliff was very dangerous, and the lad returned empty-handed. They looked for a better place to get down to the river. When they finally descended, slower than they wished, they half ran to the river and quaffed it with their hands.

Olive stopped midswallow. At first she thought it was the sound of the water she was drinking, then the river itself before her, but now that she had woken up a bit, she knew it was something else. She heard a distant sound, soft but loud in her ear, like a whisper.

They pressed on, first slithering down, then scrambling up alternating gorges, some two or three hundred feet in height, with sharp grass and jagged rocks at their bases. On one particularly high peak, Olive was convinced she could hear the whisper again.

From those hot, high rocks Olive again looked down into the chasm below her.

Heights always made her think of her friend Violet Asquith. A few years ago Violet had met a military man who was twelve years older than she. They would talk for hours, which was not something Violet normally tolerated. She loved him, and everyone expected they might get engaged. But when the man, whose name was Winston Churchill, instead proposed to a woman named Clementine Hozier (whom Violet claimed was "as stupid as an owl"), she took it very hard. Winston eventually went on holiday with Violet and her family at Slains Castle on the Scottish coast, but they could not mend their fences. When Winston and Clementine were finally married, Violet did not attend. Instead, she took a book and went to walk on some high rocks near the castle. Her family expected her back that afternoon, but by supper she had not returned.

Hours later they found Violet lying out on the beach below, unmoving. They rushed down to help her, thinking she had fallen or perhaps was dead. Thankfully, after a few moments, Violet woke, miraculously uninjured. The gossip spread fast through Olive's circle of friends: Did she fall? Did she jump? Or was it something else entirely?

Her father wouldn't hear talk of any of it. Violet returned the same as always, with her eyes on new prizes. (Her stepmother, Margot, often said that Violet, though intensely feminine, would have made a remarkable man.)

Olive paused there, in the African air. She heard the whisper beyond the rocks, and she kept looking down.

"His dwelling place is no longer to be surrounded with mystery," said Olive, mostly to herself as she turned ahead. Olive knew that this voice was what had scared away all the others. "His guardians had failed him, and the end was already near." She steeled herself, moved her feet and arms, and finished the climb.

At the summit, dense bush barred their way, but they pushed through it and saw the river beneath racing turbulently between high granite walls. Olive's eyes followed the rush of water until the ground broke, and with a roar she saw the river simply vanish into the air.

They had found the devil; they had found the falls.

They got closer and took many photographs, marveling at the power they were witnessing. The sun had finally begun its descent, and as they watched the falls with smiles and claps, the cruel force of the sun lessened, and its radiant beams lit up and flushed the dying leaves with the glowing tints of autumn.

They sought a way down the cliff. As they climbed, another strong smell of baboon wafted at them. They saw two big snakes glide away. Whether it was the sheer descent, the seething torrent below, the victory of finding the falls, or the anger of the djinn, Kukaua lifted his voice and wailed out loud. The reverberation between the walls of rock was tremendous, but they held on till they reached the bottom, where they crept out on a ledge of rock where they could look up. Spray rose in drenching clouds, and from above a beam of sunshine pierced the glistening drops, through which shone a rainbow—a messenger of peace in that stormy strife of waters.

Mr. Talbot looked at Olive. She had done it.

Full of the wonder of the scene and the magnitude of its grandeur, they all walked back to camp, passing the Saint Andrew's cross on the way. Olive's only regret was that Mrs. Talbot and M. Bertaut had not been there to share their final success.

They returned to Léré the next day. Bertaut almost wept at their victory. He assured them that no Frenchman had ever done this. That night Olive took out her diary and wrote something that she had to see on paper to believe.

> *M. Bertaut has kindly expressed his wish to name the Falls after me—"Les chutes MacLeod"—I can only say how greatly I appreciate the honor they have done me.*

Even though she was tired, Olive continued to write. She had to. It certainly helped that she was proud of the day's accomplishment.

October 30

> *We had a real hard five hours scramble before the next point was reached—up and down steep climbing over granite rocks that literally burnt like a furnace. Then our reward—two walls of water 200 ft. high, with a rainbow at the base and spray flying everywhere. We managed to slide down to take photos. . . . After that an easy route back via the same rapids we had discovered yesterday—It was fun.*
>
> *Olive:*

10

A CORRESPONDENCE,
PART 2

*January 1909, Vinters: After Telling Boyd That Her Friend
Has Released Her from a Very Difficult Situation, Olive
Begins a Regular Correspondence with Him, Writing
Letters in Advance of His Return from Africa;
She Confronts an Unspoken Problem*

Now back at Vinters, Olive had the freedom to write Mr. Alexander whenever she wished, though she was not sure when or if the letters would reach him. To educate herself on his expedition, she began to read books about Africa.

January 23, 1909

Dear Mr. Alexander

It will be too difficult writing once a fortnight, so you must put up with the patchy effect of complete letters written whenever I feel inclined. . . . I don't know what will interest you, or even how you like things, nor do I think we have any mutual friends. Still, it is very important that we should get to know each other as well as possible, I hope you are not getting a false picture of me. The ghastly thought has just struck me—I am not a prig, nor am I kind and good, I do things because they interest me. I like knowing everything I can about the different ways people live . . . as I have no other credentials. Don't you think it is very hard on the ordinary girl that they have to live at home till when they are about 40 they realize that they have nothing they can do—no ambition it is possible to satisfy—and about 30 dreary years of empty life to look forward to?

I went to the school today. Food is horrid. Hash of mixed contents that I daren't venture on—cold bacon, bananas, bread and Pepper's mixture of margarine and butter—I go there to help in the Skilled Trade & Apprenticeship Assoc. They act as a sort of employment bureau for children leaving school, getting them places that they could not get for themselves. I am so far confined to secretary work, and visiting the parents, but it is thrilling work, and the people are so friendly and nice to me. I do a little of the sort of work in connection with my branch of the Children's Happy Evenings Assoc. That is my other good work. Every Tuesday, 150 boys must be amused.

Olive:

January 30, 1909

My dearest Boyd

I had to stop my first portion abruptly as the paper gave out, but now I have a fresh stock of it and of things to say. I wonder whether we have known each other in previous existences—sometimes I think that, and I like to, because it would prove that nothing could ever really part us. At other times I feel it must be a hallucination or a dream, from which we will wake—probably when we meet.

Do you take much interest in army matters? I wonder. Being completely ignorant of them myself I can only speak like a parrot.

It is thrilling to think you have really started and I long for news of your progress . . . I want you to realize how very sad I am at having caused you so much pain. I don't know if it was necessary, but I think it was—for even now I am threatened with horrible consequences when you come home. I don't believe it, because G. is too fine a character now that the danger of shock is passed. . . . Don't let this worry you for a minute . . . Sometimes I feel I should tear this up and never write to you at all, but that is my worst self—and I want the help of our strength.

Olive MacLeod:

I am very well and the black lines under my eyes have disappeared.

February 11, 1909

Dear Mr. Alexander,

I have changed my mind again.

This time in my opinion of Mr. Savage-Landor's work about Africa, and of himself with it. I now dislike him acutely. . . . Violet recommended me strongly to just go on an expedition. The drawback of the latter being that nice, adventurous, capable ones are difficult to find on my own, or with another woman.

Quite seriously though, don't you think you might sometime take me with you? I don't think I should be a nuisance for I am very very strong and can work all day without feeling it at all—and I am sure I should love it and it would make me a much better companion for you at home too—wouldn't it? I admit this is all a little envious (especially as I often have bouts of feeling that I simply can't change my present existence).

Olive:

February 28 & March 3, 1909

Dear Mr. Alexander:

It is splendid to have got into a new month, though it has begun coldly and austerely. Snow falls more or less continuously, and we depend on the increase or decrease of a yellow fog for variety.

I try to make my letters very revealing, but then you may not get them—I shall be annoyed if you don't have patience to read them.

I went to a lecture by Reginald Farrer on 'Happiness'—it was held in such an odd place, a room of the Psychical Science society in St. Martin's Lane. Baffy Dugdale and I went together, and arrived to find them beginning some occult experiment with a tray, but unluckily they stopped when they saw us and gave us tea on it instead—at the same time apologizing for their material agency. And when they dropped some cake we had refused they said 'it is a gift from the spirits.' The audience was very peculiar, one woman was a morphine maniac, a man was a medium. The lecture was quite good, but the audience uninspiring.

I should be quite capable of taking part in an expedition . . . whites have a 99 per cent better chance than blacks—please agree. It is tiresome not being able to get answers for months.

Olive:

March 7, 1909

Dear Mr. Alexander-

I think it must be partly your doing that I should start my letter again so soon—the last few days it feels as if you had been thinking more of me.

Perhaps you have found letters, or perhaps you are writing—or more likely still it is pure imagination. It is such a bore not knowing whether it is intuition or hallucination, and consequently trying not to trust it, though somehow it is a very seizing feeling and comes on quite suddenly—when I am at a play, or reading, or doing something else active and unreflective.

Happiness—I think you have done a good deal to teach me the art—though perhaps that is not very nicely put as you are away—I mean the not very active sort of happiness, more contentment.

The only thing that at all bothers me is whether I am right in writing to you so intimately—I want to so very much, and I think you will prefer it—but . . . no doubts are unworthy and somehow I think you will be strong enough to kill them when you are here. When will that be?

Olive:

March 14, 1909

Dear Mr. Alexander–

Another busy week . . . Alice Barran's husband was tiresome in having a preconceived collective idea of woman—due to education and not to experience. True it places my sex on a pedestal but what is the fun of that when it is shared by every factory girl?—I think it really is to keep the rest of the world clear for the male sex.

We took between 70 & 80 of our boys to the zoo again yesterday, which was a wild success in spite of snowstorms. . . . By the way, I met Major Baden Powell at a lunch . . . He spoke about you. I discreetly did not—he too seems to think you are one of the few genuine and truthful explorers.

Olive:

Olive sealed and posted her letter. She had sent so many. She knew that there would be a lag in his responses. There was no mail service to the jungle, only to some of the larger outposts. That was to be expected, though she wished it were otherwise. It was a dreadful inconvenience.

Olive felt she had reason to worry, though it had nothing to do with Africa. Olive had discovered that her sister Flora had sent Boyd a letter before he left England. Olive did not know what it said but only imagined the worst. Did Flora betray the feelings that Olive had confided in her? Had she told him to stay? Or had she warned him about her somehow? Olive wondered if that was the real reason he had not written back to her. Thankfully, she received a response the very next day.

February 23, 1909

Dear Miss MacLeod,

I was very glad to get your two letters . . . I know it must be difficult to think of a person like myself who is so far away, he must by this time be a mere shadow in the gloom. But I am still confident that when I return, I shall be able to revive in you those feelings which I know I have already awakened. Being a free agent, no doubt you wonder why I do not come back at once, but that is not in my nature. When once I have started a venture, I must if possible, bring it to a successful end.

San Thomé island has not come up to my expectations, but then one must not expect new things every day. At least I think I shall have one to make your namesake, a pretty Ground Pigeon (Haplaphelia oliviae).

My work here has been rather uphill. The Portuguese have given me little or no facilities. They look upon me as a spy.

You say you do not wish to spoil my career. That is not possible. I have none—

I AM BUT A VAGABOND BORN TO WANDER
UP AND DOWN.
TO SEEK AND PROBE THE SECRETS OF THE WORLD
TO MAP THE MOUNTAINS, TO TRACE THE SILVER
STREAMS. . . .
FATHER, BEHOLD THY SON, WANDERING TO AND FRO IN THE VAST UNIVERSE
WHERE TIME'S UNDOING FINGER MARKS ITS COURSE
BY FALLING STARS

AND BURNT UP LAND.

PRETEND THY PATIENT ARM AND GUIDE HIM

TO THE HAVEN OF HIS SOUL'S DESIRE

NOW LOOK MY EYES TO RUGGED MOUNTAINS

THAT PONDER UPON THE SEA

LIKE WEARY TITANS, BEFORE THEIR TASKS ARE DONE

BUT NOT MORE WEARY THAN THE BLACK

WHO UPON THEIR LOWER SLOPES

DRIVES HIS CEASELESS TOIL

TO FREE THE BURDEN OF THE WHITE.

Boyd Alexander

Olive read the letter again. Her elation turned to a saddening curiosity. Why didn't he say anything about Flora's letter? Or was he angered that she had not simply accepted his proposal now that Mr. Hardy was out of the picture? Or was it something else entirely? What other secrets was he keeping? She wrote him back immediately.

March 17, 1909

Dear Mr. Alexander-

Last night came your letter, giving me great joy before I opened it and disappointment when I had—I had expected to be so delighted to rejoice in the prospects of a happy homecoming . . . I realize that my conduct must seem inexplicable and that you naturally expected me to say far more. . . . I am very bad at letter-writing. Because I expect everyone to see things from my point of view and I leave large blanks and unfinished sentences and thoughts, not realizing that what is dear to me cannot necessarily be so to others. Now I shall make another effort but if it turns out badly too don't condemn me for it, but wait till we meet. Even that sentence is unfair to you because you have not condemned me, only the excuse you find for me hurts almost as much—"a mere shadow in the gloom"!!!

You and I both thought it better to ignore to each other Flora's interposition, but it is that that is making trouble now. I don't know exactly what she said to you, but I expect that it was more definite than I had understood—and therefore gave you a right to expect more from me when I was free to say it than what I have said. I don't know how or why but ever since you spoke to me my personality seemed to vanish and merge into yours—it was against reason, and it defied explanation, and it frightens me. It seemed just to think that this might be due to a mesmeric influence exercised unconsciously by your superior strength and that time and absence would make it as if it never had been.

My reason said this was best, as what would cease for me would cease for you, and it would enable me to give happiness to others towards whom I was in debt. This is old history for as you know I tried it and it was literally impossible.—I was too much yours to win freedom, all I could give was myself as a sacrifice. That I should probably have done had I not met you and seen that you cared too; and the thought of your going on this dangerous expedition without your knowing how much you meant to me was hell. Then Flora intervened—I need hardly say without my knowledge. She ought not to have done it—it made it deceitful in me to carry out my contract with the Hardys, and yet I had no right to break it. I chose the latter and the lesser of two evils . . . Don't think I am not very grateful to her for having done this.

It is the right thing for us as I believe it to be, we shall not lose by waiting: and if we should find we were mistaken in each other how much better that it should be before it is too late. This winter has been a great nervous strain to us both and I am conscious of not having confidence in my judgments as I usually have—therefore I ask you to be patient with me, though I ask a great deal more too: I want your love, but I want my freedom.

It would fill me with blank panic were I to surrender it without your presence to allay my fears—To me marriage seems so sacred, so infinitely great that one hardly dares to contemplate it—think what it should mean—merging in each other then becoming one—complete love. Don't let us commit the sacrilege of marrying without the certainty that our love is not of the day but of eternity.—Do you see now why I have gone on acting towards you as if I had not known that Flora had written to you—it was a mistake and I should have faced it. It is easier to do so now because I have thought as much of you that I feel as if we were more intimate.

I don't remember how I worded my letter . . . I cried for a week consecutively. See how I humble myself giving you these humiliating details to explain away a little of my apparent coldness—Everything has got horribly mixed up. I thought the mails would take as long as you to reach San Thomé.

You have made me feel guilty which is a very bad foundation for me to start pointing out your errors to you, but I shall do it all the same-

First, please realize that though I am not worrying about you, I am very anxious—that awful climate makes me so, so please don't delay sending off letters.

Second. I don't want you to think that I do or ever have questioned your staying away for a minute. Your travelling is your career, for the present anyway, and I should despise you if you had given it up to come back to me.

Third. My last accusation against you is that you don't tell me nearly enough about yourself, either past, present, or future. I can't help longing to know when you are going to come back. Not because I want you to hurry on my account, only because I shall be so very glad to look forward to a time when it will be ended at your own wish.

I am sure you will be rewarded by useful discoveries—and any way you will be able to give valuable reports on the slave trade. It must be very very sad for you seeing so much suffering and being unable at the moment to help it.

Olive MacLeod:

Olive sealed her letter, her longest yet. She considered another revision, or yet another paragraph, but she trusted in her words to do the work of her heart. She feared what might happen next, but not enough not to send it.

INTO THE SWAMP

November 1, 1910: Somewhere in Chad, the Party
Becomes Lost and Encounters Great Peril

M r. Talbot pulled out his map and unfolded it three times. The sun lit up the dry paper, revealing a reverse image of shapes and lines. Mr. Talbot squinted as he began making connections. He wiped his brow and his eyes stung: The sun was unrelenting. Their next destination was Sulkando, a town that rested on the shores of Lake Tuburi. Once they reached the lake, they would switch to canoes, while the rest of the carriers would take the long way around on foot. After the excitement of the falls discovery, Olive looked forward to again gliding along carelessly on the water, away from all the dusty riding and marching. For this last distance toward Sulkando, the only horses they had were for carrying bags and boxes, so Olive would have to endure one more march before settling into her perfect canoe. The lake was two days away.

Before they set off, Olive noticed that Mastaba and the boys were huddled together at a distance, in a clearing just far enough for their conversation to be unheard. A few of them looked over their shoulders at Mr. Talbot. Olive found this behavior strange. Mrs. Talbot, who was still affected by her injury, noticed it too.

Olive wondered what they were saying. Was it a mutiny? Boyd had told her they were rather common, usually involving porters quitting or just running away into the bush. This would generally be very problematic for the expedition itself, especially between towns, where there were heavy things to carry. Olive tried to guess their intent. Were they not being paid enough? Had she been too trusting of their faithfulness? Mr. Talbot had been watching as well. He straightened up as Mastaba left the crowd and walked over.

Mastaba explained to Mr. Talbot that the boys had a wish. Mr. Talbot nodded. Mastaba said that they wanted to do the upcoming two days' march in one long day. They too, it seemed, were eager to get going. Olive breathed a quiet sigh of relief.

After Mastaba relayed this information, Olive sensed movement behind her. She turned to see Mrs. Talbot stand up, testing her unsteady leg. Mr. Talbot moved forward to help, but she brushed him off. Mrs. Talbot stepped forward, took a few steps, and stopped again. She lifted her head, satisfied. Her husband again walked up to her, lowered his voice, and tried to persuade her to sit back down in a sensible manner. She ignored him.

"I am," announced Mrs. Talbot rather loudly, "quite equal to the long walk."

Mr. Talbot stood back, defeated. He made a motion, and some of the boys set off to scout the coming terrain.

When the guides returned, they brought unwelcome news: There was swampland ahead. After reporting this through Momo, they looked at Mr. Talbot for direction. He could tell by their faces that the area was almost impassable. One of the scouts flattened his palm and began raising it to show how high the waters ran. Starting at his ankles, the boy's hand rose slowly upward, and Mr. Talbot turned away before the boy even finished. They would get closer and try to find a way around.

As they marched forward, at a slower pace than normal, Olive wondered if they would ever get to Fort Lamy. As she considered this very real possibility, Olive's footsteps began to squish more and more into the earth. The grasses had already gotten higher. They were nearing the swamp.

When they reached the waterline, everyone came to a halt. Olive did not find it as impressive as Mr. Talbot's fears had suggested. The green grasses sprang lightly out of the peaceful water that, based on where they stood, could not be that deep. The boys looked at one another, as one of them began walking into the green water.

The boy moved with confidence as the top half of him began to disappear, as if he were being swallowed by some great aquatic beast. Olive couldn't believe her eyes. Soon the boy glanced back with a scared look as the thick swamp water pushed up to his chest and then all the way to his chin. The boy let his head lie back on the water, lit by the sun. He blinked and looked back at the party.

Mr. Talbot said something under his breath, pulling out his maps again.

After some calculations, it was decided that the only thing to do was to cut across country and make for Sulkando by a more circuitous route. Once Mr. Talbot settled on a direction, the carriers jumped to the front and fired some loud passage shots from the guns to cut through the dense grass. Birds flew off high into the air.

As the day advanced, they marched through the grass, trying to avoid the pools of water at their feet. The sun, now fully loosed above them, began to weigh upon every open surface. Finding some scrub trees, they rested in the shade, neither awake nor asleep, only quiet and still.

After an uncertain amount of time, Kukaua's head lifted at the sound of a rustle in the outer grass.

"*Nama,*" he said. Olive knew this word well.

Animal.

Apparently not all the game had been scared away. Kukaua quickly revised his observation when he realized how loud he had said it. He knew that whatever the *nama* was, Mr. Talbot would want to hunt it to the ends of the earth, setting their arrival in Sulkando back even further.

"Small, small *nama*," he said.

But it was too late. Mr. Talbot sprang to his feet as the noise got louder. His hand stretched for his rifle. By this point on the trip, Olive had seen this maneuver dozens of times: Mr. Talbot would extend his arm and Kukaua would put the barrel of his rifle into it, almost in perfect unison. Mr. Talbot stood up, raised the rifle to his eye, and began tracking the sound.

KRAK!

He fired, seemingly at nothing.

The grass crackled, the atmosphere so dry that clouds of smoke rose into the air. But the only result was that Mr. Talbot's shot revealed more swamp ahead, to all sides of them. Olive kicked her feet. Theirs was a boggy fate they could not avoid.

Mr. Talbot sighed in a tone of acceptance. He then gave a nod and shouted something in Hausa. The boys immediately started moving, putting everything they could onto the available horses.

Olive looked around, uncomfortable at what was happening. Was she going to have to swim in this green muck or were they going to make camp? Before she could say anything, Mastaba walked up to Olive and looked down at her. He then turned his back and dropped to one knee. Aji and Kukaua similarly bowed down in front of the Talbots.

They were going to carry them.

Olive watched as Mr. Talbot placed both his legs over Aji, who then stood up, balancing him with his arms. Mrs. Talbot did the same, climbing onto Kukaua, though she was much more unsteady. When it was Olive's turn, she sprang onto Mastaba's back and scissored her legs around his neck. Mastaba stood straight up, grabbing her legs at the calves. They swayed for a moment, but Mastaba's strength compensated, keeping her steady in the air. As they advanced slowly into the swamp, Olive was surprised that it wasn't so deep that she got wet, though she feared that outcome was inevitable. What if there was a crocodile? Or a hippo? After about one hundred yards, Olive's perch became increasingly precarious. There was a division of opinion on whether the boys should instead hold their riders over their shoulders, suspended backward, but Olive resisted. She felt her position failing, but she didn't want to be carried like a sack.

Mastaba sensed Olive's unease. He stopped to give a slight heave of his shoulders to improve her steadiness. Instead of being helpful, however, this caused Olive to slide. She tried to balance herself, but it was too late. Only by tightly squeezing her knees together around Mastaba's neck was Olive able to right herself, though she heard his throat gurgle as she did so. After a while, her position once again became unbearable. Olive felt badly for Mastaba.

She said: "I will get down and walk."

Mastaba was too proud to allow her request, and therefore doubled his pace before she could scramble down. But the faster he went, the more slippery the muddy bottom of the swamp became. Soon the water crept to Mastaba's waist. He kept hitching Olive up so that her feet wouldn't get wet, but there was no denying gravity. Finally giving up, Olive swayed back, ready to fall into the swamp and its questionable waters, when Mastaba swung her around in one great motion until she lay across his shoulders, clutching at his head. Olive held on for dear life for the next four hundred yards until he placed her triumphantly on solid ground.

Mrs. Talbot was having an even worse time keeping her balance. Exasperated at her thrashing about, Kukaua finally stopped in the deepest part of the swamp and threatened to drop her. Mrs. Talbot hated getting wet, so she begged him to continue and began offering bribes. Kukaua only swayed and groaned in a way that was equal parts despair and theater. Mrs. Talbot was close to screaming, saying "I fall! I fall!," to which Kukaua replied, with true philosophy, "Never mind." Watching this unfortunate display from the opposite shore with Olive, Mastaba started back and carried Mrs. Talbot himself the rest of the way, Kukaua skulking behind him. He would probably get in trouble for this, but he didn't seem to mind.

The party continued this way in a seemingly endless march through a landscape that had begun to test their very perceptions of where—and what—they were walking on. When they touched semisolid earth again, they prayed they had left the swamp for good. Olive saw a friendly snake, slithering over the dirt, politely waiting to greet them. But a carrier picked it up and broke its neck. It seemed so defenseless and so anxious not to give offense that Olive felt very sorry for it.

But as soon as one swamp ended, another one began. The grass would part like a curtain, and Olive would see another lake of floating green. To think she had wished for this color, now forever associated with such a thick, awful smell. As Olive watched Mr. Talbot measure out the sun with his eye, she felt they must be lost. They would die here in this soft labyrinth, sinking into its endless mud.

After another respite on dry land, they came across yet another patch of swamp. They prepared to take their customary positions once again, but Olive had endured enough.

She waded right in without a second glance. The water was slow and warm.

"Wait," said Mr. Talbot.

Olive, who was now half in, was ready to tell him something bordering on the rude, when she saw the boys looking out past her. Did they spy a crocodile? Perhaps it was another needless display of flashy horsemanship come to assault their senses.

Olive tried to follow their gaze. She saw two very tall shapes making their way toward them, directly through the swamp, almost as if they were walking on its surface. Just as much as the party were hunting animals, this was the second time that people seemed to be hunting them. As they got closer, the shapes became horses. Olive saw there were two riders, two men, black as midnight.

The men approached slowly. When they dropped from their mounts, Olive looked away as neither man wore a single shred of clothing. She turned back to them. The new men stared at her with serious looks. As the only member of her party half in the swamp, she knew that she was their primary concern. She could feel Mr. Talbot edging forward on the shore behind her. Then one of the natives stepped forward and, with a gesture, presented their horses to them.

The new men spoke in low tones to Mastaba. He turned to Mr. Talbot and said the horses were a gift from the local Bamm, the chief of Sulkando. The Bamm thought they would appreciate some good horses because of the crocodiles here.

The boys looked to their gods in thanks. Olive agreed with the sentiment: Their prayers were answered. Some of the boys took the lead, saying they knew the way. As Olive mounted her new steed, she briefly wondered how the Bamm knew they were coming in the first place.

THE MEN WHO GIFTED THEIR HORSES moved ahead on foot and were quickly lost from sight. Now on horseback, the company finally began to escape the spell of the swamp. They moved with relative ease, until they heard a loud crash and saw an immense surge of water just a few yards away.

In a second Mr. Talbot was in pursuit, sliding off his horse and grabbing his rifle from Kukaua. Olive pushed herself off her horse and followed them, splashing as fast as she could through the swamp.

Olive broke through to a clearing and saw Mr. Talbot standing there, his rifle at the ready. The swamp was up to his waist, and he had his back to a tree. He pivoted in place as he took aim at different sides of the wall of tall grasses. Olive scrambled and took a spot next to him. He didn't rebuke her.

They heard the grass crash and break all around them as the unseen beast moved its great bulk, just out of their sight. They heard grunting and snorting. Olive expected it to leap at them at any moment. This went on for several agonizing minutes. Whatever it was, it was loud and getting closer.

Kukaua shouted and pointed up to the tree.

Mr. Talbot tried raising his boot out of the mud and agreed: The tree would provide a much greater vantage point. The crashing was getting closer. Kukaua pushed past Olive, thrusting the rifle into her hands. After she took it, he climbed up the tree. He rested in the topmost branches and craned his neck for a better look at their enemy.

Olive raised her rifle and looked down its long barrel. She could hear her own breathing and the sucking sound of her boots.

"Hippo!" Mr. Talbot shouted.

Olive had always thought of hippos as fat, docile creatures known more for their prodigious bellies than wanton violence. At the London Zoo they lazed away in shallow pools, crunching at lettuce with their little ears waving. The hippos were never the main attraction, not like the lions. But here in Africa, in their home, hippos were an altogether different animal. Their ferocity—and their sheer enormousness—gave them no fear of man. Their flesh was said to be delicious, but many of the boys had never eaten one, simply because they were so hard to kill. Every villager and colonial officer had urged them to avoid the hippo at all costs—to think that she had wanted to pet one!

Olive climbed up the tree and stood on its lowest bough, very conscious of the fact that a hippo could still probably reach her and engulf her in its massive jaws. Olive stood there anyway, breathing. She made no move to go higher.

On the edge of the clearing, they saw a green shape move along the water, long and curling but covered in hard armor. The crocodile cast an eye on them, then moved out of sight.

Mr. Talbot slung his rifle on his back and proceeded to climb the tree as quietly as possible. Olive did not trust Kukaua's marksmanship in this moment, no matter his reputation. From their perches they looked down to see the crocodile resurface where Mr. Talbot had just been standing. The reptile floated up slowly, then vanished again.

They waited, trying to be quiet, as the sunlight faded into a dark blue. Olive looked around. The sounds had stopped. The hippo was gone. All they heard were birds.

They clambered down the tree in silence and slogged back onto the path. They saw the dark crocodile again and gave it a wide berth.

When they rejoined Mrs. Talbot, she told them a giant hippo had doubled back to the main path and had held up the carriers for several dramatic minutes. It was colossal, its jaws half the size of a horse, its massive teeth like stone hammers. Mrs. Talbot was breathless in her description. She then asked Olive about their adventure.

"It was fun," said Olive.

WHEN THEY FINALLY RETURNED, the boys had already gone ahead to set up camp outside Sulkando, which was a bit farther on. When Olive reached camp, she went straight to bed. Her whole body finally relaxed at the thought of spending tomorrow in the idle flow of a canoe.

When she awoke, the chief of the village was there to greet the party. He started to talk, through Mastaba, to Mr. Talbot, who began to get animated.

Mrs. Talbot filled Olive in: They were not in Sulkando.

Olive's heart sank. Mr. Talbot was simmering.

"Where are we?" asked Mrs. Talbot.

"Cherijamm," her husband replied.

"How far is Sulkando?"

"Two hours," he said. "The other way."

THE TWO LAKES

November 1910: After Getting Back on Course,
the Party Explores the Tuburi Lakes and the
Strange Tribes That Live There

Mr. Talbot tried to retain his British composure. Yet he was still bristling as he silently checked his maps, confirming what the chief had told him. They had indeed missed their destination, and he knew who was to blame.

Mr. Talbot glared at their native guides, whom they had hired just before the swamps. They were already enjoying themselves, walking in and out of the open stalls of the market, which was filled with people. Olive saw a pail of butter and could almost taste it, but Mastaba restrained her. He declared it to be unfit for a white man's food. Olive couldn't help but agree—there were flies all over its surface.

Apologizing, Mastaba explained that the boys had missed the pleasures of city life and had led the party astray on purpose so they could attend the festival of the first harvest of the maize. Olive watched them happily eating and laughing and had to admit that the gladness of the place was infectious.

The Bamm, the Sulkando chief who had sent the horses through the swamp, was also waiting for them in Cherijamm. The soft-spoken chief offered to escort them to Sulkando. There was nothing to do but to pack up and go on. Olive decided to walk alongside Mrs. Talbot, who was nearly half-asleep on her horse. The Bamm, who walked along in an easygoing manner, cleared every thorn from the path as they passed, especially for Olive. He cut down even a single maize stalk if it had bent to cause her discomfort.

When they finally reached Sulkando—for what felt like the second time—they were welcomed with open arms. The harvest celebration was in full swing there as well. But after such a circuitous, nearly eternal journey, the party was eager to push off in their waiting canoes. So, after a brief respite, they all pitched in to start the next leg. Most of the party separated, taking the heavier cargo around the lake on the horses; they would rendezvous with them farther up. This way Olive and Mrs. Talbot could avoid Governor Temple's ban on being in nonauthorized areas. The party, along with their own retinue, was ready to float off onto the lake to M'burao. Olive waved silently to the Bamm, who stood on the shore like an effigy.

The canoes were going to cross two lakes: the Tuburi and the Tikem, one to the west, the other to the east, that combined when they merged in the middle. As they pushed off, Olive was immediately enchanted by the view. She saw water lilies and lotuses, coloring the heaven-reflecting waters with whites, pinks, mauves, and blues. Humbler flowers grew among them, tiny golden blossoms and the graceful water violet. Small fishing boats were scattered all over the lake. Olive watched as a waterman on a neighboring boat threw his paddle out to one of his fish traps, which was tangled in the tall grass. He then walked quickly on the floating paddle to the trap! From a little distance, he looked as if he were walking on water.

For the next few days Olive enjoyed gliding peacefully about the lake. When they were tired or wanted to stretch their legs, they would stop at one of the coastal villages. The continuous lakeshore was home to two distinct tribes, the Tuburi and the Wadama. In her journal, Olive wrote that they were "fine, well-made people, though both uncivilized."

The natives were completely unclothed save for an animal-hide loincloth that hung behind their legs. These scraps were adorned with a wisp of fur and looked, to Olive, like a tail. The women had slightly different variations. They wore long dark strands of bark around their waists that were fastened by a string and hung in a bunch at the back. Some of the bark was passed under their legs and through the string in front, so that it fell again in a fringe that reached the knee. The unmarried girls also wore a patterned blue-and-white-bead apron, four or five inches in width.

These tribes treasured finery, wearing bracelets, earrings, armlets, necklets, and anklets. Olive thought they cared just as much about personal appearance as any Parisian belle. Moussa eyed each piece with envy. Their skin was also blacker than any Olive had ever seen. As she got closer, she noticed a curious kind of strange texture to their flesh, different from the usual smooth glow. Their skin looked as if it had been painted on with thick brushstrokes. Olive realized that this tribe actually greased their skin to make it appear coal black. She deduced that a deepness of complexion was equated with stature and power.

As Olive slyly tried to inspect another group of women, one of them turned to face her. Olive tried to stifle a gasp. The woman had a large round disk, maybe four inches across, embedded in her lower lip. It was thin and shone brightly as it reflected in the sun. The disk looked unimaginably painful, though the woman did not betray any discomfort. Another woman had all four corners of her mouth studded with nails. When Olive saw her, the woman's eyes lit with delight. She posed carefully for a photograph.

For all the finery Olive witnessed, it also seemed that her and Mrs. Talbot's reputation as buyers had preceded them. At one village the women had already concealed all their treasures—not only from the visitors but also from their husbands, who were often eager profiteers. But Olive had learned from watching Mrs. Talbot how to locate a tribe's most prized and noteworthy curios. So when they entered a home that afternoon, already swept clean of interest, Olive gazed up at the ceilings and doors, though to no avail.

As they left the home Momo jumped down from the roof with a

handful of objects under his arm, pressed against his white robes. He had a great smile on his face. The valuables had been hidden on the roof. Mrs. Talbot made a quick inventory. She immediately offered a price for an iron poker. The owner refused, so Mrs. Talbot offered more until they accepted. Mrs. Talbot also bought what looked like a bird trap of attractive simplicity. Another curious article they saw consisted of two oval rings attached to opposite ends of a short piece of string, which was weighted in the center with a piece of metal. The owner said it was part of a bridle, which it obviously was not, and refused to sell it. Mrs. Talbot suggested it might be an instrument of torture.

When they got back onto the lake, they skimmed across the water for a time until Olive felt their canoe begin to slow. Olive looked down. The lake was getting shallow. The Tuburi polers they had hired sprang into the water, which was up to their knees, and made offers to carry them to the shore. Mrs. Talbot bravely balanced on her waterman's shoulder, but he looked unaccustomed to the task, and the distance to traverse was long. Olive climbed on her carrier and had barely started before her hands felt wet. She glanced nervously, first at the poler's glistening shoulders, then at her own gloves. They were not only wet through but now were splotched with black stains. Olive leaned backward and saw that her shirt bore the same marks. When dry land was reached, Olive sprang to the ground and craned her neck around. Her worst fears were realized: Her skirt was filthy and disgusting. Her carrier had been wearing the same tar-black paint she had seen before. She sniffed and detected an indescribable but horrific odor that was now attached to her.

"I feel like the proverbial dog with a tin bucket tied on to its tail," she said.

Mrs. Talbot only suffered one small patch of tar on her dress and was spared any nauseating smell, as far as Olive could detect.

They had a brief visit at the village of M'burao, whose swampy location stank even worse. Olive walked through it with a handkerchief at her nose.

"I detest M'burao," said Olive, as they left. When she wrote in her diary that night, her entry was short: "I had learnt a lesson I shall not readily forget, and that is never to let an unclothed man carry me."

THE NEXT DAY THE PARTY WAS AGAIN on the march. They made good time across a slightly drier landscape. After they stopped for the day, Olive ventured out to take some photographs. When she returned to camp, Olive walked past the boxes of supplies and the ever-present rows of dead birds. She went to her tent and lay down to rest her eyes, but was quickly awakened by loud shouting. Olive walked outside and saw a frying pan fly past her head.

Around the central firepit Cooku and Washerman were having an argument. Olive was stunned to see them both armed with cookware that they were brandishing like medieval weapons. Mrs. Talbot arrived, and Olive helped her silence the two combatants. The men kept shouting—until Mr. Talbot arrived. When they saw him, they tried to escape out past the tents, but Mr. Talbot ordered them back. They returned slowly. Mr. Talbot calmly asked them the particulars of their conflict. As they took turns pleading their case, Olive could understand only a few of their words: *"Iron," "milk," "knife,"* and *"blow"* came very frequently into the story, but she could not understand the central plot. Looking at Mr. Talbot, Olive was surprised at his aloofness. When Mr. Talbot finally passed his judgment, he neglected to mention any of the main points that Olive had caught, making her wonder if he had even been listening at all. Instead he sputtered off some biblical reference about turning the other cheek. Once he was done, Mr. Talbot regarded them with a stern eye.

"I am Master," he told them.

The men dropped their heads and nodded. There would be no more trouble.

Later Olive studied her little book of Hausa. She was tired of being left out of the conversation:

7. A noun cannot be used as the direct subject of a verb, other than the substantive verb.

A pronoun must also be used before the verb.

I am the headman, he is a slave. The boy mounted the horse. The girl went away. You are a woman. Did you (pi.) understand? We understood. The men came. The traders have a horse. The king has a slave. The headman understood. The traders have boys. I have it. The slave came. The girl has a horse. She is a girl. You (m.) are old. You (f.) are old.

shi ke nan (lit. it is this) is very commonly used to denote 'all right! that is so.'

The next day Mr. Talbot was in a mood. Everyone, including Mrs. Talbot, gave him a wide berth as he stomped around camp, muttering about this or that. Olive knew the only activity that would satisfy him: A hunt was in order. Olive and Mrs. Talbot decided to join him, if only to provide a counterweight to his predatory tendencies. He pushed himself out into the lake in a single canoe. This itself was folly, for he was now limited to shooting only what was directly in front of him: To turn around and shoot in any other direction would result in a certain soaking. Olive and Mrs. Talbot decided to follow in a separate canoe.

Hot iguanas lay sizzling upon the rocks on the lake. Olive noticed a single animal in the water, following Mr. Talbot. It raised its round head from time to time to stare at the back of his canoe.

"Look," said Olive. "A mermaid!"

Mrs. Talbot scoffed at Olive's fancy. It was a manatee. Though most made the comparison because of its long, tapering body that ended with flippers, Olive knew from their wildlife book that it was because the manatee cradled its young in its arms. Olive watched as the manatee regarded Mr. Talbot, who was oblivious to its presence, with its large, brown eyes. Then it lost interest and floated away.

The next day they camped in the Tuburi village of Yue. They were met by a couple of French officers who were stationed in the area. They escorted the party to a feast in the village in their honor. That night the natives did a great dance by the light of the full moon. Their dancing, which Olive likened to a slow cakewalk, had barely finished when the chief did the unthinkable: He turned to Olive and begged to see her hair.

Olive's red hair, piled upon her head, was both the object of her own scorn and her principal calling card. Natives ogled it sometimes more than the whiteness of her skin. Not only was its scarlet color a completely new discovery for most of them—like a never-before-seen flower or animal—it was mysterious. Anyone could tell, based on the dark arts that allowed Olive to fold and pin it up into a bun, that there was more there to see hidden under the underpinnings—possibly much, much more. Olive, in this heat, had become quite tired of her heavy head. In some places the air was so dry that when she brushed her hair at night, it set off great sheets of sparks.

The chief had asked her nicely. Olive contemplated her position.

One of the Frenchmen begged her not to.

"They will think you devils, and will treat you accordingly," he said.

Olive smiled at the chief, shook her head, and kept her hair up. As the night went on, she realized that the Tuburi had also, by their looks and gestures, detected the slight differences between her and the Talbots. Olive was sure the Tuburi knew they were of two different races, English and Scottish. The Talbot's English hair was darker, though their eyes were blue like hers. Olive wondered if it was her facial structure, or the burr in her voice.

That night Olive and Mrs. Talbot made their regular evening stroll in the long African twilight when the birds were most active. They were enjoying their walk, picking up bits of things here and there, when Mr. Talbot startled them. He was carrying his rifle.

"Keep within sight of camp," said Mr. Talbot. There was alarm in his countenance. He explained that there had been fighting in the neighboring township of Fianga. The chief there had recently forbidden his subjects to work for the white men. When two of his men served as carriers for the French, he beat them. The French sent soldiers, and there had been a fight.

Olive and Mrs. Talbot walked back quickly. Just outside camp they saw a great tree that seemed heavily loaded with full leaves. Olive had never seen its ilk before. Then she realized that these were not leaves: The tree was choked with bats.

Someone from camp fired off a shot, and twelve bats fell to the ground. Olive watched as the rest sprang to clicking, fluttering life. The bats lifted into the air as if they were one dark shape, wheeling and turning in the blue-black sky. As they took off, they blocked out all the remaining moonlight, covering Olive and the camp in shadow.

THE NEXT DAY THEY CANOED to the village of Kerra to meet the Wadama people. When they landed, the women and children fled into their huts. This was not uncommon, but the men had disappeared as well. Mr. Talbot eyed the empty village suspiciously. He thought for a moment, then directed the boys to start pitching camp. Once their peaceful intentions were apparent, the native men came down in small, tentative groups. Olive found them tall and imposing with their towering staffs. They all sat down and watched one another across a tense distance.

It was Aji, to everyone's surprise, who went across the divide first, for he was hungry and wanted to buy some corn. But because he worked for the white man, the Wadama doubted his intentions. They gripped their spears. But Aji, in his white short pants, set his jaw and ran for the biggest, tallest Wadama man he could see. Whether it was surprise or skill, Olive couldn't tell, but Aji wrestled the tribesman round the legs and threw him to the ground in a cloud of dust. Aji stood over him and brushed the dirt off his arm. The Wadama stared.

They all started laughing. Aji helped up his defeated opponent and gently passed his arm through his. The Wadama led him off in triumph to their village.

When Olive and the Talbots entered the village the next day, they were clearly welcome. They were taken on a house-to-house tour, as was becoming the custom of their visits. There were only small, and thus profound differences in each hut compared with the village before. Each Wadama home had a piece of an eggshell in it, suspended from the ceiling. Olive guessed this was a symbol of fertility because she remembered seeing something like it back in England.

The Wadama were very skilled in woodworking. Their homes had wooden doors and long beds that could be transformed into handsome tables. The men even wore bracelets and anklets made of cord and wood. As Olive admired their fashions, one of the men bared his teeth to her. Olive stared: His teeth had been filed into sharp, gleaming points. Olive averted her eyes and moved on. She and Mrs. Talbot traded with the natives, mostly with cloth, which Olive thought they would use to cover their nakedness. But the Wadama instead laid it on the roofs of their houses to make them appear fine. When Mrs. Talbot traded a native a tin of digestive biscuits, the new owner pulled out the inner lining and wound the silver foil in his hair, which brought him great acclaim.

Above all else the Wadama desired salt. Olive and Mrs. Talbot begged Mr. Talbot not to trade any more of it because their stores were very low. But Mr. Talbot wanted to deal. To show the natives what he wanted in return, Mr. Talbot took out a small silver instrument. He held it up high to show everyone it was not a weapon. He made a gesture for Mastaba to come up to him. In quick order, with flashing, fluid precision, Mr. Talbot used the tool to measure the nose, chin, forehead, and ears of his headman, who tried to be very still. Mr. Talbot then put the little tin of salt on the table in front of him.

The natives formed a line. One by one, they sat in grave seriousness as Mr. Talbot took their measurements and recorded them in his small notebook. Olive imagined the paper that would be delivered some day before the stern men of the Royal Geographic Society. As their salt began to dwindle, spoonful by spoonful, so did Olive and Mrs. Talbot's spirits, imagining the flavorless food to be prepared by Cooku in the coming days.

"I do hope the society really appreciate the measurements they ask for," said Olive slyly so that only Mrs. Talbot could hear. Her friend snorted. Neither of them understood this nonsense, especially at the expense of salt.

When Mr. Talbot was done, the Wadama were impressed enough by his acumen that they began to send him their sick. Mr. Talbot took his role very seriously. He dealt out simple but potent remedies from his personal kit that won him great respect and gratitude.

"The native likes his medicines strong," said Mr. Talbot, when he was done. One old and very poor man brought a fowl and hobbled away quickly to show he did not want payment at all.

THAT NIGHT OLIVE TOOK A STROLL with Mr. Talbot near the river. Mrs. Talbot had retired early, her injury having been reaggravated. They heard a soft splashing sound: Mr. Talbot stopped. A dark hippo had emerged about forty yards ahead of them. They both sat down under a tree to observe it quietly, lit only by the stars.

Mr. Talbot pulled up his leg with a shout. Something had bitten him. The hippo disappeared back into the water. Mr. Talbot was grimacing in pain. Olive hoped it was ants, but he said no, it was a snake.

They got back to camp in a matter of minutes, where they were met by Mrs. Talbot and Mastaba. Mr. Talbot was writhing as they laid him down and pulled off his boot. His leg was inflamed and visibly taut. Mastaba pointed at a spot below the knee, where there were two red dots.

Mr. Talbot sat up, grabbed his knife, and cut across the bite marks twice—crisscross—with the sharp point. His wife cried out in protest.

There was no blood: The poison was already inside.

Mr. Talbot called for his kit. He pulled out a small brown bottle and unscrewed the crusty black cap. Mrs. Talbot helped him pour the carbolic acid into his wounds. His teeth were gritted; there was white saliva at the corners of his lips.

"Ligatures," he growled.

As Mrs. Talbot tore up his pant leg, Olive helped tie the thin pieces of cloth around Mr. Talbot's swollen leg. Olive then fetched water bottles that the boys had already started filling. They packed it all on his leg and thigh, hoping to arrest the deadly venom before it reached his heart and stopped it cold.

Mrs. Talbot reappeared with a steaming cup of black coffee. She set it to his lips and tipped it forward until he had drunk the whole thing. She rummaged in his pack and grabbed the dark bottle of whiskey. She poured two-thirds of it down his throat in a single motion.

Mr. Talbot's eyes rolled back; he was losing consciousness.

Mrs. Talbot looked at Olive with a serious, helpless face.

No, no, no, thought Olive. Of all people, not Mr. Talbot.

Mrs. Talbot cleared the boys away. She pulled out another small leather purse and untied the leather string that held it closed. Olive saw a syringe and a small bottle marked POISON. It was a strychnine kit. Mrs. Talbot would have to inject the deadly white poison if her husband got any worse. In very low doses, it could prove helpful in getting him to rally. But far more likely, it could finish him off.

They watched Mr. Talbot for an hour as he breathed first very heavily, then in shallow gasps. Mrs. Talbot held the syringe close. But as the night pressed on, and the beasts rustled in the underbrush just beyond the fire, Mr. Talbot's pulse slowed, then steadied, then actually grew stronger.

By the early hours of the morning Mr. Talbot was awake and smiling.

"He's strong," said Mrs. Talbot to Olive.

But then, as if hearing her, Mr. Talbot began to have heavy palpitations of the heart. His eyelids fluttered and he clutched his chest. They covered his chest with compresses, and Mrs. Talbot held her husband's white hand.

Mr. Talbot, after his heart heaved, seemed to find a gentler rhythm.

He began to improve with every hour. He eventually opened his eyes again, to see his wife sitting over him.

"It was only because of leather boots and heavy trousers that he is still alive, said Mrs. Talbot later. Olive, despite the tears in her eyes, couldn't help the stray thought that she still needed new boots.

By six o'clock the next morning, they broke camp, led by Mr. Talbot, who walked with only a slight limp.

THE MAN-LEOPARD

*November 9, 1910: Bad Luck Stalks Mr. Talbot; Olive
Fears She Has Lost Something; On a Moonlit Night
in Chad, They Hear Strange Music*

There was a Frenchman waiting for them at the far shore of the
lake. They could tell by his colors and the curl of his mustache.
That, and the patience with which he watched them. When they made
land, he introduced himself as Monsieur Lasarre. He was going to help
them hire new carriers as they prepared to take to the march again.
When they got to camp, Olive saw that it had grown considerably—all
the boys who had taken the long way around the lakes had returned with
their rugged cargo of boxes, though most were awaiting dismissal.

As they made small talk about their adventures, Mr. Talbot told Lasarre about Olive and the falls. Lasarre smiled politely and said that two
Frenchmen had already discovered the Mao Kabi Falls years earlier. He
was very earnest in his delivery of this news. Olive found it impossible
that their friend M. Bertaut could not have known this and wondered
if Lasarre was lying as part of some French attempt at superiority. Lasarre only smiled and got about providing them with more carriers, at an
agreed-upon rate.

As Mr. Talbot went over to greet the new boys, Lasarre inched over to Mrs. Talbot, and in a low voice, begged her to grant him two small favors. Mr. Talbot was out of range. Unnerved, Mrs. Talbot told him to continue. Lasarre asked Mrs. Talbot not to beat the carriers herself and, if possible, use her influence with Mr. Talbot to keep him from doing so. He then smiled at her, his eyes blinking, and took his leave.

After the march began, Mrs. Talbot told her husband about the strange exchange. Mr. Talbot was furious at the man's very suggestion. Olive felt the same.

THE MOON WAS GLOWING WHEN they entered the native village of Gumun. The small, clean settlement was home to the Banana tribe, whose huts were decorated with beautiful water casks painted red and yellow. The moon revealed pumpkin gourds with bright blossoms that lay near the main trail. This was one of the prettiest settlements Olive had yet seen.

By now Olive and the Talbots had a regular rhythm when entering a new village. They would make a slow, respectful entrance, be observed from afar by slightly wary natives, and after a time the people would slowly come out to greet them, sometimes with gifts to sell or trade. If the chief was home, they would meet him, too. The farther they were from Forcados, the longer that hesitation rested in the air between trepidation and contact. But as always, that chasm to friendship inevitably closed. Having come to Africa half expecting savages approaching them at every turn, Olive had found the exact opposite.

As the people of Gumun walked into the moonlight, Olive was surprised to see the women of the tribe first. They had shaved heads and more of the large, painful-looking disks that stretched out their bottom lips. They wore no clothes.

Mastaba said it had been only three months since the white man had first come to Gumun. The French wanted carriers for their endeavors, but the Gumun people had no use for money. The French tried melting their coins down to entice the natives further, but still they refused. They wanted only the large white-and-blue beads they prized for their hair and pipe stems. So the French struck a deal: They opened a nearby store, the Compagnie française de l'Ouhame et de la Nana, and stocked it with beads, so that the natives could easily exchange their pay.

The party stayed the night in peace, then used many of their own beads to hire more Banana tribesmen for the next part of their trip. Mr. Talbot bought some provisions at the French store, including more beads. He also purchased some hammocks, though Olive wasn't sure if she could sleep well in one.

After leaving the village, the expedition came across yet another swamp. After a quick survey of its dimensions, Mr. Talbot decided he could wade through it. Olive prepared to do the same when she saw the hammocks being unrolled. Apparently there was a new plan. The Gumun boys hoisted both Olive and Mrs. Talbot in separate hammocks and then carried them aloft through the muck like Egyptian princesses. The boys were very careful, but sometimes the ground itself gave way and one of the bearers slipped and fell to the muddy swamp floor. But even as they fell with a sloshing bump, they never failed to extend their arms to their fullest so that Olive and Mrs. Talbot remained dry. Even when one of the boys did fall underwater, it only provoked much laughter, mostly from the bearers themselves.

Olive found the whole thing hopelessly uncomfortable. There was such a terrible awareness to riding in a hammock. She felt that to stir would upset all the bearers below, not to mention that the motion made her feel like a ball being bounced between four children. She was also sure she looked just as ridiculous as she felt.

They marched this way for three long hours. Olive could not believe her carriers' stamina. She observed that much of their success was because of the ways they helped one another. Most of the boys carried a small pipe, suspended on a long chain. When in danger, a boy would play some little air that would summon a comrade to his assistance, even if he was falling into a sinkhole. More than once Olive thought of the Frenchman and his ridiculous warnings.

The next spot on their map was a town called Ham. The village itself lay on a narrow ridge that rose out of the water. The huts lined along the top were clustered so thickly that there was barely room to pass between them. Plots of tobacco filled the tiny spaces in between. Mrs. Talbot explained that the name of the place was thought to be indebted to the old story in the book of Genesis: When Ham was cursed for knowing his father, Noah, in a naked state, his line was forever cursed. Because some thought that Ham was of dark skin, the "Curse of Ham" became a justification for slavery. Ham also signaled that they had finally crossed the border into French-occupied Chad.

Olive and the Talbots agreed that since the Banana tribe had been so welcoming, this small village might be a perfect spot to rest and engage in a few days' leisurely hunting. They had even seen gazelle feeding within range of the firepit. Olive could sense Mr. Talbot's excitement: He hadn't enjoyed a good hunt since his snakebite.

Once camp was made, they set upon their usual preparations for the hunt. As they were getting ready, Mr. Talbot stooped to take something from his trunk. When he stood up, his head struck a wooden beam with swift force. He blinked, swayed, and then slumped to the ground. Mrs. Talbot ran to him. He was not unconscious but dazed. Maybe it was the lingering effects of the snake's poison, but he started slurring his words, even smiling uncontrollably. They put him right to bed.

The boys said, as a matter of fact, that Mr. Talbot lived to hurt himself, and Olive had to agree. The string of bad luck that had surrounded him was like some sort of dark spell.

"What do you wish?" Mrs. Talbot asked sweetly when her husband finally woke up. He had shown no other symptoms, so they felt it safest to prescribe him bed rest.

"Sardines," said Mr. Talbot.

This was an unexpected request. Mrs. Talbot didn't know if it was her husband's delirium or a need for salt, but she was determined to find him some sardines. As Mrs. Talbot looked through their supplies, Olive looked at the medical chapter in their well-worn little medical manual.

After searching through the book, she showed a page to Mrs. Talbot, who read it with a grim face.

Mrs. Talbot called Situ over and explained that under no circumstances, no matter how sad his lamentations, was Mr. Talbot to be given sardines. The book said they could be very detrimental to his condition. In fact, any and all food orders had to go through Mrs. Talbot.

"You understand?" she asked.

Situ nodded, his mouth closed. When Mr. Talbot was unable to lead, which had been more frequent than Olive would have predicted, there was no question that his wife was in charge.

When Mrs. Talbot turned her attention back to her husband, Olive caught a fleeting look on Situ's face that looked like objection. The manual also stated that whenever possible, a wife must always tend to her husband's sickness. And if she could not, another woman should in her stead. That night Olive had dinner alone while Mrs. Talbot stayed with her husband.

Olive knew what it meant to care for the sick. When her mother first became immobilized, Olive and Flora would visit with her every afternoon and play chess with a special set for the blind. They would read to her stories from her beloved mythology books. The sisters would sometimes steal glances at each other, feeling guilty and free at the same time.

After Olive finished her dinner, she went to relieve Mrs. Talbot for the night shift. Olive told Situ to keep dinner for Mrs. Talbot, but by the time she came, her meal had been removed. Mrs. Talbot called Situ and asked him to bring it again. With a trembling voice he replied, "Master ill."

She understood what was going on.

"Yes," said Mrs. Talbot. "But Miss MacLeod is with him now. Bring my dinner, quick."

"Master live to hurt his head," repeated Situ. He would not give up his point.

Mrs. Talbot's absence from her husband's side—even if for dinner—

was unseemly, at least in Situ's eyes. He finally brought Mrs. Talbot's dinner, but for some time afterward, he marked his disapproval by drawing her disagreeable baths.

As Olive went to bed, she reached for the strongbox with her diaries— but could not find it. She rifled through her various bags and trunks but still could not find the box. Had it been stolen? A sharp pang cut into her. Had someone read them? Did someone know? She turned over some cloth she had bought in one of the markets and found the box there. It had simply been jostled on the march. She wrote inside her diary in a bleary hand, almost as if to confirm its presence. She put it back away.

A few nights later Mr. Talbot was feeling much better. Olive left him alone with his wife. Olive wandered out to the fire. It was still blazing to hold off the mosquitoes. Mastaba was sitting there, looking into the sparking wood. Olive noticed something strange in the sky: A wide nimbus of blurry light shone round the moon. The effect in the atmosphere was mesmerizing.

Olive asked Mastaba about it. She thought it looked magical.

"It is a great medicine," he said.

Mastaba explained that the moon was the work of a great medicine man, somewhere out on the plains. He crouched down, directing her attention toward the ground. He drew a large circle in the dust. Mastaba said that the medicine man had done the same, over which he muttered incantations. If his magics worked, and the nimbus appeared, the moon would stay high in the heavens for a long while.

As they sat, the river wound its way toward the great lake in waveless peace, and the shadows of the huts stood black against the brightness of the moon—but no sound broke the stillness, and theirs seemed an enchanted city. Suddenly, in the distance, a flame shot up into the sky, and another, and another, till a circle of blazing, leaping fire revealed a restless group of heaving humanity out on the low grasslands. On the breeze they heard a low chant that spoke of sadness; but a stronger note throbbed through it, that of man's power and ultimate mastery. It was a wake, said Mastaba, in honor of "one big man," which meant a chief or powerful warrior. Olive had also heard this phrase used to describe the white man.

Olive stared into the night, hearing the song out on the wind.

EARLY THE NEXT DAY Mr. Talbot stood up, went through his normal routines, and by his actions announced his intent to travel. They had miles to make up and time to reclaim. Olive regarded him, thin but upright: This man seemed able to weather everything Africa could muster. They finished a short march before switching to canoes. They would travel on the Logone River for the last journey to Fort Lamy.

They paddled all day and into the night. The moon still provided a full, hazy light, making the river and trees look ethereal. The night made every sound seem sharper. There was something in the air, and even though the sun was long gone, its heat remained as an echo.

They began to hear distant chanting. The map said that they were near the Kotoko capital of Birini, and Mrs. Talbot and Olive were excited at the prospect of meeting a new tribe. However, Mr. Talbot thought for a moment, then directed the polers to pull up on shore: He was going to investigate. As he stood up, so did the ladies. Mr. Talbot turned:

"Stay where you are," he said, "unless I send to say that it is worth your while to come."

Olive and Mrs. Talbot sat down, once again relegated to their seats as a result of their sex. Mr. Talbot disappeared into the underbrush with Mastaba and some of the boys. After a few minutes, one of them returned for a rifle. Olive and Mrs. Talbot exchanged a look and decided to follow, regardless of their orders. They were not going to miss a night hunt.

Some fifty yards from the river's edge, past a small pond, they crept up to what looked to be a clearing hidden just beyond the grass. The place was large and open, the grass having been scraped away to the hard bone of the ground. The chanting was getting much louder—had Mr.

Talbot found a rare native celebration of a successful lion hunt? Olive crept closer. As soon as she passed the grass line, the sound became even greater, almost like the waterfall. As Olive pushed through, she couldn't believe her eyes. In a great clearing, she saw a writhing circle of at least five hundred dancing tribesmen, almost every man holding an enormous wooden club in his fist.

The drumbeats were rising. Olive thought that this must be the moon dance Mastaba had been talking about, the funeral ceremony for the big man. Excited to see it up close, she spotted Mr. Talbot, who was standing outside the circle, in the open, with Mastaba. He was already attracting the attention of some of the dancers. Mrs. Talbot ran up to join her husband. Olive stayed in the shadows and observed the natives. They were tall, lithe, and the blackest people she had ever seen. The tribesmen had again used grease to darken their skin, and Olive thought the effect, especially under the moonlight, unnatural. They appeared even darker than the night sky.

The tribe, who looked somewhat similar to the Banana natives they had seen earlier, became even more curious. A few of the natives stole off, while some just stopped dancing to stare at them. They looked restless and uneasy, though Olive knew they would come around. Mr. Talbot would, as always, know how to handle the situation. Already some of them felt comfortable enough to repair to the small pond behind them to suck its water through long rushes while the rest of the tribesmen kept dancing and chanting.

When the drums finally stopped, so did the dancing. After a long moment of silence, the drums started up again, slowly at first, then faster. Soon the dancing came back to its full fervor. Between the swirling limbs and clubs, in the middle of the firelight of the central circle, Olive thought she saw an animal, pacing.

As the circle cleared a little, Olive saw that it was not a lion or ram but a man. He paced about on all fours, his head moving slowly from side to side. He was covered in thick black paint from head to toe and seemed to be wearing some sort of leopard skin over his head, like a mask. Circling slowly with a crafty, panther-like tread, he would pace, then run toward someone in the circle. When he sprang to walk upright, Olive saw that he carried a cane of some sort. He also seemed to be gripping long, sharp claws.

When he advanced on one of his fellows, his victim would run away but then turn to chase down the Man-Leopard. This maneuver was repeated again and again with increasing rhythmic intensity. The repetition carried Olive back to her old hide-and-seek days, and the sloping bank of grass dotted with great clumps of rhododendron where she used to play with her sister.

Olive began to realize that this was no game.

Dread crept over her as the Man-Leopard began moving faster, and his prey began responding in kind, swinging their clubs and missing by mere inches. But these were no symbolic gestures, and they were not missing on purpose. These were killing blows. As the drums grew faster and faster, Olive realized that a small group of natives on the outer edge of the circle had crept closer and were staring at her. She was filled with an uncomfortable feeling that the tribe was now less intent upon their dance than they were upon her and her friends.

Instinctively Olive glanced behind her to see if there was anyone between her and their canoe. She saw nothing but wondered if all the men who had gone to get a drink had returned. Olive thought it absurd to indulge in suspicions. Perhaps she was letting her imagination run away with her.

Then one of the natives, club in hand, walked right up to Olive. It happened so quickly that she could not move. His white eyes fixed on her as he clasped her hands in his own greasy ones. Other tribesmen did the same; then another, then another, until it seemed to Olive as if they would all come, not only once but again and again. She breathed easier. They had just wanted to say hello.

The voices of the tribe swelled and rose. Their limbs were covered with beads of perspiration, and their eyes were aglow with excitement. Then the circle broke, an orator began to speak, and quickly the people gathered around him. Olive was free of attention again. The spokesman was gaining power over his audience. Short, sharp exclamations garnered a howl of approval from the tribesmen, who swayed around him. Olive could tell she and her friends were the subject of his discourse, but what was the gist of it—what did he want? Olive looked over to Mastaba and the Talbots. The two boys with them had already left.

Mastaba was listening, his head inclined toward the ground. He said something to Mr. Talbot and then turned to look at Olive. Trying to stick to the shadows, he began making his way down the plain to her side. Olive watched Mr. Talbot, but he would not turn to her. His eyes were fixed on the speaker.

Then Olive saw Mr. Talbot, who had kept his face toward the natives the entire time, slowly squeeze his wife's arm.

Mastaba had reached Olive. He slid behind her and whispered in her ear.

"They mean to keep the ladies," he said.

Olive looked up to see Mr. Talbot turn to face her, his eyes flashing a mixture of fear and sadness. Mastaba seized Olive's arm.

They walked quickly, trying to keep up appearances. Olive knew that if they broke into a full-fledged run, it would be over for them in a matter of seconds. They moved briskly through the brush grass and darkness. Olive prayed that they could avoid the stray pebbles and swamp holds in their path: One fall and they would be done for.

Olive looked back to see a knot of men, unencumbered and in their prime, peeling off the main group into the side forest, moving very fast past them—one of her steps falling short of three of theirs. Olive realized that the natives were moving to cut them off at the river. If they succeeded, there would be no escape.

Olive heard the drums and thought of the clubs, the magic, and the Man-Leopard. They were behind her, hidden in the shadows beside her, and possibly already in front of her. She expected a club on her neck or a spear in her side. This was the fate of Africa that everyone had foretold for her. This was the fate she expected.

Then, unbidden, she heard M. Bertaut's words echo in her mind: *"N'ayez-pas peur."* Do not live in fear.

Olive picked up her pace until she could see the river ahead of her. The Talbots and Mastaba were right with her. The natives began to run in full chase. As Olive half jumped through the last line of grass, stretching her feet onto the short beach, she knew they were lost.

Then Olive didn't know what happened, but for whatever reason, their pursuers paused, just for a moment.

Olive and her friends jumped into the canoe as Mastaba pushed them off, splashing in behind them. As the current swept them onward, shouts of anger and disappointment were raised from the swell of natives who now appeared on the shore. Some of them ran along the riverbanks, brandishing their clubs. Olive could see their eyes even as she closed hers.

Their assailants should have prevailed. Olive wondered why they had paused. Perhaps they were afraid of some witchcraft they feared, or of Mr. Talbot's gun, which she knew would have been powerless against such numbers. Perhaps they feared the river itself. Olive did not know where that one moment came from, but she was not going to give it back.

Olive exhaled, feeling great satisfaction in being safely aboard a canoe in the center of a broad stream. She thought of the strange Man-Leopard, attacking—and being attacked—by his own people. Mrs. Talbot took her hand; she was shaking.

"We will go all the way to the fort on this canoe," said Mr. Talbot, holding his wife's hand but speaking to Olive.

Olive was very pleased to hear it.

· 14 ·

A CORRESPONDENCE,
PART 3

*March 1909, Vinters: Flora's Secret Letter to Boyd Has
Put the Fledgling Romance in Danger; A Response Finally
Comes; An Alarming Telegram Arrives*

December 29, 1909

Dear Miss MacLeod

 I meant to write a letter from the coast but did not do so as the mail boat from here takes the same letters. Everything is going well. José came on board. . . . He has been extremely kind in giving me all the help I wanted. I wonder if these letters tire you—I have no means of finding out. . . . I do hope you are well. I know there are many, who with their prayers, are helping to guard you and I hope I am not so far behind.

            Boyd Alexander

Olive studied the letter. That was it? She had been waiting on pins and needles after what she had written in her last letter. After a bit of puzzling out, she realized that she was now getting letters out of sequence. But she wasn't positive, so she decided to write again. But rather than go over the dangerous ground that was Flora's secret letter, Olive decided it best to stick (mostly) to topics at home. This was the part of life that could be understood out of context; it didn't have to be a game, one move against another.

March 18, 1909
Vinters

Dear Mr. Alexander-

When I got home last night, I found your letter from Forcados—has not it taken an age? You wonder whether I like yours—surely you can guess. You seem to think I pull everything to pieces like a sort of monkey. I lunched with the Asquiths yesterday and discovered to the Prime Minister on the evils of the slave trade.

I do hope that you agree with me in thinking my decision about waiting is right. My mother does not—she says that I am behaving very badly and that you have a right to be angry with me. Please don't be, though I am not really afraid about it as I know you want my happiness.

I don't do much. Helping wheel mother's bath chair; otherwise I plant lavender and things vigorously and practice a little music— A peaceful, uneventful life.

Everything domestic has gone wrong, the main furnace flue got out of place, as a result we are cold. Then the electric light engine stopped work altogether, we might be without light for Easter when we have people coming—then my maid has left, to marry our chauffeur, and for a week I am without one.

I went to London for a night to go to the Women's Anti-Suffrage meeting. The organizers spoke well with occasional lapses into popular clap-trap like "men are men and women are women" etc.

Olive:

April 16, 1909
Littlestone-on-Sea

Dear Mr. Alexander

 It is discouraging to write to you when you probably won't receive the letter, but I hope I shall not have many more to write—but it is partly the atmosphere of this place. As usual, I am staying with the Asquiths— a young frivolous party . . . and after an evening of romps they have gone out to play on the beach and I have stayed in to write to you. The sudden quiet and the sound of the waves on the shore and the wind sighing round the house makes me feel a little discontented and lonely—a bad mood.

 It is worrying to repeat it every letter, but before you come home, I should like you to realize that I consider you bound to nothing. I shall be sad if you don't come and see me as soon as you can on getting home, but I should be much *sadder if you came from a sense of obligation. Please promise me not to do that.*

 I have not the least idea where you mean to go, whether you do the mountains first then on to Maifoni and back further east and south— I wonder?

A month later, Olive received a brief telegram. It was from Boyd.

Telegram
April 23, 1909
To: Miss Olive MacLeod, Vinters, Maidstone, England.
From: Boyd Alexander, Africa.
EARTHQUAKE—NARROW ESCAPE.

May 4, 1909

Dear Mr. Alexander

I can't tell you what a relief your cable was saying "narrow escape." I should have cabled to you had I known where to cable to, but even this is being addressed in the dark. It is difficult to write now, partly because I am tired, and partly because this is my fourth letter to you without having received any in-between.

It would be such a relief to hear you talked about, but there is no one to do it naturally—probably you will find me in an extreme on your return, either so reserved as to be like a fossil; or broken down into torrents of emotion which will well-nigh drown you. I expect you to come back exactly as I know you, but then I don't allow imaginings about you lest they prove wrong.

Please tell me when you know your approximate dates of return. I think you will but fear I may have said foolish things to make you think it would be better for me not to know so I write this request now.

Olive MacLeod:

May 24, 1909

Dear Mr. Alexander,

I write on a gloriously hot morning under the lime trees, hoping that caterpillars won't mar my peace by falling on me. The hawthorn has suddenly burst into bloom and really burdens the air with its fragrance. Why is the season of promise nicer than the season of fulfillment?— I can understand it, but if one thinks of strawberries one realizes again that this rule too has its exceptions.

I drove our new Siddeley motor-car for the first time the other day and was astonished to find how easy it was—much less trouble than the old Sunbeam. I want father to give me a tiny one-cylinder runabout, as it is a bore having to consult everybody's schedule.

I am afraid I shall misexpress myself. How odd of you to wish me to be quite contented—I am not and shall not be—it is useless trying. One can tell oneself that worry is hurtful, and it is a relief when it turns out vain, but would you be absolutely happy if you knew me to be in danger? You seem to believe so ardently in predestination that perhaps you would, though I hope not.

Independence. Owing to my mother's ill health I have had it perhaps to a greater extent than most girls, and as you ask the question I believe this to be the main reason why I am afraid of you.—One hears such terrible tales of the tyranny of explorers, and after all you are one!— Are you sure you don't want someone who can merge their personality entirely in yours? Personally, I think it would be a bore to have a companion who did, but I am so dreadfully afraid you will expect things of me that are not in me to give.—I wish there were a more immediate prospect of you coming home to settle on this doubt—and for other reasons too, though "reason" is not quite the right word. I am rather bored with you for giving me no idea as to time.

To start with, I find life far fuller, and more thrilling, and fraught with bigger possibilities, as years advance—and if we are to spend our futures together it must be because we make life more complete and perfect for each other, and through each other for ourselves—It must not be because we need each other; and not as "a matter of course" stop on the passive unfeeling slope which leads to decline and death.

I want you to realize that I live a very active busy life of my own; the things that I do can if need be transfer to other interests but what would be harder to banish (certainly with happiness) is my activity and my life.

Olive MacLeod:

Baffy has been trying to persuade me to write but I don't think authorship is much my line. The only article I wrote took me hours and hours, which at present I cannot spare.

As summer came in glorious force to Vinters, full of flowers and insects and sunshine, Olive felt safer about her strange correspondence with Mr. Alexander. They had no commitment, but she thought they felt the same toward each other. Flora's letter had been mostly forgotten and as the months shuffled by, the once faraway point of Boyd's return seemed visible to her. Olive had been trying not to focus on a particular month, but she guessed it would be soon.

But then everything changed.

June 14, 1909

Dear Mr. Alexander

    There is a great deal that is important to tell you, and possibly you may be angry with me—though I am more vexed about it than you can be.

    Mother asked me to find out where she could get bantams—no one knew around here, so I wrote and asked your brother. That it was good to hear from you and he replied it was told in a letter that you should plan to prolong your expedition by six months more than you told me— and that you should do so without telling me, in letters written at the same date. He enclosed a note from José which said the expedition would probably last another year.

    He said you had not told him a word about our relations.

    Try to put yourself in my place.

    Mr. Herbert volunteered to come and see me and told me that I must be Spartan—and not wish you to hurry home.

    I was dancing with Mr. Brodie who had also taken me in to dinner, and who is as dull and sapless as he is nice, so I had a dreary time; but I left very early—by midnight like Cinderella. Baffy knows all about you and is very anti-you.

    We spent an evening with Mr. Gorman, who thinks aeroplanes will be an immediate feature of military use. He thrilled me by saying that telepathy is no longer questioned in scientific circles; and they are now trying to disentangle whether everything comes from the mediums or some other person supra—or sub-liminal minds; or whether anything can be infinitely traced to a world outside ours. I should love to be able to telepath, and it must be a quality one could cultivate, but I am a little afraid of what is still so little understood. It must have been something of that sort which made me so nervous about you throughout the earthquake week—three days before I saw it in the papers.

Everyone has such different standards that it is difficult to convey a meaning, but I feel that lots of cash is all important, but that it does not affect happiness if one lives in a palace or a croft.

Olive:

July 6, 1909

Dear Mr. Alexander:

Herbert came over for lunch spent the whole afternoon discussing books and art. He was contending that the landscape painter can only express his native scenery and that to do pictures of foreign lands is like speaking a language with an accent. It is an interesting theory.

Olive:

Finally, in July, he wrote back:

Buea, Cameroon
July 5, 1909

Dear Miss MacLeod

I have just received your two letters. I do not know why you should be angry with me unless it is because I have missed several mails in writing to you. If this is so—I plead guilty but find for me extenuating circumstances. You must try and remember that my lot out here is not that of the ordinary white man, seldom within touch of mails.

I did not think it necessary to tell you that your sister Flora had written to me in fact as far as I can remember she marked her letter as private, and whatever she said it only made my feelings towards you stronger if that was possible.

I have been meaning to write to her every day and I must plead the same excuse as I have done to you.

I am glad I have taught you something of the feeling of contentment. Try and cultivate it more and I think you will find that you will not imagine vain foreboding in my absence.

I was also glad when you say that you would despise me if I returned before my task was done. My work is not of much account but still that is the right spirit to regard my absence in. We have had a very exciting time in the Earthquake here and it will be a scene that is not likely to fade from my memory.

Boyd Alexander

Another letter arrived soon after.

July 26, 1909

Dear Miss MacLeod

I wonder where this letter will find you, hopefully at Vinters where I hope you have enjoyed a happy and prosperous summer. . . . I am sure by now you have regained your peace of mind. Your letters always interest me.

You know that you are country-born and therefore I always associate you with walk in the country rather than in the big towns.

I arrived here a few days ago from Kamerun after a very interesting trek . . . my arrival here completes what I call the second phase of the expedition. The last phase has come, which will be the most difficult of the three.

I never like to say too much about my future work. I am sure you understand for where plans are talked about, it seems to make failures all the more acute. José leaves tomorrow for Kano for a month's journey from here to buy camels and then he will meet me.

I am going now to Maifoni to see my brother's grave.

In one of your letters, you have misgivings that you should write to me in the way you have done because "we know so little about each other." But I shall compare our love to a seed sown in the darkness, but it is growing all the same and like the flower, will fold out into gentle bloom.

You can sever the cord. I can but go to the deep valleys and high hills—whose solitude will heal me and where I can weep undisturbed.

Boyd Alexander

Olive had to spread the letters out to determine when and where they fit in their correspondence. He was responding to things she had written several months ago. Olive found it incredibly maddening. It was not only distance that was pulling upon them, but time.

November 1909

Dear Mr. Alexander-

It is a joy to be able to write to you again after an interval of three months, I thought you must have started on your desert expedition before a letter could reach you.

I can't bear much more delay in your return.

You see it is not only anxiety, and your absence—that I will gladly fare that you may do good work—but proof positive that you don't care for me and are trying to force me to break our connection in disgust. This opinion is heightened by your writing so seldom.

If you could give me any indication as to when you are likely to return, however rough, and whatever subsequently occurs to alter it, it would help me to feel I had your confidence.

I already feel a weight off my mind and my spirits booming though you are more than likely never to get this.

Olive:

Boyd's next letter was in response to a letter Olive had written in July. She was now having a hard time locating him on her map.

December 10, 1909

Dear Miss MacLeod—

I was very pleased to get your letter of the 24ᵗʰ July which came yesterday. . . . What a number of occupations you will have now! And I wonder how you will find time to get through them all!

I arrived here in Maifoni, where I heard for the first time that the French had entered Wadai, and that the road was safe. Of course, this will make things easier for me, and I think it would be a good ending to the expedition, don't you think "From the Cameroons to Cairo" would be a good title for a book? I should be the first white man through this way, and I feel perfectly confident I could do it. I have written an official letter to Sir Edward Grey asking him to approach the French Foreign Office to give me permission to return home by Wadai and Khartoum, I wonder whether you could get your Father to back this application up? I am sure you will go heart-whole with me in this venture.

You wonder why I never gave you some idea of the length of this expedition, I did not know myself. I move slowly and allow things to shape themselves of their own accord.

I was glad to hear you have become friends with my brother Herbert. If all goes well, I should be home at the latest by the end of April.

Thou hast made my love to grow into a glorious flower,

Boyd Alexander.

Olive blinked.

He was coming home.

February 18, 1911

Dear Mr. Alexander

I am writing to you much earlier than I expect you, so as to make sure of your finding a letter to welcome you back to civilization. It is too wonderful to think that your return has come as near as that I do hope and feel that you have reaped the reward of your big difficult journey, with all that that means. I wonder whether you care how much there is to show the world (that it would understand)—of course a universal appreciation is pleasant—but it is only yourself and the few people who know that really matter, and I feel quite confident that you have once more earned that, and much much more than that.

I know you have got a very busy time before you, giving your discoveries and experiences to the world, and I can't wish you better success for "From Cameroon to Cairo" than you won in "From Niger to the Nile."

The amount of things there are to tell you are literally overwhelming . . . but I would rather wait till we meet,—In fact I am not going to write you anything personal now—it is too difficult.

We are here till March 22 or 23—then we return to Vinters.

Olive:

⸺•⸺

February 25, 1910

Violet has suddenly appealed to me to go out to the Riviera and I have promised to do so. . . . Will you therefore wire to me there when you arrive in Khartoum and if possible give me some idea of the date of your arrival in England, so I might go home at the same time—I don't know what happens—do you have to acclimate in some warmish climate or can you go straight back safely? If you have to wait somewhere why not come and join me? It depends on your dates whether I should still be there, for possibly father might come and we should all go on to Italy . . . but I will wire again before I leave.

You know that Violet is a very great friend of mine and she is very unhappy. Archie Gordon adored her, but she did not realize her own feelings and would not marry him—til they were revealed to her by his having a frightful motor accident, sustaining injuries from which he died after 17 days of agony. She was with him at the end and told him of her love, so that his last hours were radiantly happy, and he never knew he was dying to spoil it for him—You won't need to be told that she is broken in body and spirit, so I cannot fail to go to her as she wants me—You need not be shy of coming for she knows about us— . . . but wherever or whenever it is please be careful to do what is wisest and best for your own self.

Au revoir.

15

A PAINTING ON A WALL

*November 1910: Olive Spends Time at the German Fort
Bongor in Chad; She Encounters a Mysterious Painting*

The party floated into Bongor at night, the Logone River shining under the same moon that had lit their escape from the terrifying ceremony. It did not seem like a dream. Olive was aware of every sound and movement around her. Though they were safely on the canoe and she tried not to think of where they could be instead, she couldn't think of anything else.

As they reached the dock, they smelled the aroma of fresh-roasted coffee. They saw two German officers with steaming cups sitting on chairs on the dock. The officers helped them out of their canoe. When they asked how their trip had been, Mr. Talbot silenced the rest of the party with a quick motion.

"All fine," he said.

When the German resident appeared to welcome them, he told them more about Fort Bongor. Details were given, but Olive didn't remember them. She didn't even get his name. When the resident warned them about the local tribes, she perked up.

"You cannot depend upon the friendliness of the natives here," the resident said, shaking his head. "Though it is unlikely they would attack so large a party as yours."

Neither Olive nor the Talbots responded.

The Germans received them with genial hospitality. While the party rested and refreshed their supplies, Mr. Talbot was informed that the nearby village of Musgum was holding a festival. The natives told Mastaba that it was a wake for "one big man," though no one seemed to know who it was.

"Your boys might be speared on sight," the resident said, warning them again. This did nothing to alleviate Olive's fears. Mr. Talbot politely declined the invitation.

Olive could hear the revelry from her tent that night. To be fair, it sounded nothing like their experience of the previous night, but that didn't change her mind about going. By the fourth day she again remembered M. Bertaut's mantra about not living in fear. She and the Talbots left their tents and walked into the village. The natives saw them and rushed at them with great speed. Olive's heartbeat quickened at the sound of footsteps running toward her. But this feeling disappeared when the villagers met them with smiles and hand-shaking. Olive looked down to find her own hands once again thickly coated with the black tar. When they got back to Bongor, she and Mrs. Talbot sat with a basin of disinfectant between them for a good twenty minutes, trying to wash it all away.

The native village itself was remarkable, notably for its thirty-foot-high conical buildings, interspersed with palm trees in a very aesthetically pleasing arrangement. The low doorways were richly ornamented on the inside by small, cresent-shaped impressions made in the soft mud by fingertips. Olive and Mrs. Talbot found various treasures in the houses that the people consented to give them in exchange for cloth and beads. Olive spied leather armor sets and small bags filled with reeds or rush. Mastaba told them that every woman owned one, and if she were to part with it, she would die, for her life was woven into its mesh.

Even with the welcoming nature of the tribe, the party was still on edge. None more than Kukaua, who had seen the leopard tribe bearing down on them from the terrifying view of the canoe. He knew how close they had come. Though a few days had now passed, his nerves were still raw. That night, engaged in his customary chore of cleaning the guns, Kukaua was early in the process when a deft flick of his thumb detached the gun's safety. He flipped over the rifle:

KRAK!

The gun went off with a loud explosion. Kukaua raised his head with a blank look. In his haste he had somehow forgotten to unload the bullets.

The breath went out of Kukaua's body as his eyes looked to see where the gun had fired. A few of the boys were standing outside a tent. They looked down at their bodies and started patting their chests and bellies. Kukaua gasped—he saw a clean round hole in the middle of the tent's doorflap. It was Olive's tent.

Olive appeared on the other side of Kukaua. She had been on the other side of the camp and had heard the shot. She followed everyone's pointing fingers. She saw the hole in her tent. Then Mr. Talbot came. He saw the bullet hole, then looked swiftly back at a shaking Kukaua.

Kukaua was immediately relieved of his position as gun boy and demoted to the rank of general laborer. Mr. Talbot searched the growing crowd. He nodded at Aji, who instantly stepped in as Kukaua's replacement. Proud of his new calling, Aji immediately proclaimed himself a Mohammedan. Olive couldn't understand this and asked him why.

"More is expected of me," he told her.

THEY LEFT BONGOR THE WAY THEY entered, on the Logone River. The sandbanks were covered by a living mass of birds. They saw egrets, plovers, waders, crowned cranes, storklike jabirus, pelicans with flesh-pink breasts; geese, herons, fish eagles, fish hawks, and ducks that rose in clouds of nearly two thousand at a time. There were other animals that they couldn't even find in their book of African wildlife.

Sometimes the temptation was more than they could resist. Mr. Talbot would bark the command and they would land—and the hunt would start again. There were no paths in this region, only tracks and sounds and spoor. Instinctively Mr. Talbot would bring his rifle to his shoulder and pause and peer, but his prey was usually just wind in the grass. If Mr. Talbot had the good fortune to see an antelope or wild boar, it was not often that it escaped with its life. Hunting had become not only a habit for Mr. Talbot, but a sort of involuntary action. They ate what they caught and stuffed the poor unnamed for the British Museum. Sometimes they had to stalk a beast for half a mile or more, tracking it by the blood marks on the reeds as it pushed its way inside the endless maze—for even when the wound was mortal, the tenacity of life of these animals was extraordinary. Olive learned it was necessary to follow a wounded animal, for its fate in that country of beasts and ants would be unthinkably worse. Olive was resolved that for this reason, she would not herself attempt to shoot.

The headman of the canoe polers they had hired had brought his wife with him, and she would chant while on the river, supported at brief intervals by a chorus. They were not songs, and though the effect was repetition, each phrase varied in some tiny way. Olive listened and puzzled over these ditties, but they went by so fast that there was no chance of hearing the exact thing repeated, only something like it. Olive jotted down a few notes, to give at least a general impression of the song:

SOLO,

REFRAIN

IN YA VELLE BONGOR TA VA TA TO I TA VA TA TAA. AH AH AH EH.

SOLO REFRAIN SOLO REFRAIN^

AY A DI TA DI-TA

AH, EH AY A DI TA DI TA AH, AH, AH, EH.

SOLO. STACCATO AND VERY QUICK. CHORUS SLOWER.

As they entered the shallows, Olive saw angular bugs skimming over the flowers. She saw a small island of sand, complete with two gray pebbles and some small pinkish flowers. When the pebbles blinked to life, Olive realized what she was actually looking at. The hippopotamus, submerged in the water, was almost wholly hidden. Though Olive knew what was going to happen next, she relished the second or two of complete intimacy, as she thought the hippo looked the height of liquid comfort in the blazing heat.

"Don't move," said Mr. Talbot.

Olive followed him as he swiveled his head and pointed at another spot in the water.

Olive began to count more eyes, snouts, and bald, soft heads that were making themselves visible from the water. Three, four, five; the boys joined in the pointing until a grand total of nine were counted.

There were nine hippos. They were surrounded.

Olive's heart raced. They had been lucky so far, having chased (with little success) a single hippo here and there, but never more than one. With maws that dwarfed the lion's, even one hippo was a formidable enemy. But nine? In their fragile canoe, in the hippos' watery den, they were at the animals' mercy. Olive knew they were in significant danger when she saw Mr. Talbot begin to take aim. There were no trees to climb.

They had no choice but to kill them all. Olive knew the water was low enough that they could retrieve the bodies for food. This was now a hunt.

Mr. Talbot wasted no time—*KRAK! KRAK! KRAK!*—as he pivoted his body and aimed and fired at as many of the animals as he could. At the loud sound the terrified polers flung themselves into the bottom of the canoe. Blood filled the swamp as four hippos began to sink like slow, heavy stones. Five more pairs of eyes rose up to stare. The hippos began swimming swiftly toward the canoe.

Mr. Talbot nodded at Olive, who grabbed her own rifle. Mr. Talbot then motioned for the remaining boys to push their canoe out of the contested waters. They started drifting toward the shore. Mr. Talbot looked at the land and let his gaze linger there, just for a moment. "If we hit that sandbank, we'll be helpless!" he shouted. "Turn around!"

Some of the hippos began to open their jaws. As if on some great hinge, they revealed pink mouths studded with ivory teeth. As Mr. Talbot shot, the canoe still had nowhere to go. They were being penned inside the quickly tightening circle of animals, all in a haze of smoke and heat. One of the hippos opened its mouth right next to the canoe. Olive believed he would shatter it in two.

Olive pulled her gun open.

"Now!" Mr. Talbot roared.

Olive wasn't sure if it was the huge, jagged teeth, slowly being revealed by the gigantic mouths of their attackers, or the surprise at her own rifle at the ready, but the boys finally leaped up and began to push the canoe downstream. Olive turned to look at the hippos, who were swimming after them. How could they move so fast?

Finally the last hippo gave up and the canoe slowed down. They were safe. The boys were almost completely out of breath. Olive sat down and handed her gun away.

Mr. Talbot's mood was dark. Olive guessed that he was angry because of all the kills they had left floating behind them. She knew he wanted to go back to retrieve the fat, slickened bodies, but it was too dangerous.

"I didn't fear the hippos," Mr. Talbot told Olive, reading her face.

He explained that during the fight, he had seen natives waiting for them in the bush by the shoreline. That is why he directed them back toward the hippos. He had been told by the Germans that there were dangerous men along the river who had recently murdered two white men. They might be a cannibal tribe.

"Since they've seen us, it is too late to go back," he said.

AFTER SEVERAL DAYS ON THE RIVER, a great sunburned wall, made of mud baked into hard rock by the African heat, appeared before them on the riverbank. They estimated that the structure was nearly fifty feet high. There were some trees peeking out behind it, but little else. But as they floated closer, they could see dark figures moving along the top of the wall. There were only a few feet of dirt between the riverline and the wall. This was the city of Musgum, known throughout the region for its unparalleled beauty.

They brought the canoes ashore and prepared to enter the city. A gateway opened onto a narrow street that skirted the edge of a water meadow. Behind it rose the mud wall, built in narrowing tiers to only a single layer at the top to better repel attacks from raiders. Inside, tall, picturesque houses also tapered upward, and women and children peeped out like flowers from behind them. Olive noted a peculiar smell but attributed it to the closeness of the river.

The inhabitants of Musgum had recently converted to the Mohammedan faith, but they still engaged in very ancient tribal practices. Olive found that all the little girls between eight and ten had the outer skin of their lips slit open, and light metal disks, with rounded grooves—like bicycle wheels—inserted between the cut and the flesh. This was done both in the lower and upper lips, and often in the earlobes as well. As the girls grew up, the size of their disks would be gradually increased. As adults the women learned to use them as a sort of sounding board, over which they trilled their tongues in terrible shrill cries that curdled the blood.

Unfortunately their everday speech was so distorted that their own people often found it hard to understand them. A steady stream of saliva also constantly dribbled from their open mouths. To accommodate an even bigger disk, some of the lower teeth were sometimes pulled. Mesmerized by these objects, Mrs. Talbot offered to buy some spare disks. Almost immediately one woman after another took the grisly objects from their lips and handed them to Mrs. Talbot, leaving visible their own gaping fissures and loosely hanging half wheels of skin.

Olive did not agree with Musgum's reputation as the loveliest city in creation. She found herself downright nauseated, but it wasn't just because of the appearance of the women. The town's odor had become overpowering.

"This is the foulest town one can possibly imagine," Olive said. "The stench passes all bearing." By the time they were ready to leave, Olive was holding a handkerchief drenched in eau de cologne tightly to her nose, so that she might conceal an expression of disgust she did not wish to share.

Invited to camp inside the town, they were told the Germans had done so numerous times. Olive could only admire their endurance. Instead they withdrew to a spot nearly half a mile to the windward side of the town, where they could escape the smell.

Their respite was short, for the wind changed, and nauseating odors wafted over their camp. Olive had already prepared for bed, but sleep would have been impossible, so she and Mrs. Talbot wrapped themselves in their dressing gowns and took to the canoe. They crossed to an island of green grass in midstream, where they tied up, and spent at least a healthy night, lulled by the lap of water as it washed against the boat, the peace broken only by the occasional quacking of ducks, as one of their number fell victim to a crocodile.

THE NEXT DAY, Olive decided to give the city another chance. Musgum was not overly crowded, though there were many small homes. Residents ran nimbly up and down the walls of the round-roofed huts, using built-in footholds. The ornamentation on the fireplaces was also very fine; Mrs. Talbot sat down to replicate it in her notebook.

Olive walked by the houses, enjoying the feeling of the ground beneath her boots. She stopped, her attention arrested by a large, primitive painting on one of the outer walls of a normal-looking house. The images were done in black and red paint with cuts of bright white chalk across them. The scene depicted a rolling wall that was most likely Musgum itself, complete with a narrow, ornamented entryway that was oval-shaped, like the eye of a needle. Scattered over the right section were horsemen, thundering after game that looked like hippos and even giraffes. The figures themselves were simply drawn but strangely powerful in their mystery. Olive noticed a curious detail. Not only did the riders have both legs on the same side of their horses, as was common in primitive art, but some were depicted with their legs on the farther side—the way women rode. Mrs. Talbot, who had finished sketching her fireplace, arrived and was similarly struck by the painting. The owner of the fresco came outside, obviously very proud of the ancient work that had been there when he moved in. The man and his friends sat around on the low mud rail around the house and watched Mrs. Talbot sketch the painting. The man said that the early Musgumites used to be pagans and were subject to constant slave raids. They were attacked from all sides, so they built the wall.

Olive studied the work more intently. In one corner was a man in what looked to be a helmet. He was three times larger than any of the other men and was colored in black. Above this figure was a woman milking what was probably a cow—Olive was not sure. There were sheep, ostriches, gazelles, and possibly an anteater. On the opposite end of the painting was a canoe full of people looking up at a great bird. Meandering through the whole work was a tail that looked very much like a snake, but it had no apparent head.

The mysterious painting was one of the most sublime things Olive had seen in Africa. Its presence and age filled her with a deep sense of connection. As she left it, she looked back and felt great remorse that she would most likely never stand before it again.

THE NEXT DAY THEY AGAIN floated down the Logone on canoes. As they neared another small village, Olive looked to the opposite bank and saw white clothes scattered everywhere. She saw a native girl on the ground, thrashing about strangely. The girl was in the grip of a crocodile. There was blood. The monster began pulling the girl backward into the red water. Mr. Talbot asked for his gun, but Olive knew he would be too late. The girl was screaming.

As the crocodile slowly pulled her into the dark water, the girl went still. It was over. Then the girl's arms flapped wildly about the crocodile's head. Her hands somehow found its reptile eyes and her thumbs plunged into the soft flesh under the monster's hard brow. The girl pushed and pushed as the creature continued to back down into the water. Then it was the crocodile's turn to thrash as the girl pushed harder, screaming. Olive saw more blood—darker and thicker—as the crocodile finally pulled her down beneath the surface.

Mr. Talbot raised his gun but there was nothing there.

Soon, as they knew it would, something floated to the surface, slowly and sadly.

It was the crocodile, dead, its eyes blighted and caked in blood.

The girl rose up beneath it with a great breath. Some of her tribe had by now arrived and jumped into the water to help her to the shore. Though she had been bitten, she was walking under her own power.

Olive tried to look back as their canoe kept going. They stayed on the lookout for more crocodiles, but saw only a pelican. Mr. Talbot shot it. When he brought the bird aboard, Olive noted that it had a beautiful pink breast.

AS THEY PASSED TIME ON the river, their party was not alone. Roan antelopes and gazelles stood on the bank, gazing at them, and monkeys would swing themselves down from branches and grin as they went by. Red-stemmed mimosas, covered with a wealth of golden blossom, scented the air with a delicious fragrance. The water was half-disguised by thick grass, which for hundreds of yards together waved above Olive's head and enclosed them with a terrifying completeness.

One night they had hunted late and were still on their canoe when they were approached by a rugged steel canoe. A white man was inside, wearing a rumpled German uniform. His canoe was filled with cages. He told them that he was the head of the German carrier-pigeon department. A year before he had brought his birds from Germany, and was training them to make the flight between Kusseri and Garua, a distance of nearly two hundred miles. He took out one of his birds, a small gray lump with soft eyes. The German puffed his chest and told them that his pigeons could fly at almost forty miles an hour and could outdistance any African bird of prey. The man almost covered his little bird's ears when he shared that there had been only three casualties, and from other causes, anyway. The German said that pigeons would hopefully one day replace the telegraph, which was obviously problematic in Africa. He gave a quick sad glance to the skinned dead birds that Mr. Talbot had near him.

"Where are you going?" the German asked, putting his pigeon away.

"Kusseri," replied Mr. Talbot.

"Ah," he said. The German took out a little pad, scribbled some pages, and rolled them up into very small scrolls. He whistled, opened another cage, and gathered up four new birds as if they were scoops of ice cream. He affixed the tiny papers to the birds' legs with very precise motions. When they were freed, the birds rose in the air, circled around the canoes two or three times to get their bearings, and flew away. As they went, a hawk darted in pursuit, but the pigeons eluded it with ease.

"Now they will know you are coming," he said.

THE NEXT PLACE THEY VISITED was called Karnak, which meant "great." The richly appointed city boasted two-story houses with outdoor staircases and was largely Mohammedan. When they walked into the center square, they saw some three hundred men, many of them soldiers armed with rifles, the greatest among them wearing brilliantly colored cartridge belts. A considerable band was playing. Among the court of the chief, the Mai—was a jester, who bounced over to Olive and the Talbots and described them as the "three biggest white men." The flattery seemed excessive, but it was due, Olive learned later, to Mr. Talbot being the only European who had ever brought his "wives" with him.

They met the Mai on the outdoor roof of his home, where three deck chairs were laid out for them. They conversed through two interpreters and in three tongues. Olive found that the Mai was the ninth successive chief in his line. After directing them to sit, the chief asked Mr. Talbot if

Olive was his *piccan*? Olive stifled a laugh as Mr. Talbot leaned forward to correct him.

The Mai then took them to see the women's quarters. His ten principal wives were of different races, and each had their own apartment. In the presence of one poor woman, the Mai said that though she had once been his favorite, her health had not been good, and so she was no longer. He summoned his many lesser wives in batches of fourteen or sixteen so that Olive might photograph them. They huddled humbly together, walking with bent carriage and downcast eyes, not daring to look at their lord, though they shot many furtive glances at Olive. It felt like a sad occasion.

Mrs. Talbot walked over to Olive and whispered into her ear.

"Let down your hair," she said.

Olive agreed that it seemed like the right time. She took out her pins, and her long red hair came down. The wives stared at its length and fineness with great awe. The Mai was also immediately struck by it.

"I wish to have an English wife," he announced. "She would take precedence over all the rest. The Mai then turned to Mr. Talbot and asked if he might procure him one. When Mr. Talbot rebuffed him, the *Mai* called for an enormous and beautiful straw hat that he at once gave to Olive as a reward for having shown her hair.

The moment was cut short when the Mai's successor was announced. A superb little personage about six years old was carried before them, his mouth muffled in a turban, his rich brocade dress standing out stiffly around him. Olive thought he looked like the very model of a Van Dyck portrait. The first son born after his father's accession to the throne, he therefore took precedence over his elder brothers. The little boy regarded them in silence.

The party left through the water-gate, after being escorted there in great style with music and wonderful costumes. The polers were waiting for them, though a little worse for wear after having enjoyed the good things of town life, including *pito*, their homemade native liquor. The party made a start on the river but could not get far, and took comfort in the thought that at least the boys were removed from further temptation.

"Drink water," said Mr. Talbot to anyone who listened.

These words resonated with Olive. Her mother had always forbidden her and Flora from drinking water, so they were often given stranger things. While in Vienna to visit their aunt Hanna, Olive and Flora had lunch at a charming outdoor café under a blazing sun. When they were served tankards of ice-cold beer, the girls drank them, though they found the claret that was served next much more to their liking. Some champagne and after-meal liqueur later, they went to the lovely gardens of Schönbrunn Palace. Olive was giddy and fixated on a little girl and her hoop, which was going around and around and around.

Watching the little girl, Olive's face suddenly fell, and she turned to her sister and began weeping. Olive took Flora's face in her hands and said: "How miserable I would be if you died."

Flora, scared out of her wits, fetched their father, who took a long look at Olive:

"We must go home," he said.

AS THEY MADE THEIR FINAL PADDLE to Kusseri, they passed flowering acacia and convolvulus trees, all filled with brilliant birds and many monkeys. When they reached its deserted shore, they found a lonely fort surrounded by only a few houses. The commandant, Herr von Raben, gave them a delightful welcome. He was short, his round face set off by a remarkably curling mustache. With his stature and in his military finery, he reminded Olive of a happy Napoleon. He showed them to their rooms, and Olive stopped in astonishment. Her room was furnished with a bed with sheets and pillows, a washstand with a china basin and soap, and a chest of drawers, chairs, tables; and in the dining room tea was already laid, with rusks and cake and a bowl full of limes.

Olive scrubbed off the scent of dead birds, hippos, and general swamp as best she could. She emerged refreshed, though she barely recognized the creature in the mirror. She sat, ate, but still found herself restless. They were so near Fort Lamy. In fact Olive had seen it when they arrived at Kusseri, just beyond the bend in the river. Olive looked at all the pleasant amenities supplied by the Germans. She then gathered her things and left.

The commandant understood. He watched from the dock as the party got back into their foul-smelling canoes and paddled off to Fort Lamy.

Olive's heart beat like a drum in her chest. She knew that in a half hour she would find out everything she needed to know.

On that last leg, Olive thought of the whale and the kraken; of the Lamido and his wives. All the hippos, snakes, and injuries—they had all borne her here. Or she had borne them. She had been told Boyd was dead. She had been told many things.

Olive would be overjoyed but not surprised to float into Lamy, and see her Boyd, with his arm in a sling, waving and smiling at her.

She could see him.

16

FORT LAMY

*November 25, 1910: The Expedition Finally Reaches
Fort Lamy, the French Outpost from Which
Boyd Alexander Set Off on His Trip East; Dire News
and an Incredible Surprise Await*

As they pushed into the dock at Fort Lamy, the place was frantic with French soldiers. A man in a smart blue uniform waited for them on the dock. This must be the famous Colonel Moll, thought Olive.

"I am Captain Lancrenon," said the man, as he helped Mr. Talbot up. His face wore a serious look.

"There is news," he said, "from Wadai."

OLIVE AND THE TALBOTS WALKED UP from the riverbank past a tree-shaded garden containing many flower beds, and up to the big house of the commandant. The immediate grounds looked just like a riverside lawn in the Thames Valley. There were trees, but they were low, and sand was already encroaching from the east. Upon entering the white house, they followed Captain Lancrenon from one room to another. Each was outfitted with European luxury, including fine tablecloths, glass lamps, and vases.

The final room they entered was filled with soldiers. Olive looked at each in turn very quickly: Things were moving so fast. The captain walked to the big wooden table before them. He directed their attention to the map on it.

"Three days before your arrival," he said, "a runner came from Wadai with letters that told of a terrible disaster to the French force at the battle of Dorote, in Dar Massalit.

"Out of a total of three hundred and ten native troops, seventy-three men were wounded. Thirty-one were killed."

Olive searched the map for words. She saw "Dar Fur," "Sudan," "Abechir," "Khartoum."

"The white officers suffered more heavily," said the captain. "Eight out of twenty were wounded and eight killed." He paused. "Amongst them, Colonel Moll."

Mr. Talbot bowed his head. Moll was very well-regarded as an excellent leader and a fair and just man. Olive could tell by the faces in the room that this tragic news would have far-reaching consequences.

The captain explained that Wadai was the last holdout to French rule in the area. The last French attempt to take Abechir, the seat of Wadai power, was in June 1909. The leader at the time was the sultan-king Moude Mourra, known by the French as the Lion of Mourm, as well as the Black Knight. The French were finally able to expel him by sheer force of men. They appointed Assil, his half brother, as replacement. The Abechirans hated Moude Mourra because of his cruelty and wantonness, making the shift in power easier for them to accept.

But Moude Mourra escaped capture, hiding in the murky corners of his former kingdom and waging a guerrilla war with the French. After some small victories, Mourra began getting converts to his cause. Though Abechir still despised him, the natives of Wadai and Dar Fur dreaded the white man even more. Many of the big men in the area had gained their power from the slave trade that the French had shut down. So, they joined Moude Mourra and began to wage open armed rebellion.

Captain Lancrenon explained that this most recent battle had taken place on November 9. In its wake Captain Chauvelot remained in Massalit, the scene of the disaster, with one or two hundred soldiers to hold the entire country. This was a handful of water against an ocean.

The worry was that other chiefs who had bowed to white rule would now feel emboldened to fight against it. On the next action hung, perhaps, the fate of the whole French dominion in central Africa.

Captain Lancrenon explained that Moll's successor at Lamy was Commandant Maillard. But he was not to stay long; he was set to ride to Abechir and leave Captain Facon in control. Captain Lancrenon stood up straight as the very men he was speaking of—Commandant Maillard and Captain Facon—briskly entered the room. Maillard looked about, then nodded to Lancrenon. He was stocky and wore white pants and a long, downward curling mustache. He saw Olive.

"Mademoiselle MacLeod," he said, bowing.

In that instant Olive knew. All those miles, all those footsteps, all the swamp and the dirt; the victories and failures she had waded through and climbed over on her impossible trek across Africa all shrank down to that very instant. She didn't know the final answer would come with a look from a Frenchman. But it had. Her heart stopped in her chest. Though she couldn't name the emotion exactly, she knew. As anyone would, she had clung to some gossamer hope that Boyd was still alive.

She now knew he was not.

She hated the Frenchman for this truth, just for a moment, even though it was not at all his fault.

The room was cleared as the captains talked among themselves. One of them motioned to a remaining soldier who left and returned with a dented iron box. The soldier set it on the table and left. Maillard was staring at Olive.

"We are going to tell you everything," he said.

He began with an official report that gave a more detailed timeline to the last days of Boyd Alexander. Maillard read the report aloud, as if it were some sort of ceremony. Olive quickly located her notebook and began taking furious notes.

After he left Fort Lamy, Boyd had indeed made it to Abechir before he attempted to reach el-Fachir, the seat of Ali Dinar in the desert of the Sudan, but he disappeared somewhere along the way. A week or so later, on April 7, Captain Chauvelot engaged the Furians in Guéréda, partially in response to an earlier raid in January. Chauvelot's forces annihilated the native army. Afterward, as they searched the battlefield, they found a strongbox. Maillard pointed to the one on the table.

It was Boyd's.

They brought the box to Captain Chauvelot. It had been broken open and looted. The captain squinted through the sun and looked inside. He saw a few items hiding in a crumpled corner and put them in his bag.

Captain Chauvelot knew that something was dreadfully wrong. He had some of the natives questioned as to the whereabouts of Boyd Alexander. All they would say was "Dar Tama." The captain took his fastest men and made for Dar Tama with the greatest possible haste.

On his arrival at the village of Ilarne in Dar Tama, Captain Chauvelot searched the outskirts. He got down on his haunches and surveyed the ground with a sharp eye. On the dirt path leading to the main hut he found trampled grass. It looked as if something heavy had been dragged through the brush, possibly the iron box. Chauvelot followed the path to a small shape just inside the encroaching trees.

It was a pile of stones.

Captain Chauvelot slowly began taking the stones away, one at a time, until he saw a matted tuft of chestnut-brown hair.

"Death was due to a rifle shot," Maillard said, lowering his tone, "and to blows from clubs and stones." Olive steadied herself but kept writing. "For fifty yards the ground bore marks of resistance," Maillard said proudly, "then they ceased, and the track of the body on the earth was even, showing that the struggle was at an end. Part of the body lay half-buried under a pile of stones, while some of the bones had been scattered . . . by wild animals." Chauvelot said that he took a piece of Boyd's hair and a thread of bandage from around his finger as proof. His full remains were later recovered by José Lopez, who carried them back to Fort Lamy.

"He was then buried in Maifoni," said Maillard. "With full military honors. Next to his brother, Claud."

He nodded, and two books were taken out of the box.

"We are going to send them home to his family but thought you might want them first. Route maps were made from Maifoni to Fort Lamy, but these were sadly not recovered."

Olive took the books in her hands and held them. They were heavy and dirty. Olive stared at them as if they were a sleeping child placed in her arms.

These were the last diaries of Boyd Alexander.

TWO DAYS LATER COMMANDANT Maillard was set to ride off on his dangerous mission toward Abechir. Olive didn't know when they would see him again, so they lunched together outdoors and strove to be gay. Olive felt close to the captain now, not only for his help and consideration, but because he had officially confirmed that the MacLeod Falls were her discovery: The French rumor had been false after all. Jokes and laughter echoed around the table, but a pall was present nonetheless. When the revelries drew to a close, Maillard spoke very simply of his fear of defeat and death, and what a victory would mean to the glory of France. Olive thought him a very brave man, but he was too human not to take account of the chances of failure. She could sense that life was dear to him.

"I have one more gift," said Commandant Maillard, smiling.

Something moved from behind the house, led slowly by one of Maillard's men. The shape was small and angular in its motion and full of legs. It was a baby giraffe.

The creature walked out, knock-kneed and wobbling, its longish face trying to stay steady as it moved in midair. Its large brown eyes set on Olive as she walked up and began stroking its fine black hair, placing her hand over its head and its small pointed ears.

"Her name is Josephine," said Maillard. She was three years old, and she was now Olive's pet.

For the rest of the day Olive watched Josephine float out into the short trees and crop the smaller ones, her head moving perpendicular to the juicy leaves. Olive watched her as she ate, one patchy eye turned back toward her. Josephine quickly endeared herself to all. She had no fear of walking up and demanding something, usually a handful of salt, or even tobacco, of which she seemed particularly fond. When night came the baby giraffe returned home, alone, at dusk, to seek shelter from the wild foes of the forest. Olive found Josephine to be a beast of great ability. She easily followed white men, even when they had guns. But the moment they would raise them to shoot anything, Josephine would attack them with her feet. Olive was quite proud of her.

THE ENTIRE FORT GATHERED to see Commandant Maillard go. The camels, kneeling, were still being loaded with cargo. Arabs led them away by the cords passed through their noses as they first lurched, then walked with swaying ease. Most of them were indifferent, but one overburdened creature simply shrugged off his cargo, including his rider. The weirdness of the scene was enhanced by the strange cries of the camels, a high sound full of eerie quavering. These sandy-colored beasts had a hard time before them, for the rainy season was not so long over and their big rounded feet were not well fitted for the swamp.

When Commandant Maillard arrived, he attempted to bring order to the confusion. Somehow he got nearly all of them out of the gate and on their long, slow way. The square was now nearly empty save for the few soldiers that Fort Lamy could spare for the mission. The force consisted of fifteen Senegalese and one white officer. They were not an orderly group, but their reputation on the battlefield was superb. As they marched off, their wives walked with them, just for a little while.

Commandant Maillard could not leave without ceremony. The Mohammedan religious leader of Fort Lamy, the sharif, his chief *mallam* beside him with some sixty headmen, came to wish the commandant godspeed. Even an exiled sultan who lived at Fort Lamy as a prisoner of state, came to offer his respects. As they stood in a row facing the commandant, the *mallam* folded his hands and began mouthing a swift, fast-moving prayer; he then made his prayer aloud. Everyone said "Amen." It was the only word Olive understood.

As the sharif joined his hands in prayer, his cap fell from his head. It was returned to him in an instant, but the people believed it to be a bad omen. More good-byes were offered until Commandant Maillard turned to leave. His horse was already kicking, and as he mounted it, the animal reared up and threw the commandant into the air. But Maillard never let go of the reins and swung himself back on his horse. *"La première victoire!"* declared some of the soldiers as he rode away.

THE ENTIRE FORT WAS SADDENED by Commandant Maillard's departure, especially in the face of the grim odds in Wadai. As the party moped about, an envoy group from Kusseri arrived with a little basket from Herr von Raben. Olive expected fine foods, even sweet-smelling soaps. But when she started to open the basket, it moved.

Olive backed away. As the basket began to sway to and fro, it fell over and out spilled two round, fluffy lion cubs. The boys called them *zakoki*—*zaki* being the Hausa word for "lion." Olive named them Lamy and Kusseri in honor of the two friendly forts. They were only three weeks old and rolled rather than walked, and Olive found them utterly charming. Raben enclosed a letter in which he expressed the hope that the little lions might buoy their spirits. Mandara volunteered to care for them and got a milch goat to be their wet nurse. Olive was overwhelmed: This gift was very much needed.

Kusseri was the runt, but he was the first to kill, having stalked a pigeon the very next day. Mr. Talbot saw the crime and smacked the little lion, hoping to teach him not to be bloodthirsty. But Kusseri would not let go of his prize. Mr. Talbot boxed his ears, and the poor fellow took very ill. The poor cub could hardly move and dragged his limbs as if paralyzed. Mastaba seized him by the wounded ear and shook him violently.

Olive almost screamed in anger at such cruelty, but Kusseri leaped up and walked around, seemingly cured.

Olive was already starting to worry about what to do with her menagerie, when Captain Facon showed up the next day with his own gift: a pretty little harnessed antelope. But, taken too young from its mother, it perished. So he sent a tiny kob of a mousy color and with tender brown eyes. The animal was very friendly and was quickly made welcome. But when Mandara saw the kob, he stopped in his tracks. After the kob walked farther off, Mandara told Olive that if the kob stayed, the *zakis* would die. Olive assumed he meant the opposite, so she asked Situ to act as interpreter.

Situ listened to Mandara and stared at the kob. The small animal was eating grass.

"Bad juju for head," explained Situ, still staring at the kob. "It was fit to kill."

"Kill what?" asked Olive.

"Everything."

They stared at the silent little animal, looking back at them with still, flashing eyes.

Mandara believed it was a demon. He said, via Situ, that the beast had the power of assuming all sorts of shapes, that of a snake or any other animal. He said that nothing could kill it except a dog specially prepared for the purpose by magic. Situ said that first the demon would kill the *zakoki*, and then it would kill them all.

Olive did not feel she could doubt him, so they mournfully refused the little animal their hospitality, and it disappeared soon after, somewhere in the sand.

17

A CORRESPONDENCE, PART 4

*June 6, 1910: A Few Months After Boyd Was
Found Dead in Africa; Olive Travels with Her Friend to
Littlestone-on-Sea to Escape, But as She Mourns,
She Begins to Make a Plan*

Olive sat in a chair facing the gray sea. The waters crashed, white and wet, against the sandy shore, pushed forward and pulled back in ceaseless flow. The ocean had a faraway roar.

Violet had gone off. Olive felt alone. Her black suit was billowy, and her black hat covered her face. She told Herbert a few days before that she hated the sun and the spring and the brightness, and though that was true, and would always be, she was glad to be at the seashore.

Olive saw a young couple emerge near one of the bathing machines. Olive felt intrusive, watching them, but still did not look away. The girl was young and laughing and her hair was covered so it wouldn't get wet. The man was wearing a striped suit and had strong features and a mustache. Olive looked up. In the west the sky was getting dark.

Violet returned and they went inside. They sat in silence, Violet doing

Dunvegan Castle on the Isle of Skye

Sir Reginald MacLeod, Flora, and Olive

Boyd Alexander

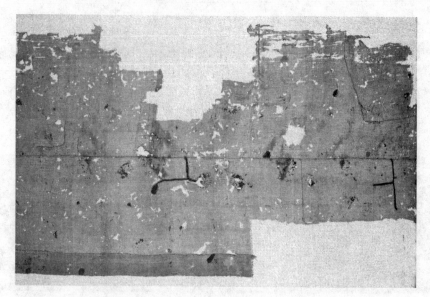

The Fairy Flag

Mr. P. A. Talbot

Mrs. Dorothy Talbot

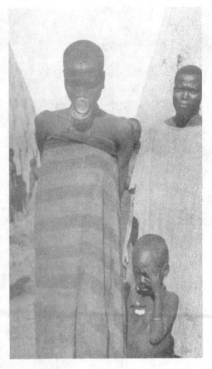

Chief Abbiga

Banana woman with a lip-disc

Mastaba, Washerman, his wife, Situ, Cookoo,
Small Boy, Mandara, and Moussa

The Devil Falls

The Black Magira

The Great Gauaronga

Boyd Alexander and his dog,
San Thome

José Lopez

The little zakis

Josephine

Lamy embracing Mr. Talbot

ABOVE:
Hajer-Hamis from
across Lake Chad

LEFT:
Olive in the
sacrificial cave

The ancient hall

A Buduma mother with her children

Buduma men

The Talbots on an elephant killed in Southern Nigeria

Olive MacLeod

embroidery and Olive cutting out press clippings to put them into a book. She looked at the one in her fingers:

A BRITISH EXPLORER KILLED
LIEUT. BOYD ALEXANDER MURDERED
IN CENTRAL AFRICA

They were mostly the same, these articles, but she still carefully read them, clipped them out, and pasted them into her book. After hours of this Olive looked at her watch to see that the afternoon had only just begun.

That night a thunderstorm raged outside Olive's window. The lightning flashed, followed by deep crashes over the sea. Violet had left again, this time to return to London life for a few days. Olive was alone.

Olive started to write a letter:

Dearest Boyd:

I am sure you would be kinder about the honeymoon couple than I am. They do make me sick, and one overhears so terribly much from the bath—After having been really abstentious about the sitting-room, the man is indulging an orgy of taste for it—synonymous with Violet's departure—I suppose as a protest of my still being here.

As I write I feel you are with me and that the veil that divides us is less thick with my returning sentience. I have got lots of work to do in life to attain to heaven and you, and only if I can do it quickly perhaps God will see that I am ready for the call and will spare me a few years of toil here.

Your longing, striving, and oh so sad,
Your intensely loving
Olive:

A few days later Olive couldn't believe that a fortnight had gone by since she first received the news from Africa. "Each day had been like a year with great stretches of space between each," she wrote that night to Boyd. "The meals of the day marked epochs."

Olive hired a new beach room. It was blazing hot, so she went outside to bathe. Olive saw the honeymoon couple again. Wishing the lightning would come back for them, she immediately scolded herself for such a thought. Olive swam exhaustingly without any progress and then took a chair to her deliciously scented enclosure. She reclined, with Housman's *The Cloak of Friendship* open before her. She felt peaceful for the first time in weeks, until one single massive drop of rain landed on her page. She went inside as the storm came again. She looked at the small photograph she had of him, as a darling little Eton-jacketed boy. His mother had given it to her.

She wrote another letter.

Oh Boyd darling. We have grown together during the time of our absence—haven't we and then comes our most perfect reunion for time without end. Beloved, beloved—I want you so and crave for you.

In perfect love yours,
Olive:

Violet eventually returned. On the beach she asked Olive what she thought of remarriage. After some discussion, they agreed that it was all right provided the second husband understood it was an arrangement for this life with no complications about the next. But both Olive and Violet agreed that it was not practically possible in their circumstances.

"One might as well consider marrying another woman," said Olive.

Violet quite agreed. She then told Olive that she wished her dear Archie could talk to her, if just a few words. Olive didn't tell her friend that Archie had talked to her and told her to take care of Violet. Olive wrote Boyd to say that she wished she could tell Violet about "the revelation you have given me." But she knew she couldn't offer any proof, "especially at a time when they think me likely to be hysterical." Olive didn't tell her of the vision she had before Boyd died, of his carriers looking at her, their eyes moving from side to side.

June 17, 1910
Wilsley

Olive stood and looked out onto Lake Chad. The sky was cloudy, and the waters had thin ripples from the wind. She saw Boyd on the far side of the lake. He was coming closer to her.

But it wasn't Boyd. It was Robin, his twin. From far across the lawn there were some similarities to the photos that Olive had in her room. He looked like Boyd but was thinner and sad. And it wasn't Lake Chad, only a facsimile. Olive was at Swifts Place to see Boyd's father, Colonel Alexander. This Lake Chad, though magnificent, was only a replica, carved into the parklands south of the mansion as a tribute to Boyd's brother Claud, who had died in Africa. On its islands and banks were reproductions of thatched native huts that looked quite picturesque. On the adjoining lawn was an old boat, one of the original vessels from the fated Alexander-Gosling expedition.

Olive walked around the false shoreline. The grasses were tall and thick. Olive saw the dog—Maifoni was a good boy—running by Robin, who had stopped along the far edge. Olive was staying for a few days. Robin was terribly isolated, but Boyd's father, his brother Herbert, and others came and went to keep her company.

Olive thought the best part of the lake's enchantment was the falls where the replica Yo River fell into the water. It produced such a wonderful impression of sublime wildness that she was sure it accurately captured the majesty of the lake itself. She walked slowly.

Olive went to Wilsley for the afternoon. Marion Davis, Boyd's married sister, met her and they walked to his outhouse museum. Olive did not know Marion very well, other than she adored Boyd, and seemed to harbor a slight dislike of José Lopez. Marion explained that

Boyd and José would sometimes drive to Bath to visit her family, where José's complexion would always cause a bit of a stir. Boyd would bring an enormous box of chocolates and tease Marion's daughter Ursula—whom he nicknamed "Little Bear" because of her name—that they had visited the London Zoo on the way down to see the cage they were preparing for her. Her daughter almost believed it, said Marion, but Boyd made up for it later when he told her he was getting her a real pet bear to live at Wilsley. Boyd and José met Ursula at the train station with a truck holding a large box with thick chains around it. Ursula was wide-eyed; when the box was opened, out bounded a fuzzy and black little Schipperke puppy. Marion smiled. She handed Olive the keys and left her to her grief.

Olive closed herself in and saw the same birds that would never move. She luxuriated in the memory of their first long talk there. The room was dark and musty.

Olive wrote Boyd another letter, as she did every night:

I loved your visit last night it was so gloriously living—please be with me today—with your betrothed not till death us do part but till death us do unite. What a glad triumph that will be. Boyd—your love for me has taught me everything I know—oh to be reunited speedily. . . . I love you and we are one.

The next day Olive went to church with the Alexanders. She sat next to Herbert but kept turning to gaze at a row just behind them. She imagined Boyd there. She heard him ask her a question there. She could see it. Later on, someone saw Olive's scrapbook and remarked that she should organize a book about Boyd. Marion told her she had many letters that would help illustrate his life.

Back at Vinters, Lady Balfour came for a visit. Olive wrote to Boyd about it.

Lady Balfour came down. She says I look different.

Lady Balfour talked about how her mother's one son (father's great friend) shot himself—and her eldest boy went off to sea, and just after an absence of two years was drowned. His mother having heard nothing of him for months, but she like me, had a vision.

Your always loving
Olive:

She continued to write him every day, even when the days were long and bleak.

Best beloved Boyd

There is so little to tell you—only my own utter desolation—but it gives me a little courage to sit where you and I sat together at the end of the lime avenue, looking into the lake. Oh Boyd I can't believe that you aren't coming back to me. Let me feel that you are very near to me. For Beloved, I am very lonely.

I am too tired with sobbing to write more now—I only want you to know how I love you.

Very lovingly yours
Olive:

Sometimes Olive overheard others talking about what had happened. They would quiet down when she walked into the room. They were exceedingly stupid. Did they not know she could read? Sometimes she would go to her book and look at the articles, though not very often.

The full details of Boyd's fate did not come to the papers until midsummer. The French Colonial Ministry fixed a date of April 2 for when the incident occurred, three-quarters of a mile west of Nyeri, the capital of Tama. This area, the Dar Tama, was stretched to high tension since the French had captured the main city of Abechir.

Lt. Childers Thompson, a British soldier, gave the full story he heard from the French. Olive found it difficult to reread, but since she had read it so many times, she knew almost every word by heart.

Boyd was delayed for a long time at Abechir, in Wadai, due to French disturbance. About two months ago he left with his Portuguese collector, José Lopez, in a northeasterly direction, arriving at Tama, a place that is under the Ali Dinar of Dar Fur, a chieftain owing allegiance to the Anglo-Egyptian government. They reached the place late at night, and on their arrival, the local chief summoned them to his presence. Boyd said he would see him the following morning. They camped near trees outside town, surrounded by people from town. One laid on hands, but Boyd naturally pushed them off. A small boy who was standing by seized a gun and blazed at the explorer, who instantly fell. The crowd then set upon him and killed him out of hand.

They fell on José, trying to get his ring. When they could not, he offered to take it off for them, and when they backed off, he fired shots at them and ran away. José escaped.

The bad luck of the whole thing is that two days after the explorer's murder, Ali Dinar of Dar Fur, to whom Boyd had sent his boys (presumably to announce his arrival and to ask for guides), sent an escort for the British officer to give him safe passage across Dar Fur. Two days later would have made all the difference.

When Olive first read the article, through stinging eyes, she was confused and angry. A small boy? Abechir? Ali Dinar? Though Olive knew Boyd was going to traverse the desert, she had not imagined that he could be involved in such conflict. She kept thinking of his little birds. Since his death, Olive had been rereading Boyd's books. In *From the Niger to the Nile*, he praised Ali Dinar as an example of a ruler who paid tribute to the British, but was not ruled by them:

It is doubtful if Wadai will be able to disregard the White Man much longer, and if his capitulation can be brought about by peaceful mea-

sures, so much the better for all concerned. A military expedition pa-
ralyses a country for several years, and it should be the endeavour of
all Governments, especially in the Mohammedan provinces of Africa,
to sheathe the sword as much as possible, and by propitious and kindly
means win over the independent potentates and chiefs, and through
them rule their people. After all, they are the rightful owners of the
country, and the only excuse for interfering can be on the grounds of
protecting the community of trade interests. Wadai may yet save his
skin, if he chooses to follow the example of Ali Dinar.

Ali Dinar's men had been almost in time to save him. Olive was saddened that he had gotten so close to rescue.

A month later José Lopez's version of the attack appeared in the
papers. He was an eyewitness. He said they arrived at Dar Tama at six
thirty in the evening. It was too late to see the king, but a headman
came to them and said that if they were English all would be well, for
Englishmen were their friends. The headman asked them to come with
him to the chief, but Mr. Alexander, who was tired, said they would do
so the following morning.

Two hours later the headman returned and insisted they come see the
chief. Mr. Alexander thanked the headman but reiterated that they were
tired and had already unloaded their camels.

The natives returned even later that night, with soldiers.

Four men seized José by the arms and led him away. Other men had
seized Mr. Alexander. He freed his right arm but in the struggle struck
one of the native soldiers. Another of the soldiers pulled his gun and shot
Boyd dead. The servants ran away screaming. José later learned that the
soldiers had come to take them away because they thought they were
French spies.

"They did not mean to kill Mr. Alexander," José said. "It was just bad
luck." The account differed, but Olive trusted José because he had been
there. And the story didn't really matter to her. The outcome remained
the same.

June 20, 1910
Vinters

There was talk of Olive going to Maifoni to pay her respects at Boyd's grave. A man named Mr. Talbot, who knew Boyd, offered to take her after being contacted by Herbert. Olive had been to a few places, but never to Africa. The idea seemed outlandish. The acting governor of Nigeria, a Mr. Temple, wrote to Mr. Talbot, urging them to wait because of the rainy season. Robin tried to persuade Olive not to go because she would return "withered and desiccated." Olive gave him a photograph of herself to remind him that she was, in her words, "once juicily plump."

The trip began to excite Olive. But every day was different. She wrote to Boyd again:

> *Such a terrible feeling of isolation from all, where one had thought one-self close—a horror of the gulf that divides—and a great sense of left-behindness. . . . It seems so hard to try and fail, and I have struggled very persistently to keep a brave front before the world; and at the same time reveal how my soul is one with yours.*
>
> *This evening I have broken down and sobbed for an hour for the whole household to hear—and I am ashamed—I had hoped that the quiet tears I had shed at intervals throughout the day would have re-lieved the physical strain, but it was not so.—Each day proves me un-worthy of you, but I shall struggle yet.*
>
> *I wonder if it would be very bad to pretend it is all right and that you are coming really—it is weak to shelter behind subterfuges I sup-pose, if one can't have joy in actuality why not in fancy?*

Olive also found opposition from her father and Herbert, who had changed his mind about the expedition. Olive's father eventually agreed and said he would pay for it, but that she needed a female chaperone. He finally relented when Mr. Talbot's wife agreed to go, but he still wanted Olive to get final permission from other competent persons, including Herbert and Colonel Alexander. She wrote to Boyd:

I want to get permission to settle about Maifoni—first I must see Her-bert alone and then explain to your father how should Death come to me there it would be the greatest gift God could make me—think of our reunion and help me to look upon it as near.

Herbert told her there was no reason whatsoever to hurry. He told her that once José returned, he would be happy to escort her. Herbert told her that if she stayed, they could write a book about Boyd together. This was a tempting offer. But Olive knew her path now. It had crept up on her slowly, without warning. It was whispering in her ear.

She wrote to Boyd for advice.

I felt so gloriously that you were with me again this evening and even as I write that you are now: also curiously as if there were something you wished me to understand and at last that you were asking if I were ready to go to you. Oh so badly—yes—but I can't see how anything so glorious could come to me out of the Blue, and I think perhaps it is the higher test. I must live each day as if it were the last.

I can't think how I can bear the ordinary burden of life again—I do so long for the time to be short. Yours impatiently and oh so lovingly.

Olive's mother thought the trip an excellent idea. She then told Olive that that if a child did not marry, they caused only misery. This brought a pang to Olive, but she knew her mother was ill, so she tried not to take it personally. The other remaining obstacle to Africa was getting an official reason to be there. Herbert thought they should collect pot-tery. Mr. Talbot thought he could map, but Acting Governor Temple said they had enough mappers already. Mr. Talbot was going to consult the British government. He told Olive not to worry about it. Olive felt slightly bad about the whole affair, but she understood it intimately.

All they needed was a purpose to mask their true one.

Olive eventually received final consent from Herbert—she was going to Africa. Herbert surprised her by taking her to the Kodak company and buying her a camera with a Goerz lens, the finest money could buy. She bought more supplies and boots and planned for her adventure. She told Boyd how she imagined herself there, in Africa:

> *Mounted on the dearest little astride saddle, with a holster in front containing amongst other necessities my revolver. The drawback will be that I have never fired one. I am more than doubtful that I will be able to mount much less stay on.*
>
> *I got delicious soft mock-antelope boots, which are to do both for riding and for camp life—and heavy fieldboots as well.*

Olive was coming alive again, and her family and friends were pleased. She passed the time before they left by reading bad detective novels to her mother. Mr. Hale, the vicar, came to give Olive's mother Holy Communion. Olive joined in to give her mother pleasure, which it did, though Olive felt a sense of artificiality because she was self-conscious and not true about it all.

She spent time with her friends, too. She and Baffy went to see the Chinese pictures at the British Museum. They raved over them. Olive was especially struck by a painting showing a man descending a valley amid high winds, apparently accepting of the elements around him.

"It moved me for there was no resignation," wrote Olive, "no making the best of things, simply (as I said before) acceptance. That is the spirit I should like to attain to for in it there is no make-believe." Olive took care of practicalities as well. One afternoon she wrote some business letters, ordered some new photographs for her family and friends, and wrote her own last will and testament.

"Isn't that absurd?" she asked Boyd that night.

As their plans began to proceed, Olive entered a dual life. She stumbled through the day, sometimes excited, sometimes distraught, all the while waiting for the night, when she could correspond with Boyd again. It became not a habit, but a sacrament. She rarely mentioned him to her circle of friends because it made them sad. But Olive did not seem as sad anymore.

Olive was now writing Boyd every night, but she was worried that she would be found out. People would not understand. The next night Olive confided in Boyd about a piece of equipment she had purchased for the trip.

There are things I long to consult you about, but I daren't explain them before my box has arrived to secure this perfect privacy. Goodnight.

When she finally received her small strongbox, she took it upstairs and put her diary with her letters to Boyd in it. She didn't want others to see them. As she placed it carefully inside, she looked over some of the last entries. They were about the subject she wished to consult Boyd about. "I am wanting you ever so badly and it seems as if there is nothing to cling to," she wrote. "I don't ask for anything in life, but I do so long for the prospect of death." In another letter she wrote that "I am so utterly tired that I must just shut my eyes and be in the dark—be with me." She saw only one hope for happiness: "How I long that our time and parting may be short: the hope that each day may be the last is what gives me most help."

Olive, lost in the darkness of loss and affliction, was contemplating her own secret reason for going to Africa.

By the end of July, Olive was still consulting Boyd about her plan. On July 26 she wrote:

Shall I find you—or is it not to be for a while yet? I would be cowardly to seek it, but I long for our reunion—all the same I am a physical coward and you must come to meet me and help me at the hour of death.

Goodnight
Olive:

Marion had sent Olive a lock of his hair from childhood. Olive placed it softly in her locket, with the heather that Boyd had sent her before. Her box was locked beside her.

. . .

AS SHE PREPARED TO SET SAIL, Olive wrote to Boyd and said: "I want dreadfully to do something and prove myself. To be not just an idler." She explained:

> *There are some things that one can't bear to contemplate and what our life together would have been is one of them, but there again I find myself following the cul-de-sac of the might-have-beens, and I must look to the open road looking not at what was nor what is, but straight ahead to the yet dim what will be—oh Boyd it is so difficult to be courageous—please help me.*

On August 9 Olive was in Liverpool. She opened her diary to write in it one last time on English soil:

> *This is the last letter I write in this book, for some time at any rate . . . What a good thing it will be when the pain of farewells is over—and I know a time of loneliness lies before me on board; but it is to be our honeymoon and you will make it easy for me, won't you?*
>
> Olive:

18

THE WANDERER

*November 1910, Fort Lamy: Olive Reads Boyd's
Diaries and Learns Several New Truths*

Olive retired to the hut provided to them by the French. The fort was so busy—it was accommodating sixty men instead of the usual twenty-five—that the party was given a separate place near the camp prison. Occasionally Olive could hear sharp commands and clanking chains through the walls. The captain told her that sometimes the prisoners made a great show of their condition, especially when marching through the streets, so that the women might pity them. Some local wives even suspected that their husbands wished to go to prison to enjoy regular food, good conversation, and to escape the endless toil of Africa.

Olive sat down and regarded the two books in front of her, their bindings dusty with sand. She was alone now. She thought of them sitting untouched for long days, shut up in the trunk as a bloody battle raged outside. The books were there when Boyd died. She touched them.

Olive knew that the French had given her a great gift. They wanted the diaries back, but she had been given time to read and copy them. Olive opened her own notebook and found her pencil. Then she opened the first diary and saw Boyd's handwriting, long and dark. She brushed her fingers over it.

She started reading and copying the words, in her own straight, tidy hand. She had to get the important parts, but she didn't want to miss anything. As she read and wrote, the words became something more as they moved from the original diary to her own hand. Even though she was committing these words as is—as facts—something inevitable happened as they passed through her: She could see them play out in her mind. Though she knew that diaries were sacred things, they didn't always reveal everything. Taken together, the facts of the diary and the words themselves—some worthless, others full of longed-for meaning—finally became a story:

A MASSIVE, RESOUNDING *BOOM!* sounded from the top of the mountain. Boyd Alexander stuck his head out of his tent. He looked down at the ground—was it moving? He looked across the pitch-dark camp. He could see José, though barely. Without a word, they understood each other. He had felt it too.

Earthquake.

A new explosion bellowed from the top of the mountain on which they had made their camp. Boyd heard small sounds all around him. He couldn't quite see what was happening. One of the boys rubbed his head in pain and picked something off the ground. He had been struck by a rock.

Stones began to pelt them from the sky. As they headed for cover, Boyd made sure his dog, San Thomé—white, scruffy, and altogether fearless—was safe with him.

Boyd and his dog dropped into the forest and saw trees crashing around them like matchsticks. He heard monkeys howling as they fled past him in the trees above. Every five or ten minutes another shock came. As they ran, Boyd heard a strange sound coming from farther down the mountain. Hymns were being raised by the missionary group camped near the base. This kind of thing could only happen in Africa, thought Boyd.

The shocks finally subsided, but when the rains came, Boyd sounded the retreat. Their small company of Boyd, José, and their few boys scrambled down the mountain to the spot already prepared for their next camp. When they reached the clearing, Boyd sent the boys back for more of their things. Returning, they said they had barely escaped with their lives from the shower of stones. They all moved down the mountain and finally escaped to the small village of Buea below. When they touched level ground in Kamerun at last, dawn had finally come.

Four days later a native from the village looked up the mountain and saw a rich red glow from the opposite side of the peak.

This was not the dawn.

"The fire is coming! The fire is coming!" the man began to shout.

As the mountain—the volcano—exploded once again, the village was seized with panic. People surged from their homes. Boyd noted that the British officials had already left for the nearby town of Victoria on boats. Thousands of natives spent the night on the beach.

Boyd stayed in the area several days and even got to survey the crater, once it calmed down, though it was still hissing. He laughed because the natives all thought him responsible for the eruption. They thought he had climbed the mountain and fired his gun into the crater itself, enraging the devil inside. According to the locals, the devil in the mountain was half man, half beast, and had one eye. The grass on the mountainsides was the hair that hung from his limbs.

BOYD'S DAYS ON THE MARCH were repetitious, but only because over the years he had found a schedule that suited him. Every day he rose at five thirty when his boy brought him a cup of boiling coffee. Boyd would then go hunting for birds, before coming back at nine for breakfast. José did the same. After breakfast Boyd would skin what he had found and go out again until midday. Then he would have his lunch and rest until two o'clock before heading out till five. After a refreshing warm bath, he enjoyed a whiskey and sour to set his brain cogs in motion. On this day Boyd watched as José was trying to teach the men football, who took to it very well. Boyd smiled at the "capital" sight.

Every night they would all have supper at six thirty, either something they had shot or slices of ham they had carried, accompanied by cold tea. Then Boyd would sit down to write. He tried to find a shade-giving tree, preferably with a view and a lean to it. Sometimes he felt he could see the whole country mapped out before him, even imagining the sea just beyond the vista. Boyd believed that a good view stimulated the brain, which was helpful when there was writing to do.

"And so the days pass," Boyd wrote one night, "but they are always delightful, since I feel that I am in close touch with Nature."

By May they had arrived in Ninong, in southern Sudan. José was sick; a bad worm had left his foot, but he still had a very high temperature. Boyd treated him for rheumatic fever, but as José recuperated, Boyd himself came down with an attack of ague, a sharp form of fever he had never experienced before. Boyd thought the mountain mists might have gotten into his bones. He was looking forward to lower altitudes and warmer temperatures. He was shivering.

As they marched, morale began to flag. One of the boys, a member of the Mendi tribe, complained they had not enough food and threatened to desert the expedition. "We are still hungry," he said. "It is always a Mendi," Boyd muttered, as he reached for his stick. He stood up as the boy cowered. As Boyd flogged the boy's back until it bled, he saw the looks the other men gave him. He felt that they had been brought to their senses. José watched from the edge of camp.

"A tight hold is necessary with these people," wrote Boyd. He believed that Africans offered the finest labor in Africa, but he felt the British were spoiling them with overpay. Workers were often paid at the same rate as private soldiers at home! Boyd couldn't believe this, especially since when they were paid, the natives usually gambled it away in games with the cowrie shell: "The Government really should do something to stop this," he wrote. "The next thing that always follows is that the winners lend their gains to the losers at exorbitant rates."

SAN THOMÉ, WHO WAS NAMED after the island where Boyd had found him, sprang ahead of the marchers on the trail. Though they were tired, the boys smiled at the dog's familiar display of enthusiasm. Boyd heard a splash of water ahead and ran up to see where his friend had gotten to. There, sitting in the shallow water of a large pool, was Boyd's very happy dog, his tongue hanging out in triumph. There were other bathers in the pool, though they were staying more to the center. Boyd saw why. Two feet away from San Thomé was a massive, grinning crocodile.

Boyd knew this place. It was the Crocodile Pool, a sacred bath that was rumored to have healing powers. He had visited it before on an earlier expedition. San Thomé let out an excited yip at the sight of his master. The dog was oblivious to the monster behind him, whose eyes had now slid open. The other bathers shouted at Boyd to call his dog out. As the crocodile began to move, its body like a mass of prehistoric rock, Boyd swiftly took his stick and batted his sad dog out.

As they approached the city of Ibi, José left to get the camels they would need to reach Abechir. Boyd said they would meet again in six weeks' time, in Maifoni. Entering Ibi, Boyd took great pleasure in the fact that no one knew he was coming. In the old days, when white men in Africa were few and far between, one's approach was heralded at least three days ahead. Now his arrival was met with normalcy. As Boyd approached the market, men sitting by the side of the street stood up when he passed. Natives in togas and turbans even paused to take off their sandals or bent themselves to the ground. Boyd thought this deference wonderful.

Suddenly Boyd heard an unearthly scream. He jumped into a side street and stopped to listen. When he heard the wail again, he looked through the matting of a nearby *zana* hut. In the middle of the dirt floor a sheep lay on its side, flanked by a woman and a juju man. The sheep's throat had been cut, and its blood was flowing down a hole in the ground. The woman was on her hands and knees, beating the dirt with her hands. The juju man was crouched down, lapping up the blood, performing silent incantations with his lips and hands between each sip.

Boyd got his camera out and took pictures.

As he made his way back through the market, Boyd bought a sheep for San Thomé, who he felt was in need of some meat. His dog had been shivering of late, and had seemed very thirsty. That night, as he tried to get his dog to eat, Boyd wrote his father, his brother, Herbie, and O.M.

OLIVE CONTINUED READING AND copying Boyd's diary under the lamp-light, now buzzing with insects who had somehow gotten in. She read every word, as fast as she could write them.

When Boyd reached Maifoni in September, he entered the city with a tornado at his back. Captain Knox generously offered him his own house for shelter. It wasn't until Boyd was shut up in the dark that he realized this was the very room where his brother Claud had died on their last expedition. Boyd sat on the bed for a long time, thinking about Pickles—his childhood nickname for Claud—as the storm outside howled and wept.

During dinner the storm was still in full sway. Captain Knox told Boyd the surprising news that the French had taken Abechir. The road east was now perfectly safe, he said. Bolstered by this news, Boyd knew he still had to get permission from the French to travel there. That night Boyd received a telegram. It was from Boyd's brother Herbie, asking, "When home?" Boyd's reply was simple: "Well . . . not yet."

The next day Boyd visited Claud's grave for the first time since 1904. He found it very poor indeed. The stone cross that had been sculpted by Alexander Fisher in London was crooked, propped up by a makeshift pillar. A low wall of crumbling cement marked the borders of the grave itself, and a solid sheet of cement covered it. The mud wall of the small cemetery was in places almost washed away. Boyd tracked down the master of works and set upon a plan to repair the cross. He also wanted to break apart the awful cement floor that covered his poor brother.

Before leaving, Boyd visited the grave again. Around him all the mimosa trees were a vivid green, bursting over a flat country burned brown as far as the eye could reach. He gazed at the little river; it was full now.

On October 6, Boyd was sleeping in his tent outside Bomu when he was awakened by his dog. San Thomé raised his head from his familiar spot at his master's feet, growled, then dashed off like a streak of lightning into the darkness. It was three o'clock in the morning. Boyd sat up, rubbed his eyes, and reached for his gun. On the sides of his tent he saw immense, swaying forms that suggested the heads of gargoyles. Then he heard a very welcome voice indeed: José had returned! As Boyd stepped outside, he saw his true friend, who was nursing a finger that San Thomé had done his best to take off. He had the camels. They were going to Abechir.

Within weeks, Boyd and José had reached Gubduri. The harmattan had begun to blow, and the sun was a red orb. They again lived the life of the march, though with a much smaller retinue. In villages they would trade and buffer themselves for the next leg. Sometimes after trading, Boyd would treat the natives for various ailments. A man came to him, carrying his little son, who was probably six years old. The boy had a look of distress on his face. His father explained that for the past few days his son had been unable to pass any water. Boyd nodded to José, who spread out a blanket. Boyd chose one of his instruments, a very thin steel tool, and as the boy first struggled, then screamed, they were able to pass it through.

Though Boyd made several attempts, he failed to induce a proper flow. The child's legs were twisted since birth and he could not walk, so Boyd concluded he had a malformation of some kind. They stayed an extra day and Boyd tried again, but he was not successful.

Several days later they were on the soaked road to Fort Lamy. As they took a detour to avoid the water, José shot two gazelles at two hundred yards, which was very difficult considering the slenderness of the animals. Boyd told him he was a fine shot. One could not beat the Mauser carbine for that kind of work.

Around four o'clock that afternoon San Thomé died.

His poor friend had been getting sicker. He had been coughing, and often swayed to and fro before collapsing into a dark corner. Boyd feared it was madness, and knew what was going to happen, but the little dog's death was still a terrible shock. Boyd put his feelings into words that night, in the heavy rain:

> *It will be difficult for me to find such another companion. He was always faithful, and never left my side. Even at night he used to come of his own accord to sleep as close as possible to my bed, and he kept his watch well.*
>
> *Goodbye, faithful friend! Many days have you shared with me my tent and the toil of the day's march over mountain passes, through rivers, and through the desert heat. And where have you gone to now? Perhaps I shall know one of these days!*
>
> *Africa is a sad place; here all things seem to die before their time, and the span of life can be reckoned only by the hour and day. The native mother is seldom destined to see the survival of all her children, for so many are cut short by fever in the early days. The favorite horse that has carried one over many miles suddenly collapses and dies from the deadly fly. Yes, all things die in Africa before their time.*

Boyd buried his beloved dog under a tree whose leaves would never fall. "There will always be shade here," he wrote, "as there will always be darkness."

Boyd turned his head to hear a yipping sound. Two hours before, as they marched out toward Gallwui, one of the boys had called attention to a heap of dry grass. Peeping out of it was the head of a small puppy that could not have been more than a few days old. Boyd took him along. "It almost seems," he wrote, "as if the spirit of poor San Thomé had passed into the little puppy."

It was a strange coincidence indeed. He named the dog Maifoni.

Boyd reached Fort Kusseri by early December. The Germans, especially the resident, Raben, gave him a rousing welcome. After they got settled, Boyd sent José to nearby Fort Lamy to ask the French commandant's leave to travel through Wadai. Boyd waited anxiously for José's return. When he did, it was with a kind invitation and full permission to travel.

THE NEXT DAY BOYD MET WITH Colonel Moll at Fort Lamy, who shook his hand and put him at ease. "Everything is at your disposition," the colonel said, though he cautioned that almost nothing was known of the country between Abechir and el-Fachir. If Boyd could make that trek, he would be the first white man to do so since the days of the great German explorer, Gustav Nachtigal, who was once lost in the Sudan. "You will have a most interesting time," said Colonel Moll.

Having feared a French refusal for many months, Boyd was elated. Now he would not have to attempt his secondary plan, which involved staining his face and limbs with a dark permanganate of potash to pass as an Arab. The dye he had been developing was quite promising, but he was glad he would not have to use it.

That night Boyd and José celebrated with the Germans over excellent food and drink. After dinner Raben led Boyd into the next room, where a miniature Christmas tree stood on a table, its branches gay with many-colored candles. At each corner of the table, under the shade of the tree, were groups of presents for each of them. Boyd's, which were clearly the most substantial, consisted of three bottles of whiskey, a Huntley & Palmer's fruitcake, and a variety of well-timed jests. It was a wonderfully festive Christmas.

Before New Year's, they left for Abechir. The expedition was compact, consisting of four camels, seven horses, and some boys.

Two weeks into the march, however, Boyd grew sick with fever and vomiting. He was inclined to blame the north winds but conceded it might be a form of influenza. They lost two men in short order: One ran away in fear of there being no water ahead; the other had to be dismissed by Boyd for insubordination. When the boy turned to go, he said good-bye to his old comrades with tears in his eyes, before taking the road back alone. Boyd wrote: "An incident of this kind always upsets me for some days to follow. Our numbers are now reduced to eight."

By February the road emerged onto an open plain, a great straw-colored expanse of sandy ground. Crested cranes flew here and there, while overhead in the far distance, flights of plovers and redshanks kept passing from the north. The way had been hard to find, but Boyd had been making a good map. He gazed up at the great boundless tract of the sky above as it moved slowly with them.

They eventually arrived at the French post of Yao. All they found was dust and silence; the fort was almost deserted. They found an officer who told them that everyone had been recalled to Abechir. Captain Fiegenschuh had been on a reconnaissance into a kingdom four days to the southeast, to make peace with a renegade sultan. After a friendly exchange and agreeing to talks, Fiegenschuh, in his white pants and short blond hair, made camp. But the sultan and his men crept near them in the dead of night, and at his signal they massacred the French expedition, including their captain, with only nine men escaping to tell the tale.

Boyd could barely believe this news. By this foolhardy action, the sultan of Dar Massalit would gain in power and Abechir could rise in rebellion. "It seems that the French have made a mess of it," he wrote. Abechir had always been the refuge of all the "bad hats" who had no use for the new Africa, but they had been driven out when the French arrived. Now they would return with spears and guns to retake the city. Boyd was furious: What were the French even doing out there? Dar Massalit was technically under British influence.

Before Boyd left Yao, the old *mallam* of the city gave him a gift of some dates from Abechir. Boyd had never tasted the strange fruit before and was surprised to find them delicious. In addition to being most nourishing and invaluable for the long desert journey to come, Boyd found the dates could be a first-rate medicine.

Their little band marched through the low thorns for what seemed like forever. The background receded into a hazy russet band, the only growth shabby, with stunted leafless trees. Some others were half-decayed, and all prey to the ravages of ants. The branches of many of these trees had fallen and lay bleached to the color of bones.

By March, José went ahead to arrange their quarters in Abechir. Boyd rode along the Kachemere range of small hills, which ran in a southeasterly direction. Of a reddish color, they were bare but for a little grass and scattered trees. Boyd noted that as he moved, these forms rapidly altered and got disconnected, making mapping them from a road no easy task.

THE FIRST SIGHT OF ABECHIR was very disappointing, and Boyd wondered if he had expected too much. Against the orange sunset, there was almost no outline to the town. The sandy coloring of the mud houses was in complete agreement with its surroundings, and probably the reason why it was so unremarkable.

The French commandant, Julien—a man of stout proportions—met Boyd at the city gates. Boyd knew immediately from shaking his hand that the commandant was a man of rough manners. Presenting his letter from Lamy allowing him further passage, Boyd then put himself—as a soldier—at the commandant's disposal to assist in their present difficulties with Wadai.

Both subjects were immediately dismissed. Regardless of the letter from Fort Lamy, Julien said that he could not take the responsibility of allowing Boyd to pass by the road to el-Fachir. And he did not need the help of an Englishman in French matters. There was nothing to be done.

Boyd felt shipwrecked. All was lost.

That night in his quarters, Boyd weighed his options. "The French have not a leg to stand upon as regards the Massalit affair," he wrote.

They were going to war against a chief of Ali Dinar's in Dar Fur. This was unfortunate. Ali Dinar was the man Boyd was hoping to meet.

Boyd knew that his arrival in Abechir was anything but pleasing to the French. He guessed that they were probably making plans for an expedition to punish Fiegenschuh's killers, which meant another step into British-held territory. Boyd's presence complicated that, with Julien fearing that Boyd would alert the British. After all, Boyd had mapped his way there.

"I think he looks upon me as a secret agent," Boyd wrote in his diary. Olive read this line, wondering who he was writing to.

Boyd's lodgings had been provided by Sultan Assil of Abechir, who also gave Boyd and José a Sara boy as an attendant. He was the body servant of the sultan and was very useful. Boyd found him to be very bright, always laughing and dancing and picturesque with his matted hair.

As Boyd walked through the market the next day, he talked—and listened—to its people. Able to move quite freely in Abechir, Boyd found himself treated with the greatest deference. He wondered if the people might be clinging to the hope that the English would take their country from the French. As for the market's fare, he found nothing of novelty or taste. Apparently the adage held that Wadai could boast of little except its beer and skill with the knife.

Boyd walked by the sultan's palace. Sultan Assil was recognized by the French, but he did not preach rebellion. There were whispers that in the dungeons under the palace tower, slaves were immured for months at a time, in total darkness, till they grew tame or died from their suffering. Others were heavily chained and forced into painful postures until they starved to death.

A FEW DAYS LATER THE COMMANDANT asked Boyd to join him for dinner. Julien told Boyd that if he could provide assurance of safety from Ali Dinar himself, the French would allow him to leave Abechir. Overjoyed at this news, Boyd knew it would take a good month before he could get an answer from Ali Dinar. A quick runner could reach el-Fachir, due east, in sixteen days. The next day Boyd got the head *mallam* to write the letter. Dictating that he was English and was asking for protection to el-Fachir, Boyd also offered gifts to Ali Dinar of one hundred pounds, a horse, and a gun. The *mallam* finished the letter, and they found two volunteer runners who set off the following morning. As a final hope, Boyd wrote Commandant Julien with one last proposal:

> *My courier leaves tomorrow, and I write to ask again if it would be possible that you would change your idea and allow me to depart from here under my own responsibility in five or six days. I would save time and money, and I would like to return home in May.*

Boyd received no answer.

ON MARCH 17 NEWS CAME FROM the frontier. A large force from Ali Dinar was within a day of Abechir. They had burned to embers several towns along the way. Boyd was told that his couriers had been taken prisoner, that his letter had been sent forward to Ali Dinar. Julien called Boyd in and told him that the force now occupied Nyeri, the capital of Dar Tama near the border of Dar Fur in the Sudan.

That night five chiefs loyal to the sultan of Abechir left the city under cover of night to join Ali Dinar's force, along with more than two hundred riflemen. Abechir was now a place of great unrest.

As he restlessly awaited a response from Ali Dinar, Boyd had been spending time with the historian of Abechir, Mahamud Bamba, who claimed to be more than one hundred years old. He had "a pug-nose like India rubber," wrote Boyd in his diary, "much splayed out at the nostrils, and thick lips." The historian's hands were big and bony, the left never leaving his praying beads, which were large on account of his rheumy eyes. His forehead was deeply furrowed; his white mustache and little beard were sparse, and his shiny head was almost hairless. He wore a capacious leather reach-me-down coat, ruddy with age. When he met with Boyd, he would take his hand and beg him to sit upon his mat, a long process punctuated with many "Dear, oh dears!" But as old as he was, there was a method in Bamba's recounting of his facts. When asked a question that stretched far back through time, he would spread out his bumpy hand to smooth the gravel; then, with his forefinger, he would make strokes as he remembered the various names or points in the story. And then, the tale finished, his fingers spread out once more to smooth over the surface again.

He told Boyd the history of the Wadai. They claimed to have originally come from Mecca. They were led by King Abdul Kerim, who founded Wara, a day's march to the north of Abechir. It was there the Wadai dynasty began. After the death of Abdul Kerim, the next sultan was Sarbun, whose reign began about 1770, and lasted for thirty-three years. Under his rule there was great peace. The herds increased, and there was much prosperity and no molestation at the hands of the Arabs.

On the death of Sarbun, Harrifen, one of his three sons, succeeded him as sultan. His reign lasted for fifteen years. He gained popularity with his subjects by drawing upon the wealth of his father's reign. He was generous and gave away fine presents; he played and feasted, and meat could be had by anyone for the asking. In those days, a Kano gown would fetch twelve cows in the market, an indication of the great value of the herds.

Olive blinked.

The diary had ended.

She flipped the pages to the end. She turned over the flyleaf and spied some writing in Boyd's hand. It was unsteady and almost illegible.

January 3, 1910.

Am feeling very bad; it must be the results of the poisoning, but never say die!

Olive turned back to that date in the diary. There was no mention of sickness on that or any of the following days.

Olive had expected to find peace and sadness in Boyd's diaries. But as she stared at the pages, she grew aware of two very hurtful truths: that the man who did not write her very much wrote every single day, and that in his own diary, he had mentioned her only once, and only in passing, by her initials.

She looked back at the first diary. There, folded inside, was a bundle of letters.

They were hers.

19

THE GREAT GAUARONGA, PART 1

December 12, 1910: The Party Journeys from Fort Lamy to Tchenka to Meet a Mighty Chief; They Encounter a Mysterious Figure on Horseback; Danger Strikes

Gloomy weather only magnified the downcast atmosphere at Fort Lamy. Even Josephine seemed to want to be left alone. Now that the commandant had left, the party struggled with what to do next. They would go to Maifoni, of course, but beyond that they were not sure. Some of them harbored their own ideas.

When a messenger came on horseback to invite them to attend a fete in the local chief's honor, Captain Facon urged Mr. Talbot to go. The village was only a three-day march south, and the visit might help lift their spirits. The festival, called a fantasia, promised to be a singular display of horsemanship involving all the local tribes. Mr. Talbot looked at Olive, who wasn't saying much, and agreed. They began the trek to Tchenka, the capital of the Bagirmi tribe, on horses and oxen. Olive rode in back, a blank look on her face.

They rode across flat plains and watery swamps. They watched a primitive Punch and Judy show in one village and saw electric-blue birds in the trees. They saw countless giraffes, slow and majestic and much taller than Josephine. On the third day, when they got within a mile of Tchenka, they realized—as the sun got higher and warmer—that they couldn't go on riding in their best attire, which they had donned for the fantasia. So they began walking, knowing full well that they were going to be late yet again.

Captain Lucas, the French resident at Tchenka, rode out to greet them. His uniform wasn't as immaculate as those of his fellows at Fort Lamy. Though he was probably younger than Mr. Talbot, he looked every bit the seasoned soldier, albeit a little dusty and rough. He found the travelers to be in similar straits. Dismounting his own proud horse, the captain walked alongside them. The Bagirmi messenger turned and stared: It was probably the first time the native had seen a "big man" walk on the road. Olive wished she had realized this effect before they had decided to get off their horses. She would have risked slits in her dress and a fall from her horse not to lower white prestige for a captain. But it was too late, so they walked in the dust. Captain Lucas began to tell them about the chief they were going to meet. His name was Gauaronga. Olive still thought of the first chief they had encountered months ago, Abbiga, who had met famous explorers and even Queen Victoria herself. How long ago that seemed.

Gauaronga's story began when the city of Massenia was razed to the ground by the savage Wadai, who slaughtered more than thirty thousand members of his tribe, the Bagirmi. Gauaronga was captured and taken in chains to Abechir, their capital. He was seven years old.

After many years the young Gauaronga was permitted to return to his kingdom on the stipulation that he send tribute every three years. He had, of course, to pledge himself to Abechir. This toll required Gauaronga to blind his brothers upon his ascension to the Bagirmi throne, to which he still held claim. But when he came of age, the sultan of Wadai felt a rare mercy and demanded only a single eye.

As ruler of Massenia, Gauaronga personally supervised the rebuilding of his city. But his rule was not without contest. A Furian warlord named Rabeh, who was born into slavery, had escaped his shackles and was much feared. Rabeh had killed his way to the self-appointed rulership of a section of Nigeria known as Bornu. On most European maps the territory he had conquered was marked "Uninhabited." His name was a shadow over hundreds of miles. There were rumors that the dry bed of the Yo River was filled with tangled skeletons of his enemies.

Rabeh was a slim man with a shaved head. His brows were always furrowed, and he often wore a uniform. He whipped Bornu into a military dictatorship based on the sharia law of the Koran. In addition to his military ruthlessness, he was known for his personal brutality. He had one of his concubines executed because she kept a secret talisman that had been enchanted to win Rabeh's love. He listened to poets and paraded across battlegrounds carrying the heads of his enemies. He captured and sold thousands of slaves.

Rabeh expanded his army by offering everyone he defeated in battle—who still drew breath—the same choice: Serve him or die. Since the latter often included the grisly process of having one's head removed, placed in a box, and then sent back to his home village—and his body thrown into the river—Rabeh had no difficulty finding soldiers. New recruits were assigned to the different flags of his army. If they proved themselves, they were given guns and a payment of seven dollars a month. This was the army that allowed Rabeh to establish a vast kingdom from Kano to Wadai. The French called him the Black Napoleon.

In 1893 Rabeh laid siege to Gauaronga's kingdom of Massenia. After resisting for months, when supplies ran low, Gauaronga abandoned the city of his birth, burning it behind him rather than letting it fall into Rabeh's hands. Gauaronga had also trafficked in slaves, and when Rabeh took over his supply lines, Gauaronga's retinue was down to only a few servants and eunuchs. He spent two years starving in exile; only the French would help him.

The French returned to the region with a smaller force to rally the Bagirmi. Gauaronga joined them, but Rabeh again emerged victorious, forcing a twice-wounded Gauaronga to flee once more. Rabeh exterminated the entire French force. Swollen with the pride of his victories, Rabeh expanded his desires. Beyond the conquest of his neighbors, he wished to eliminate the white man from his gaze forever.

The French returned in 1899 with more men, but Gauaronga wanted no more part of fighting Rabeh. The French force produced a stalemate, but it was two secret French battalions, one from Senegal, the other from Algiers under Commandant François-Joseph-Amédée Lamy, that surprised Rabeh and boxed him in. Sensing victory, Gauaronga rallied the Bagirmi under his flag and attacked his dreaded foe. A seer had foretold of Rabeh's demise, and the rumor surged through Gauaronga's forces, giving them renewed strength.

Rabeh, shaken by the prophecy himself, retreated down the river. The French force under Commandant Lamy finally overtook him in April 1900 at Kusseri. In a bloody battle, Rabeh's followers were destroyed, but no one could find their leader. Anxious to see his infamous opponent, Lamy crept among the wounded, asking each man if he was their king. He put the question many times in vain, when at last a large figure sprang from the ground and cried: "I am Rabeh!" before driving a dagger through the Frenchman's heart. The other French officers immediately avenged their leader. Rabeh, pierced by a dozen swords, fell lifeless at the feet of his equally dead conqueror.

The French gave Gauaronga the full rights of an independent sovereign. For some years he was allowed complete liberty of action, but it was found that he used it to secretly manage an immense traffic in slaves. Gauaronga was taking as many as five thousand men from neighboring territories to sell into slavery in the Libyan region of Cyrenaica. Since then the French had established three outposts to guard against such activity.

Captain Lucas, in a tone that was more surrender than braggadocio, said that he was in charge of the outposts. He was assisted by three noncommissioned officers, one of whom constantly traveled between the forts, in accordance with the French system that no one man should be left long alone.

As they walked alongside their horses and heard the story, Olive couldn't help but feel sorry for this king, who had been kidnapped as a child and sold into a life of terror. At the same time, she wondered why they were being sent to meet him. When Olive later spoke with the Talbots, she wondered if the French weren't trying to scare them into obedience. Perhaps they were trying to deter them from making a dash to Abechir.

Olive noted that Aji looked downcast. Mrs. Talbot walked up next to Olive and spoke softly.

"He served under Rabeh," she said, pointing to Aji.

Olive watched him leading the horse. She thought of how desperate he had been not to serve a woman, and she looked at this boy—this young boy—reminding herself of the adage that to know is to sympathize.

WHEN THEY FINALLY REACHED the capital, they were, as they feared, undeniably late. As they approached, they heard the salaam to Allah being loudly chanted from somewhere up ahead. But something was wrong: There was no one else on the road. The hour was apparently even later than they thought.

Olive wondered if the Bagirmi had told them the wrong time on purpose so as not to sully the proceedings with nonbelievers. She knew that the salaam signaled a moment of great importance when the chief would turn and kneel to Allah in a gesture of peace. Olive stepped up her pace, determined not to miss this ritual. The chanting seemed to be coming from about a mile ahead, from an open area on the far side of town.

When they finally reached the large road that led into the clearing, Olive realized they were not late after all. The chanting had stopped, but the participants were just making their way from the village to the fantasia. Captain Lucas found them a spot to observe from. They tied up the horses and set out their wooden chairs.

The first marchers were a handful of black soldiers carrying a French flag. Then, from the wide road behind them, came the slow rumble of countless horsemen. Olive was again overwhelmed by how a simple turn in Africa could result in such drastic and sudden change. Despite Africa's great scale, its massive capacities for both man and animal, it was still experienced step-by-step. The war chiefs were followed by their own private companies. Men rode by who held offices that Olive could only guess at, their costumes colorful and layered with leather and skins. The king's heavily guarded daughters followed. Olive was already excited by the display.

Turning the corner, its feet kicking up dust, was a horse that bore a woman as its single rider. Even in the midday sun the woman was cloaked in black from head to toe. She was perfectly still, almost like a tree. A long dark veil ran from her head all the way to the ground. Olive didn't know the material; it seemed heavy and flat with a kind of deep reflection to it. Even the woman's face was covered. Olive could not see her eyes.

Olive wondered if this was indeed a person at all. It was more a shape really, more of a creature than a human being.

"It is she!" said Mastaba, swiftly lowering his gaze. "The Magira!"

Olive caught the feminine form, but the actual word escaped her. She had no idea what this was, this unnatural-seeming *thing* she was looking at. However, Olive knew she must be held in the highest esteem in the court because of her location in the parade. She wasn't a wife, because Olive knew there were many. Then she remembered the word.

Magira. "Mother."

The thing swayed. Olive could see no eyes. It was clearly a woman, though she couldn't see her face. Olive could tell she was powerful because of the reverence she received from the crowd.

"The king's mother?" guessed Olive.

"Yes and no," Captain Lucas said. "She died some years ago."

Olive's face turned to horror. She looked again at the Magira. Was she watching a corpse that had been propped onto a horse? The thought chilled her. Or had the hallowed mother been somehow animated by some secret potion or fire? Olive studied its face, pointed straight forward and unmoving. The creature was motionless. Then Olive finally understood. This was just a totem, like a statue.

Then the Magira turned its head and gazed at Olive.

Olive felt all feeling leave her legs as the black-garbed woman rode slowly past. Mastaba saw Olive and guessed her thoughts: "He live to be Sultan's mother," he said, "though he be man."

Olive considered his words carefully. This was not the great chief's mother after all, but one of his men disguised as her, perhaps even wearing her clothes. Olive was still as she watched others bow before the Black Magira. Olive took a photograph, but was worried she had missed her chance.

"In her name she takes precedence over all," said Captain Lucas, "even over the Great Chief himself."

Gauaronga then appeared upon his warhorse. A huge tentlike umbrella, symbolic of his royal power, was held over him. Cabochon garnets, aquamarines, topazes, pale amethysts, and turquoises were studded into his high saddle. His head was shrouded in a turban that came down over his forehead. A set of oversize motorcycle goggles covered his eyes. He was a thickset man, and Olive thought that his gorgeous robe was shown to little advantage. He did not look like the warrior who had evaded Rabeh three times.

When Gauaronga saw Captain Lucas, he stopped the entire procession with his hand. Captain Lucas stepped forward and indicated that Olive and the Talbots should do the same. The captain returned the king's salute. The king stared at Olive. She knew then that what the commandant had told her was true: Gauaronga was looking on the first white women to enter his kingdom. Gauaronga rode slowly on, greeted by shrill cries of applause from his subjects. He glanced back curiously.

Olive and the Talbots followed them into the great clearing, where Captain Lucas brought them closer to the front. After being helped off his horse with some difficulty, Gauaronga collapsed onto a stool, his legs bent and spread. He was wearing black-striped, tentlike pants, straw sandals, and a massive cartridge belt. He held a sword between his legs, its angled point thrust into the dirt. He had a pinky ring on his left hand and wore a white scarf. He put on a tall, colorful headdress, his goggles remaining firmly in place. Behind him boys sat in the sand.

Gauaronga watched the fantasia and continued to receive the salutes of his people. The crowd was motley—here a prince or some great chief mounted on his favorite horse, there a group of Arabs clad in rags that seemed barely held together. Splendid high-spirited stallions jostled alongside hungry ponies. Olive observed that everyone had brought the best they could muster. Among mingled crowds of Bornuese and Kanuri came a line of men, waving ostrich-feather fans above their heads and dancing forward, to make an escort for the princess royal, whom Olive could not really see. Though the show was still proceeding, Gauaronga left early with a selection of his men. Olive studied their dark, serious features. After they had gone, she and the Talbots returned to camp.

Captain Lucas told them that stringent times had come to the village of late. The French believed that Gauaronga's coffers were empty, largely due to their checking of his slave trade. Gauaronga was now forced to find revenue in other ways. Pronouncing it a grave threat that women of marriageable age should remain unwed, in his great goodness and kindness, he arranged marriages for all. Those who were grateful for the sultan's interest in their romantic life would naturally be expected to express their thanks by some gift worthy of his acceptance—while those who did not like the choice selected for them used the same means to get let off.

THE PALACE WAS THE CENTRAL BUILDING of the town, occupying the whole length of the great square and enclosed by a high mud wall. The mosque stood next to it. The sandy square was shaded by some big trees, where women bearing heavy water pots paused to exchange greetings. Men gathered there to rest and talk. The huts were largely *zana*, while those belonging to important men had tall clay walls. Just outside the palace, the party saw a freshly killed ox, crumpled onto the ground, its large eye clouded in the sun.

Olive, the Talbots, Captain Lucas, and Mastaba stood outside the palace. In case they met the queen, they would need a female translator, so they brought along the wife of Mohmaduba, who was Captain Facon's chief interpreter. Lucas told Olive that next to nothing was known about the queen other than she was from Wadai, and had married Gauaronga when he was a captive at Abechir. The queen had never borne him any children, but in gratitude for their past, he retained her as his principal wife. The others bore the lesser title of *Leli*—"princess." If they were lucky enough to meet the queen, said the captain, they would be the first white people to enter her presence.

They were received in an inner court, approached through a gate kept by immensely tall guards. Olive and the Talbots rode into the first court, walked through the next, and were then divided from the royal presence by a gate made of flashing tin. The gleaming door was thrown open, and behind a screen sat Gauaronga himself. He was seated on a deck chair, his turban and goggles concealing his face. He seemed taller and stronger close up, observed Olive. She searched around with a mixture of curiosity and fear, looking for the Magira.

The king took a moment before he rose to greet them and motioned with his hand to where two more deck chairs had been placed opposite him.

Olive and Mrs. Talbot bowed and sat down, leaving the men to stand. As Olive gathered her skirts and settled into the chair, she looked up.

The Great Chief Gauaronga—the *Mbang Ngoolo*—was staring directly at her.

There was an awful pause, reminiscent of the Lamido when he considered Olive's outstretched hand. But this was very different: Gauaronga was bristling with fury. Olive knew she had made a grave mistake in sitting in that chair, but she didn't get up. The whole court stood transfixed.

In a moment additional chairs were brought in, and the men were all seated. They immediately started talking to the king through Mastaba. Everyone acted as if the incident had never happened. As the men conversed, Olive looked up at the chief.

He was still glaring at their chairs.

Only Mohmaduba's wife stood, creeping along the outside wall with averted eyes, in an effort to efface her miserable person before the Great Gauaronga. Soon after, two eunuchs appeared and conducted the three women to an inner door. As they pulled them off the chairs, Olive had a moment of fear, but Captain Lucas told her not to worry: They were going to see the queen. As the ladies moved to a secret room, the eunuchs went back to bring along their two chairs. The sultan's harem was housed in strict seclusion.

In the open-air inner courtyard, children were playing happily as goats and ducks wandered about at will. Slave women worked at washing and cooking. The only sign of riches was a water basin made of copper and brass that had been lowered onto the ground for the goats to drink from. They passed through another tin gate and finally came upon Gumsu, Gauaronga's queen. She was sitting on a Persian rug and was dressed in a beautiful robe of blue brocade. Her hair hung in tight brown ringlets around her head and she was adorned with richly chased ornaments of gold and coral. Old and very shy, she kept her hands before her face so that Olive could not really see her features. Olive asked questions through Mrs. Mohmaduba; she especially wanted to hear more about Wadai.

But the queen did not answer a single question, and Olive began to think of her as ugly. After more silence she was glad that it was time to say good-bye.

The eunuchs then led them to the *Leli* Bondigul. She was sitting in a quaint little circular vestibule, with a long, narrow passage at the end of it. Her dress was a gorgeous cerise-colored robe of Arabic work, and she glittered with jewels. There was just enough room for her and her two principal attendants. She was a pleasant, intelligent woman, and seemed very happy to see Olive and Mrs. Talbot, and was not unnerved by their appearance.

Her one son was the heir apparent to Gauaronga and bore a title, Churoma, that was equivalent to that of the Prince of Wales. She told them that her son had spent six months in France. When he returned, said his mother, all he could talk about was the French ladies and their wonderful hair.

Olive knew what was being hinted at. She had been asked many times, but this was the first time she had been asked in Africa by a woman. And though the *Leli* was not the queen, it was clear that she was Gauaronga's true love. Mrs. Talbot gave her a look of agreement. Olive stood up, tilted her head forward, unpinned it at the top, and swept her head forward and to the side until her hair fell, red and long, all the way down to her legs.

Olive felt a little sheepish. In her mind the hot climate had left her little hair to display, though no one there would agree. After a moment Olive rolled it up again with hairpins in the space of about a minute. She thought that this quick transformation must have been a marvel, since some of the natives' own elaborate coiffures often took hours to arrange and were left standing sometimes for two or three months. Olive's trusty British hairpins must have seemed like miraculous instruments.

As they left the women's quarters, they were each given a finely woven white burnoose, made by Gauaronga's wives. In a remarkable tradition, these were given not only to honored guests but also to beggars. The beautifully made cloaks were often brought to a house of mourning, so that the dead man could be buried honorably. The *agid*, or messenger, would then remark to the bereaved family that they must make some acknowledgment of the sultan's sympathy. The *agid* returned to his royal master laden with all that he could lay hands on—sometimes the dead man's whole fortune.

THE EUNUCHS LED THEM BACK to the throne room. When the tin gate clanged shut behind them, they found Captain Lucas and Mr. Talbot slowly munching on kola nuts. They both clearly disliked them but must have felt obliged to eat lest a refusal displease their royal host. Olive did not care for the nuts either. They had a bitter taste at first and sweetened upon chewing, but then only slightly. As the men tried not to make faces, Olive noticed that she and Mrs. Talbot had not been given anything. She was disappointed because she was hungry for real food and had, on their last march, dreamed of roasted royal pigeon on skewers, which she imagined holding delicately in her fingers.

Others began to join them in the room, curious about the white newcomers. One of the men announced the arrival of Gauaronga's son Churoma and Ngarh Moriba, his half brother. Olive noted that everyone who entered the presence of the chief afforded him overwhelming respect. These were his royal sons, but even they came in and stood quietly against the outer wall until the chief very lightly waved his hand, permitting them to sit on the ground around him. Churoma, a heavy youth of about seventeen, seemed suspicious of everyone. Perhaps it was being in France had given him such an unpleasing expression; that, or his return to Tchenka. Moriba, on the other hand, looked full of life and spirit, and seemed as sharp as a needle.

Mr. Talbot began talking, which Olive knew meant one thing: They were going to trade. Soon enough Gauaronga gave a command, and two fine suits of chain armor were brought in. They looked to be of native workmanship and very valuable. Through a translator, Gauaronga said that the more impressive set was what he wore in Abechir. He said that he had seen five hundred men dressed in the very same kind of impregnable armor march against Rabeh. No one made the point that Rabeh had defeated them all.

Now that Gauaronga had presented his treasures, it was Mr. Talbot's turn. The chief seemed to make the choice for him as his eyes rested on one particular object in the room.

He was looking at Mr. Talbot's rifle.

Mr. Talbot sighed. The man had no dog, no favored horse, and though Mrs. Talbot was his confidante, his rifle was as important to him as his own arm. Still, the society back home would prize the armor from Dar Fur. Mr. Talbot had never seen anything like it.

When their interview was concluded, Olive and the Talbots left the palace, some boys carrying both sets of armor behind them. Mr. Talbot was lighter both on his back and in the weight of his purse. When they got back to camp, Captain Lucas was greatly surprised: Never had Gauaronga wanted to trade before. They felt victorious. Mr. Talbot was happy to be in possession of the relics but knew that a rifle in central Africa was almost priceless.

Olive smelled something that she hoped was not just a product of a hungry imagination. Waiting for them at camp, they found a spread of food to welcome them. There were calabashes full of delicious pigeons, honey cakes, eggs, honey, some strange plants, and livestock. This was a gift from the chief. Captain Lucas was unsurprised. He said that everyone in Tchenka was sent food from the royal table. Even Fort Lamy got a delivery from time to time.

But, Captain Lucas said, this munificence was not practiced toward the poorer residents of the town; in fact, a beggar received alms only if a crowd of spectators was there to witness it. Gauaronga liked to feel that all were dependent on him, the supreme monarch—the birds of the air as much as the men and beasts of the earth. Every week one or two oxen were slaughtered outside the palace, that the vultures might come and feed.

THE NEXT DAY THEY WERE invited to another outdoor affair in the sultan's honor. The event began quite unceremoniously. The staging ground was filled with people—troops and chiefs and other groups—but no one moved to pay homage to Gauaronga himself, who again sat lazily at the front. Olive sensed that something was wrong. A man came in dressed up as a woman, and fooled about, but nobody laughed. A soloist then played a small sweet-toned pipe—till the whole band cut in and drowned him out. Behind them danced more than one hundred women, waving stiff ostrich-feather fans. These were Gauaronga's slaves and accompanied him everywhere, even into battle, where their duty was to taunt cowards into an assumption of courage. Olive noted that most of them were very old and ugly.

Olive was beginning to feel sympathy for the neglected Gauaronga when Captain Lucas told her that this was all by design. Apparently there was a high dignitary, the keeper of the palace, the Bata Kuji, who had the privilege of being the first to present his homage. But this man was so conscious of his own unworthiness to enter the kingly presence that he remained at home until the sultan sent for him many times. His position was so important that it took precedence even over that of the Magira, the incarnate ghost of the queen mother, whom Olive did not see, much to her relief.

Apparently the unworthy keeper felt very worthless this day, because many messengers were dispatched and still he would not come. Finally Gauaronga stood up and fired a pistol into the air. Within several minutes two horsemen in armor announced that the keeper was outside. Suddenly a great number of retainers appeared at the gate, walking backward toward the king. At the end of the strange procession was the keeper, who turned and bowed deeply.

Then a quaint figure advanced. It was a woman clad in long, trailing garments. Her face was shrouded beneath a heavy veil, but the texture was not so thick as to wholly conceal her gaunt features. Captain Lucas said this was Miramiza, aunt of the sovereigns of Wadai. She was attended by her women and paid the sultan her duty with considerable dignity. She had not found life easy in her native land, and lived here in Tchenka, the grateful recipient of Gauaronga's hospitality. A good many Wadaians came with her. They were easily distinguishable from the Bagirmi by the light brown ringlets that hung around their heads and faces. Though they were impoverished, they walked with power.

All the chiefs came and bowed, each attended by their own followers, all the way down to a few naked boys who kept a far distance. Olive, from her folding chair under a tent, guessed the crowd might number two thousand people. When the musical salute was done, each man waved his dagger or spear aloft, while the Bata Kuji dropped to his knees and crawled to the sultan's feet, prostrating himself in the dust. As soon as the ceremony was over, the keeper seated himself humbly on the edge of the rug beside the sultan.

The Magira then appeared and passed immediately by the Bata Kuji, swaying and twisting before taking a seat. Next came representatives of all the sultan's wives, sons, and daughters. Captain Lucas explained that these chiefs, and others who held posts of authority, were mostly from nearby tribes, for the sultan feared giving an office of power to men whose birth and position might tempt them to power. He took even further precautions: Many of the sons of influential men were castrated.

The captain pointed out a man from one of the smaller tribes. Olive saw that his nose was slit and his eyes torn out. Lucas told them that he had been one of the king's war chiefs until he ran from a battle with Rabeh. He had been physically reprimanded and dismissed from office, but he had worked his way back into comparative favor and was now chief of one of the river towns. Olive watched the man turning his head from side to side.

The event lasted about three hours, ending in an unceremonious rush for the door, while Gauaronga remained to watch the exit.

The affair was so long that it reminded Olive of another performance she attended, over ten years ago. In 1896, Olive's father confronted her and Flora with a wide grin. He told them he was taking them to Germany to see a once-in-a-lifetime opera. Their lives had always been filled by music, so they were ecstatic when he revealed they were going to Bayreuth to see Wagner's *Der Ring des Nibelungen*, which was going to play in its entirety for the first time in twenty years.

Olive and Flora studied the score for months and played the parts on their own instruments. Flora played the male singers on her viola; Olive played the women's parts on her flute. When they finally took their seats in the massive, gilded rotunda, far from home, Olive fell silent as the lights cut out and all was plunged into darkness. Then a lone horn sounded, heralding the birth of the universe. As the music began to flow like a cascade, the lights came up, and the opera began. It was one of the most unforgettable nights of Olive's life.

They begged their father to stay another day for the second cycle, but all the seats were sold out. The theater officials smiled at the girls so moved by the *Ring*. Somehow they were able to locate some seats, and they stayed another day to see the second cycle. For months afterward, Olive and Flora acted out the scenes in their room.

The Rhine maidens were Olive's favorites: elusive and beautiful and strong, but not without fault. Olive hated the lame dwarf, Alberich, who came to the Rhine maidens and tried to woo them, only to hear them laugh at him. But when he found the magical Rhinegold, the treasure of the maidens, they revealed its secret: Only one who had foresworn love could forge a shining ring of ultimate power from the gold. Cursing love, the dwarf stole away with the treasure.

Olive and Flora had to imagine the next operas, which they did to the music as they spun throughout their room. The ring was forged, eventually ending up in the hoard of the serpent-dragon Fafner. A young hero named Siegfried was trained to destroy the dragon, but he was young and foolish. Only after being trained by the mysterious Wanderer did Siegfried slay the dragon and take the ring.

THE NEXT WOMAN OLIVE WANTED to meet was the princess royal. All the sultan's married daughters were known as *maiarami*. Olive learned that each princess had her own house, which the husband was not allowed to share. The princesses sent for their husbands when they wanted them, but the men had no right to enter their presence without an invitation. Being chosen to marry a princess was so much dreaded that a man who thought such an honor was imminent would often flee the country. If one of Gauaronga's choices was already married, then the man had to divorce his other wives and live forever after with the *maiarami* as his sole wife.

The princess royal was seated on her mat, in her home off the palace square. When Olive, Mrs. Talbot, and Mrs. Mohmaduba greeted her, the princess just stared. Not only did she not send for chairs for her visitors, but she did not exchange a single word with them. Olive had had enough. She walked right past her and toured her house, the only two-story building in the city. The mud staircase led to two rooms with a good view onto the square, where the princess could watch without being seen. As Olive came back, she met the younger princess, the *Maiarami* Lamina, who was a bright, cheerful girl, like her mother, the *Leli* Bondigul. Lamina at once sent for a new mat for Olive and Mrs. Talbot to sit on. She showed Olive some rare jewels. In return she asked to see her hair, whose fame had apparently preceded her. Olive complied. When they got back to camp, they were surprised to see that the princess royal had acknowledged their visit by sending some eighty eggs as a parting gift, though since seventy-nine of them were spoiled, Olive felt little gratitude and begrudged having to make a return present.

The last visit they paid was to Miramiza, the elder princess of Wadai they had seen at the celebration. Her house was a tiny little hut and contained nothing except a blue-and-white earthenware teapot. The place was so thickly infested with flies that it was difficult to see. Miramiza was very much pleased to see them. She pulled Olive close, her eyes glistening and voice quavering with excitement.

"Don't go, don't go, don't go," she repeated.

"Where?" asked Olive.

"Don't go to Abechir," she implored.

When the princess paused to listen to Mrs. Talbot's assurance that they were not going to do so, the old woman patted them on the shoulders, shook both their hands, and showed immense relief. She too asked to see Olive's hair. She unpinned it, and down it fell again. The old lady stroked it in silence, then sighed and said that she had longed to see hair like that of French women. The resident had told her that they could wrap their toes in it. Olive refrained from comment on this, but when she told Captain Lucas at camp, he half denied it. Olive blushed as he said: *"Mais, Madame, elle exagère."*

That night Mr. Talbot got word that the king had apparently been feeling remorse over selling his armor. He now wanted Mr. Talbot to sell him his remaining rifles in recompense. This, of course, was an impossibility. Captain Lucas again expressed his surprise that Gauaronga sold his armor in the first place but assuaged their fears by saying that Gauaronga knew his place and held no ill will toward the French. Still, he warned that a devoted subject of the king might try to bring these treasures back to him in a more surreptitious manner. The Bagirmi, he warned, regarded skillful theft as a virtue. So they took apart the armor and hid it in different places among their clothes and luggage.

Olive noticed that soldiers were now on guard around their rest house all day and all night. She couldn't remember when this started. The fort was within sight, and only a few yards away, so they did not feel in danger. Still, Olive again slept with a loaded revolver under her pillow.

Olive did not worry. For all her fears after hearing the captain's stories, this was one of the most pleasantly civilized places they had been to. This was most apparent at night, in the first cool hours after sundown that Olive had grown to love in Africa. Then, with the orange tailings of the sun disappearing into purple twilight, they pushed out all the tables and chairs and ate and talked under a staked tent, with good food on their table.

They sipped lime juice from clean glasses and talked of Gauaronga, his wives, and even the Magira.

Olive and Mr. Talbot were engaged in laughing conversation when Mrs. Talbot announced she would dress for dinner. As she left, Mr. Talbot placed their lamp on a table to provide a bright glow against the slowly flooding dark. As they continued to talk, Mr. Talbot jumped back.

"Run away," he said, pointing.

Olive jumped and sprinted, but not before catching, in the corner of her eye, a matte gray cobra unspooling from under the table.

Mr. Talbot froze in place and watched as the cobra slithered over the edge of his boot. He held his breath. The serpent was a very slow five feet long.

When the cobra finally slid off his foot, Mr. Talbot looked quickly, but couldn't see a stick or knife within reach. The cobra was headed straight toward the small hut where Mrs. Talbot was changing. They could hear her humming a tune.

There was no time to lose. Mr. Talbot shouted to his wife and seized a tent pole, sending the canvas down and striking the snake in the same movement. But the pole bent, and the cobra spun about in a blur and slowly rose off the ground. Its hooded head floated and swayed in the air as it set its gaze upon Mr. Talbot. The serpent's mouth opened, revealing two scimitar-shaped fangs.

Before Mr. Talbot could even think of moving, the snake seemed to choke and cough. Mr. Talbot covered his face and screamed. Only then did Olive realize that the serpent had spat its deadly venom into his face. Mr. Talbot roared, then brought the tent pole down on the snake with such anguished force that the stake instantly broke its back. The cobra lay unmoving as Mr. Talbot collapsed into the dust, his hands over his eyes, bellowing in pain.

Mrs. Talbot came out, took one look at the scene, and ran to grab her husband's bag. When she came back, the boys had eased Mr. Talbot, still crying in pain, into a chair. What ill fortune this good man had! thought Olive.

Olive consulted their manual again. Mrs. Talbot bathed his eyes, first with salad oil and then boric acid, but otherwise there was nothing to be done. The chemical seemed to help as Mr. Talbot began to quiet down. He was breathing evenly and seemed to be past the worst suffering. "Thank heavens," said Mrs. Talbot. Her husband began to whisper.

"My dear," he said. "I can . . ." His voice trailed off.

He looked out past his wife's shoulder.

"I'm blind."

20

THE GREAT GAUARONGA, PART 2

December 1910: Still in Tchenka, Mr. Talbot Is Blind;
More Gifts Are Exchanged; a Tall Man Appears;
a Choice Is Made

Captain Lucas rushed into camp and dropped to his knees. Mr. Talbot's purpled eye was so swollen that he couldn't even open it. Mrs. Talbot held her husband's hands.

"Percy," she said.

Captain Lucas examined the rest of him, looking for the telltale signs—swollen flesh and dual pinpricks—of the cobra's bite. He looked twice. Satisfied, he sat back.

"It will just be a matter of time," said Captain Lucas.

Mrs. Talbot gasped.

"No, no," he added swiftly, shaking his head. "I'm sorry. I meant it will just be a matter of time before his recovery will be complete. Permanent blindness does not result from snake poison." Mrs. Talbot caught her breath again.

The captain looked around the edges of the table, poking at the dust with his shoe.

"It was unlucky that the snake should have come," he said. "They are not common here. And made its way straight to the one spot of light in the place . . . almost uncanny."

All that night Olive could not help wondering whether the snake had come by chance, or whether there had been an evil agency at work. But their boxes were secure, and she repressed her speculations as unjust.

THE NIGHT WAS A HARD ONE, as was the next, but the following morning Mr. Talbot's eye was much reduced in size and he could open it without too much discomfort. When he announced that Africa was getting to be less and less of a blur, Olive reflected on the constant, almost insurmountable obstacles that had befallen him.

It was now already mid-December. Their brief jaunt south had turned into what felt like an eternity. Though Gauaronga had been most hospitable after the cobra incident—sending them food and help—Olive was eager to return to Fort Lamy as soon as possible. She was looking forward to spending Christmas at Kusseri around Herr von Raben's merry little tree, just as Boyd had. Olive also desperately wanted to see her Josephine and the little rolling *zakis*. These beasts, though small and new to her life, brought her mind great happiness. But Olive knew they couldn't leave Tchenka until Mr. Talbot's sight returned.

The day finally came when Mr. Talbot could once again count fingers and point out mountains on the horizon. As they packed hurriedly to leave, one of Gauaronga's emissaries appeared at their door. He had his hands behind his back. Olive froze for a moment, but the man revealed gifts from the chief: a cowrie-bedecked clarinet and a long wooden trumpet, two royal treasures that they had highly desired. Mr. Talbot met their price, and they packed the instruments into the luggage.

Captain Lucas was a bit less happy at this late turn of events because it meant they would have to indulge Gauaronga in a ceremonial visit of thanks. He and Mr. Talbot went to the palace as Olive and Mrs. Talbot continued to pack. As Mr. Talbot put on his hat and moved to leave, his wife looked concerned, as if a thought had come to her.

"Mr. Talbot," she said. "I beg you not . . . to accept anything to eat or drink from him."

Her husband stared at her. And though they had not conferred, Olive found herself in agreement.

"That's absurd," said Mr. Talbot, sharply.

The visit was a predictably long one. Gauaronga shared a long, excellent tea with them and insisted on hearing more about England. He then offered his guests some dates, which had come from across the desert. Mr. Talbot and Captain Lucas ate some, and Mr. Talbot put the rest in his pocket, remembering his wife's words.

When they came back to camp, Mrs. Talbot questioned her husband about the visit. He pulled out the dates and explained that everyone had eaten them. Satisfied, Mrs. Talbot ate three. Olive ate only one, out of curiosity. Someone made a joke about the carefully concocted emetic they carried and how it could be used on an unwilling companion if needed.

They finally left Tchenka in the afternoon, after a long good-bye with what seemed to be the entirety of the sultan's inner circle. Captain Lucas escorted them out, but then rode on ahead, as he had business. The Grand Duke of Mecklenburg-Schwerin was expected on a visit and the French had to begin preparations. The captain rode off, his mighty horse kicking up dust behind him. He had helped them a great deal, and Olive watched him go with sadness.

It was already night, but they wanted to press forward. They saw a bright fire they thought was the next outpost, but it was just a campfire by the road. As they approached, Olive saw a school of little boys gathered in a circle, one of whom would continually jump up to add twigs or straw to the flames. A *mallam* was squatting by them. He had a prayer board, on which some verses of the Koran were written, and he intoned them for the children to repeat. Olive found the scene—of the children reciting the strange words by the flickering light—picturesque. She stood and watched for some time. Just then, a tall man rose from the background of the fire and began to walk away. As he stood to leave, the boy put on fresh twigs and Olive could see the man's face for a moment by the light of the flame. He was one of the henchmen Olive had seen at the fantasia. He was one of Gauaronga's, she was sure of it. Once they took their leave of the group, Olive told Mr. Talbot. That night they took care to have their boxes placed close around the tents. However, Olive eventually convinced herself that she had been imagining things, so she slept rather easily.

After a second day of marching, they camped at the Arab town of Abugher under a massive tamarind tree, which filled the sky with its curved, blanched fruit. Since it wasn't even night yet, Olive and Mrs. Talbot set about their normal camp activities. Olive then realized that Mr. Talbot was still standing there, rigid as a pole, staring off into space. He finally dropped his head, muttered something about rest, and climbed into his tent.

Mrs. Talbot didn't know what to say. This was something her husband had never done in all their married life, in the jungle or at home. Olive volunteered that it was probably the glare of the fierce sun that had tried his weakened eyes. Mrs. Talbot thought that sounded right. They retired for the night. Olive was elated that they had finally left Tchenka, but a deeper worry wrapped itself around her.

The next day Mr. Talbot woke up fully refreshed and ready to lead. After a time it was Mrs. Talbot who lagged. Olive dropped back and found her friend sweating profusely.

"I am feeling very ill," she said.

It was midday, so they stopped at a house in Ngama, a small Arab town on the border of the Bagirmi tribe. Mrs. Talbot nearly collapsed onto a hard wooden bed. Mr. Talbot bent down to her, but she begged to be left alone. She wanted to rest to be ready for the three-hour jaunt that afternoon. She wanted to get to Maiashe, the last town they would camp at before Fort Lamy.

Olive and Mr. Talbot agreed that rest would be the best medicine for her. But ill news came when Momo informed them that there was no water in Maiashe. Olive was surprised, for there had been plenty of water ten days before. That meant they would have to remain in Ngama, then make a long march to Fort Lamy tomorrow. At least this delay would give Mrs. Talbot more hours to rest.

Making the best of his time, Mr. Talbot produced his silver instrument and took measurements of the Ngama villagers, but there were not enough of them to make up the full twenty he always tried to achieve for scientific purposes. He was just one short. Olive was helping half-heartedly when a tall figure blocked out the sun. It was the man she had seen at the fire.

"I will complete your number," he said.

Olive was now sure it was the man she had seen in Tchenka. She was positive he was Gauaronga's agent. Mr. Talbot didn't seem to recognize him. He dutifully measured him, then gave him the same payment he had all the others. But the man refused the payment. Olive stepped forward.

"Why are you here?" she asked. "When we said good-bye to you at Tchenka, we little expected to see you again so soon."

The tall man smiled with a strange expression.

"I have come to act escort to a great stranger at the bidding of the Sultan."

Olive considered his words. The grand duke was coming, so he must be referring to that. They smiled and said their good-byes before Olive watched the tall man walk away. That night Olive had the uncomfortable feeling of being watched. She knew it was ridiculous thinking, but she felt she was caught in the land of her enemies. She longed to get to Fort Lamy.

The next day's march started with the sun. Mrs. Talbot felt much better and kept up her usual pace. When they reached Maiashe, they beheld a pool full of clear, refreshing water. Mr. Talbot looked at Momo, who had said the village was dry.

"It must be a mirage," said Mr. Talbot, and he walked right up to the pool, scattering a noisy flock of sacred ibis that quickly took to the air. Mr. Talbot dropped to his knees and palmed the cool water to his lips—it was real. He turned to look at Momo. He was soon dismissed.

The next part of their march was through the lower Sudanese desert, which was very arid and hot. They were headed toward the two pools of Bokkoiyu. Mrs. Talbot was once again tired, so was propped up on her horse in a way that reminded Olive of the Black Magira, though she hated herself for thinking it. When they reached the water, the sky was pitch-black. Exhausted, the party ate a quick supper and went to bed.

The next morning Olive woke to see kob drinking from the pool only a few yards away. She pointed them out to Mr. Talbot, who was already up, standing and staring out past the water. But he made no response; he didn't even look.

"Might I ask leave to lie in your tent?" he asked. This was astoundingly uncharacteristic. "I do not wish to disturb my wife," he added. She had not yet awoken.

Olive was greatly alarmed. She searched his face. Mr. Talbot did not look well, and he knew it.

"The symptoms I have," he said, "are those of dysentery."

MR. TALBOT'S ILLNESS PRESENTED very similar to his wife's. Olive hunted through their two medical books, but no one disease fit all their maladies. This didn't seem like dysentery at all. Their hearts were weak, and internal pain racked their bodies. Then a thought occurred to Olive that terrified her:

Poison.

This idea made her the most anxious because she had no idea how to treat it—with the syringe? With medicine? But as Olive tried to research a cure, she began to feel sick herself.

Olive denied the aches in her body and her own shortness of breath until it became impossible to do so. Though she continued to run the camp, it was growing more difficult. When Flora was sick with scarlet fever as a child, their mother made her get out of bed and attend to her lessons and chores. As her sister stumbled around in delirium, Olive watched with sympathy. It was their father who had to beg his wife to let Flora go to bed. She finally relented, and Flora slept for days. Olive now felt in need of a similar reprieve. Luckily Mrs. Talbot finally began to feel better, so she could help. But her husband grew worse.

Facing growing despair, Olive sent a boy for help. He returned with cows and milk. There was no shade near the water—there was no shade anywhere—so Mr. Talbot lay in a tent covered with three canvas sheets. But nothing could keep out the merciless sun, and by day the atmosphere was like a furnace. At night they had cool breezes but had to sleep within a sheltering circle of huge fires lit by the boys, lest a lion or leopard penetrate their circle. As Mr. Talbot groaned and slept, Olive copied Boyd's diary in earnest, trying to finish up the early entries, which included a great deal of writing about birds. As antelopes poked their heads into their tent, Olive wrote in her own diary. She felt so hot and desperate that she did not bother to conceal her actions. She was onto her second volume now, and like every single page before it, the daily entry took the form of a personal letter to someone who was gone.

> *Dearly beloved Boyd*
>
> *I had a vision of you waiting for me, I knew I could never not come to you hereafter—it was glorious, but oh the suffering of this world. What is right? What is wrong?*
>
>

Your always devoted,
Olive:
>

Three days passed in fever and heat. On the third day Olive realized it was Christmas. She again thought of her home, both at Vinters and in the little houses of her youth in London and Scotland, and even in drafty Dunvegan. She thought of decorations and songs and snow. And she also thought of her mother. Throughout their childhood their mother never gave them one Christmas gift. She showed them books rather than embraces, offered lessons on duty rather than flowers. Their father was often away but always returned with barrel hugs and presents.

On Christmas Day, Mr. Talbot seemed to improve. Olive even went for a walk around the oasis, promising to keep within sight of the camp. The farther out she went, the smaller it became. Mastaba joined her on her Christmas march; in fact Olive had a feeling that he would not leave her alone. There was no apparent cause for fear, but perhaps he had seen or heard something. When they returned, Mr. Talbot had suffered a significant relapse. Once more his illness seemed very grave, and Mrs. Talbot sat very close to him, refusing food or sleep.

Whatever had befallen Mr. Talbot, it was not a normal ailment. Olive kept thinking of the sultan's dates. Mr. Talbot had admitted to eating about ten of them. When he awoke for a time, Olive told him of her suspicions. He remembered that the sultan had handed him dates from one end of the box, while he had taken those for Captain Lucas and himself from the other end. Olive cursed the old beast who had done this to them. Was he so angry over his rusty, bartered possessions? Or was something deeper at play?

The next day was one that Olive feared would be sad beyond measure. But Mr. Talbot again improved. Late that morning one of the boys pointed to the road. There was Captain Lucas, riding by at a stately pace, on his way to Fort Lamy. Olive's heart leaped as she waved him down.

The captain seemed very surprised to see his friends. He had thought they would have made Fort Lamy long before. Olive and Mrs. Talbot said nothing of their fears about Gauaronga, though they did not know why.

"How have you been?" asked Olive. He said he had been in perfect health.

Olive told Captain Lucas that Mr. Talbot was getting better and they would be right behind him. They gave him a short good-bye, and he left. She wasn't sure why she didn't ask his help. She just wasn't sure.

On December 28, the party set out again. Mr. Talbot was indeed better but still weak. When they reached the next pool at Bamboiyu, the water there was foul and there was no milk to be found. Mr. Talbot got worse again. Olive ordered a move ahead to Bahr Alienya. It was a risky decision, but she knew that if they stayed, Mr. Talbot would die. They pressed on through the sand, and when the sun rose, they could see Fort Lamy in the hazy distance. They arrived by New Year's Day. It felt like coming home.

Olive smiled and laughed when the little *zakis* ran to her and she could pat them and scratch them behind their soft ears. Mr. Talbot was getting better. Olive decided not to tell Captain Facon about her suspicions. She thought about the missing maps and how the French did not wish to provoke Ali Dinar. She couldn't trust anyone. "Don't go to el-Fachir!" the old woman had said. Olive secured the remaining dates carefully in a pouch and hid it away. When she wrote Boyd that night, as she did every night, the only light on was hers:

Jan 1, 1911
Fort Lamy

Very dear Boyd–
    The first words I address this new year are to you. Pray God that you are having a higher happiness than we can imagine. Perhaps I shall join you soon for life here is very difficult. I had meant to write last night, but we came in late.
    I hate this place though I like its inhabitants. I long to get to Lake Chad and Maifoni,
    Then I can die happy.

                               Lovingly yours,
                                   Olive:

THE FRENCH REPORT

*January 1911: Back at Fort Lamy, Olive Struggles
to Finish a Full Copy of Boyd's Diaries;
She Receives a Secret Report*

Olive stretched out her hands and fingers until they tingled back to life. As Mr. Talbot healed, she had buried herself in the task of copying Boyd's diaries. She had copied the last part first and was now backtracking through the earlier entries. One night, after finding Olive slumped asleep over her pages, Mrs. Talbot put her hand on Olive's shoulder and offered to help. Olive was surprised by this offer, but knew she needed the aid. It was odd, at first, but the work soon overcame any awkwardness. They would work sometimes until eleven at night, though Olive suspected Mrs. Talbot of sometimes staying up all night to lessen her own portion. The diaries had not given her answers, but Olive felt energized by the fact that the information they contained would be put to good use. Mr. Talbot had told her that the War Office must see them first; then he could find use for the scientific parts.

On January 6 Captain Facon met with Olive and gave her some further materials. He was almost secretive about it, which Olive found curious until she realized what he was giving her—the official French report of the incident, including a map. She was very surprised by this.

She quietly accepted the papers, knowing that she would have to return them as soon as possible.

Olive began going through the report with measured exhilaration, her fingers lightly passing over and moving the pages to find the right spot to plunge into. At first glance, the reports seemed to be cobbled together from eyewitnesses, official records, and notes from the commandant himself. More important, it seemed to fill in the gaps left by the end of Boyd's own account. She could wait no longer. Olive started reading, copying the pages in the same manner she did his diary.

When Boyd was in Abechir, waiting for the letter from Ali Dinar that would allow him passage, he went to Commandant Julien and told him that he must get a report through to Khartoum. He leaned forward, saying that he had a mission to carry out for the Foreign Office. This was news to the commandant. Boyd asked if he might visit the villages that had been razed by the Furians. He had to "ascertain the facts and investigate the amount of damage done, in order that he might draw up a report on the subject."

Julien, who had before refused Boyd passage because it was so dangerous—and so potentially explosive to the region—agreed. He had previously suspected Boyd of being a spy—was this confirmation or just a ruse to leave the city? Julien's only stipulation was that Boyd must return by the end of the week.

On the morning of March 18 Boyd set out with an escort of four, including Fatcha, the headman of Sultan Assil, along with José and a cook. They had five horses and two camels between them. Boyd carried his trusty Lee-Metford rifle with two hundred cartridges and a .303 BSA sporting rifle. José had a revolver. Boyd left some of his luggage behind. The French kept meticulous records of this.

On Sunday April 3, 1910, assuming he had returned, Commandant Julien sent for Boyd to join him for dinner. He never received a reply. Julien went to Sultan Assil, who informed him that his headman had returned, saying that he had to leave Boyd in Dar Fur. Boyd had been very well received in the villages of Wadai and had gone on to el-Fachir, said the headman. Julien was angry because he had explicitly forbidden this action.

Julien knew that even if Boyd reached el-Fachir, he could not control Dinar. He also knew that Chauvelot was mounting a strike against the Furians—what if Boyd saw it? As he spoke with Assil, José Lopez was announced. He walked in, dusty and in torn, dirty clothes. With sweat pouring down his face, in trembling Arabic, he told them what happened. When José finished, he wept.

"Is he dead or alive?" barked Julien.

"I don't know," said José.

Days earlier, at Nyeri, the two men who were carrying Boyd's letter to Ali Dinar had been seized. One was sent in chains to el-Fachir; the other disappeared. When the carrier brought the letter before the sultan himself, on his throne in his palace, he shivered with fear.

Ali Dinar looked at him with inscrutable dark eyes. Rifles were propped up behind him, and his sword lay against his leg.

"Is it true there are only two Frenchmen in Abechir?" asked Ali Dinar.

"There are certainly more than that," the carrier responded softly.

"Is it true the sender of the letter is English?"

"Yes."

"Is he coming to el-Fachir?"

"If he receives your permission."

Ali Dinar regarded the runner. Making a motion for him to be brought forward, Ali Dinar rose and started walking. His guards pushed the man to follow through a door and into a larger room, where Ali Dinar showed the messenger a good part of his war arsenal. Ali Dinar had twenty guns, eighty carbines, ninety carbines with bayonets, and a great many pistols. He had thirty-six golden swords.

"Has Assil anything like this?" he asked. The carrier said no.

Ali Dinar made his prisoner tremble in anticipation for three days. On the fourth Ali Dinar gave him four letters: one for one of his generals, one for an exiled sultan who supported him, one for Sultan Assil in Abechir, and the last for Boyd Alexander.

Ali Dinar said that if Boyd Alexander was truly English, he had nothing to fear:

"Come to el-Fachir," he wrote to Boyd.

The runner traveled as fast as he could, going four days with water and two without. He delivered his other letters along the way to Abechir. When he finally arrived in Abechir, Boyd was three days dead.

OLIVE WAS STUNNED BY THESE revelations. Had the French been observing Boyd? That made sense, but the level of detail here was still staggering. He was so close to receiving that letter.

As Olive reached the end of the report, she realized that it contained a transcript of some sort from someone she had been yearning to talk to since this whole nightmare began. When José Lopez rode into Abechir after escaping the assault that killed Boyd, he found the commandant and gave an immediate deposition as to what happened. Here, in the sweltering African darkness, was that very deposition. Olive felt as if she had found gold. She had been chasing Lopez forever. Finally it seemed that she would hear his story.

In the French report José said that once Boyd made up his mind to go beyond the Wadaian frontier and into Dar Fur, he tried to convince him to turn back. They had not yet received a letter of safe passage from Ali Dinar and the region they were to enter, Dar Tama, was boiling over with unrest. But Boyd pressed on. It was, said José, like talking to a deaf man.

Boyd sensed his old friend's unease, and made the proclamation that "Anyone who wishes may return to Abechir." After a few silent minutes, José and the remaining boys watched their master walk out toward the horizon alone.

After waiting two hours for his friend to return, José spat and realized he should have known better. He rounded up the boys and they saddled up the camels in an attempt to catch up to Boyd. When they did, he barely acknowledged them. The unrelenting sun muddled everything.

They rode as a group into the village of Ilarne at dusk, where Boyd hoped to find an emissary of Ali Dinar waiting with his letter. The party camped under a wide tree. The sultan sent two men to greet them. Exhausted, Boyd told them he would see the sultan in the morning.

The next morning, Boyd was finishing his coffee when the two men returned. There were others with them. They were armed with guns and swords. Boyd went to his trunk and pulled out his Union Jack flag. He billowed its weight into the air, proof that he was an Englishman. The sultan's men muttered.

José could not understand what the men—who were Furians—were saying, but he knew they had murder in their hearts. He begged Boyd to leave. "They are bad men," he said, "bad men who will return to kill us!"

But Boyd had confidence in his flag.

When it turned completely dark, the two Furians returned and demanded that Boyd go before the sultan immediately. Boyd refused. One of the men put a hand on him and a fistfight ensued. A little boy stood and watched the whole thing, astounded at seeing a white man being attacked. The boy was holding a gun. Excited, the boy accidentally pulled the trigger and the gun fired, hitting Boyd in the body. Wounded, he fell to the ground. In an instant the crowd flung themselves at José, while the rest made off with the horses, camels, and baggage.

Boyd was crying: "José! José! José!" as his assailants began to drag him by his feet. He put his arms over his head to protect himself from their blows while his elbows dragged along the ground.

José was powerless. Four men had seized him and were greedily pulling at a ring on his finger. He offered to remove it himself, and in the split second in which they released him he sprang away to grab the Lee-Metford rifle, but he had no cartridges. The only other gun they had was the revolver, and it was with the cook, who had already fled. Jose held the rifle to his shoulder and faced the men scrambling at him. He tried to fool them. They hesitated.

On the ground Boyd was being ruthlessly hit with spears. José shouted to him from a distance.

José backed up with the gun still pointed at his attackers. If he moved it off them, he would be dead. Another of their boys used a sword to fake his own death. Once the soldiers realized that José was not trying to save his friend, and that he had no ammunition, he began to flee with bullets whizzing by him, one hitting him on the hand. In the forest José met up with the cook and took his revolver. José found his horse on the side of the road and rode back to Abechir.

Olive stopped copying. This version was different—very different—from the one José had given the British newspapers in the wake of Boyd's death. In addition to many details that did not reconcile—from the number of people involved, to the small boy, to who had the revolver, to the Lee-Metford rifle, which José had told the papers was not only loaded but was used by him to shoot at his attackers—the most important, glaring difference was that according to the French report, Boyd was still alive when José escaped. Boyd was calling his friend's name when José deserted him.

In the report José also said that Boyd was extremely ill with blackwater fever, even suggesting that the illness had given him a feverish, exalted state of mind that only contributed to his death. Olive couldn't believe what she was reading. There was only a slight intimation of this illness in the diaries. Boyd had taken José as a boy from poverty to help him become one of the most seasoned guides and skilled taxidermists in Africa. After José saved Boyd's life from a hungry lion, Boyd welcomed him to his country home in England as family, even letting him drive his car. They were inseparable companions; there was no obstacle they could not overcome together. How, then, could a man of such character and so thoroughly experienced in the worst dangers of Africa have run when his friend was screaming for help?

Olive was so disturbed that she wrote to Herbert:

> *It grieves me terribly that José should have given such contradictory reports, for it looks as if the French must be correct in saying that he deserted his master. It certainly is odd that he should have given the*

cook his revolver—had no ammunition for the Lee-Metford—and
was lucky enough to happen upon his horse in the bush the next day. I
can't bear to think of Boyd calling to him in vain.

As Olive closed her letter and tried to fall asleep, that call was the
only thing she could hear.

ONCE EVERYTHING WAS COPIED and quietly returned, it was time to
begin the stretch to Maifoni, through Lake Chad and into the very heart
of Africa. Their first march would be overland to Gulfei in the Kamerun
region, traveling along the right bank of the Chari River. Meanwhile, the
mass of carriers would head straight to Maifoni. Olive and the Talbots
said good-bye to their French friends, who once again warned them
about the east. Two French soldiers were going to accompany them to
Lake Chad, but Olive didn't know if they were for protection or to ensure
they stayed on their prescribed path.

Before leaving, Olive set about one final task that she had been dread-
ing. She slowly walked to the low trees outside the resident house. There
she found Josephine, her baby giraffe, nibbling happily on the leaves of
the smallest trees. Josephine walked over to Olive and put her nose in
her hands. She was getting taller every day. Olive patted her on the head
and pulled some of the low leaves to feed her. Josephine ate them right
out of her hand, her long purple tongue curling around Olive's wrist. She
couldn't bear to part with the gentle animal, but she knew that the journey ahead was no place for the young and defenseless, even if they were
Africa incarnate. Olive knew that Josephine would be much happier at
Fort Lamy, where she could live out her days as a beloved and well-fed
friend of the soldiers. These were the men who had avenged Boyd. No
matter what else, she would never forget that. She tarried a moment,
feeling the animal's nose and mouth slowly moving side to side in her
hands. When they left the fort, Olive felt very sad.

The lions were going with them. The *zakis* were bundled into a little wicker cage that they had habitually tried to climb in a sort of never-ending game of King of the Castle. Mandara carried their cage, and the lions accepted their position quite philosophically, looking out with wondering eyes at the incidents of the road, then falling asleep curled up against each other when bored. Olive called them her little lords. When they made camp, the lions were let out and immediately started to explore, usually in opposite directions, for they were afraid of nothing. Olive took some photos of the cubs as they growled in celebration of their limited freedom. At night they slept side by side with Mandara around huge fires, for there was danger from leopards and jackals.

On the march the lions were always free and scampered about, jumping up and kissing anyone nearby, especially Mr. Talbot, whom Olive knew they adored. Their only annoyance came from the round burrs that could be found in the low grasses. The cubs would get full of them and would attend to each other by pulling them out with their teeth. They loved to play with any round fruit that they might use for a ball, and did a kind of tightrope walking on the edge of low village walls. Sometimes they climbed trees, or at least tried to.

As they marched, Olive caught Lamy staring at her pony's tail, his head cocked to one side. The lion started to bat at the swishing brush and Olive feared the worst, but her horse—that ornery, obstinate horse—took it all in good fun. The only nuisance the lions afforded was when they, like cats, would bring their masters gifts of the beasts they had murdered. One night Olive lifted her bedsheet to see a mangled pigeon, a night gift from Kusseri. They also tended to favor the taste of clothing. One time Lamy drew Olive's attention as Kusseri jumped on her back to take a generous bite of her shirt. Olive yelled their command word, "*Kai!,*" meaning "You!" but it was too late. The mischievous cub had already taken a morsel from an irreplaceable section.

At Gulfei the party was given two superb canoes to cross the Shari River in. The *zakis* were much puzzled by the water and jumped into it again and again to test its nature, though they expressed a strong disapproval of its wetness when they had done so. Olive allowed them to indulge their curiosity by the shore, but kept them close by in the canoe, where they continually tried to scramble up its steep sides. The canoes stopped at a coastal village named Kotoko where Olive brought some instruments, including a snakeskin guitar, from a group of musicians in a hut. When she tried to play the guitar, the *zakis* hid away in a corner.

Later that day Mr. Talbot left camp. He took his rifle and some of the boys to hunt hartebeest. Mrs. Talbot, though an evergreen supporter of her husband, had most recently begun to tire of Mr. Talbot's endless hunting. Nonetheless she waited and watched diligently under the cover of some bushes that offered slight respite from the sun.

As Mrs. Talbot sat there on the grass, she watched her husband begin to move, crouch, stop, then move again through the brush. It was then that she saw a gleam. She thought it a trick of her imagination or a by-product of the sunshine, but the next time her husband got up and moved, the gleam appeared again, behind him in the grass, seemingly moving at the same pace.

Mrs. Talbot sat to attention. She watched as it happened again. Olive came to her side and started to speak, but Mrs. Talbot silenced her, pointing to the light. It wasn't the glint that worried Mrs. Talbot but the undeniable fact that its movement was married to Mr. Talbot's. When he moved forward, the light moved as well; when he stopped, so it did, coming in and out of sight as it shifted against the sun. Mrs. Talbot realized it was a spear.

The French authorities had told them that the lands just east of the lake were dangerous. White men had been found murdered there, individually or in small numbers. They were encroaching on the blurry line of Wadai.

Mrs. Talbot called for her horse. She knew her husband would be furious with her, but both he and his pursuers were now out of sight. She galloped out and rode toward him at the best speed she could muster, with Olive quick behind. When they reached Mr. Talbot, he was walking toward them in complete ignorance that he was being followed. He and the boys did a quick sweep of the area but found nothing. Mrs. Talbot persuaded her husband to abandon the day's hunt, and he reluctantly agreed. Olive looked out to the flat east, in the direction where Mrs. Talbot had seen the reflection. There were some trees in the distance, and the soft indentation of what might be three or four mountains, looking more like watercolors in the late afternoon. But mostly it was the overwhelming flatness that took hold of her; she felt as if she could see all the way to Abechir. Whoever these pursuers were, they had been moving from the east, the direction of someone who might be looking in their own direction right now. Olive wondered about Ali Dinar—the man who had never been seen by the white man; the man who held a magic sword.

AS THEY MARCHED ON, the landscape became entangled in low woods that distorted their perspective. They could no longer see the low hills that Olive first spotted. The mimosa wood closed in, and branches stretched out from either side. Olive felt that the twisting trees seemed ready to catch hold of them as they made their way through the narrow forest path. The thicket ended suddenly, and she saw a sheet of water lapping lazily on a sandy bank. A bar of glittering beams flashed on its surface where the setting sun touched it with its golden light. Across the little bay, Mr. Talbot pointed out the hills of Hajer-el-Hamis, which had reappeared in shadow.

They had made it to Lake Chad.

They pitched camp on the open sand, next to the sparkling water. This mysterious inland sea, fed by the waters of east and west, and inhabited by mysterious tribes, had drawn the adventurous of the world. For centuries the lake was the polestar of African explorers. Many had come, but no one had truly lifted the shroud of enchantment from it. From hearing Boyd, Olive knew that the riddle of the lake's shallow waters, of its uncharted islands, and of its mysterious inhabitants, were awaiting her.

Olive wrote of the lake that night:

Very dear Boyd

The Spirit of the Lake is Loneliness, and she is clad in grey. Her spell is over all: in the shallows, and the depths; in the sunshine, and in the darkness; in the tracts of water that stretch to the horizon, and on the sandy islands. There is nothing that does not yield allegiance to her sway.

We are starting next a.m. after a day of writing, as I have begun the book. You know what that means.

Your greatly loving,
Olive:

22

VALKYRIE

January 23, 1911: Near Lake Chad,
Olive Finds the Four Fabled Peaks of
Hajer-el-Hamis, Where She Has a Vision

When the sun rose, Olive slid out of her tent to get a better view of the mountains. She pulled her shawl close. The air here was colder. There were four hills in total, each of a different height and rounded at the top. They had been told that each was only about a hundred feet high, but from the endless sandy plain they looked like mountains. The highest hill stood alone and was so close to the lake it appeared as if it were floating upon its mirror surface. The other three were clustered a way off, as if in quiet observation of the tallest one, called Hajer-el-Hamis. According to legend, this hill was the final resting place of Noah's ark.

They set their march. The French soldiers who accompanied them walked in step as the rest of the expedition moved at their usual ramshackle pace. As she walked, Olive felt the magic of the place. She tried to picture the plain around her as a drowned world. The Lord rewarded Noah's patience by sending him a single white dove as proof of his covenant. When the Flood receded, this is where the ark, with its great ribs of oak, had rotted down and mixed with the dust of the earth to make a most secret and sacred place. Olive looked around and imagined the high black water covering everything in sight. She thought of their trip here on the *Dakar*.

Olive noticed the abundant wildlife around them. There were so many different varieties of animals in the vicinity that they seemed their own evidence that this was where the beasts came spilling down off the mountain, two by two and eager to populate the new world. The name of the surrounding country also bore witness to the past: "Bornu" was short for "Bur-Noah," which meant "the land of Noah."

They stopped at a small village of the Mani people, the last settlement before the hills. The chief came to greet them, accompanied by a small band playing clarinets, drums, and a snakeskin guitar. He wished to join them on their trip to the mountains and brought two guides to help. As they started out, one of the guides told them that the main peak had been a place of pilgrimage for centuries. He said there was once a group of pilgrims who went on *hajj* from Chad all the way to the Kaaba, the black cube in Mecca—for Mohammedans, nothing less than a journey to the very House of God. When the pilgrims finally came back after months of hard travel, the *mallam* pointed toward Hajer-el-Hamis.

"You could have gone there," he said.

As they got closer, one of the French soldiers pointed to one of the smaller hills. Olive saw a dark shape there, near the top. It was the opening to a cave.

"Very long ago," the Mani chief explained via Mastaba, "it was a place of human sacrifice." Olive hoped that was no longer the case.

One of the French soldiers explained that these mountains had been, until very recently, surrounded by Lake Chad. The hill they were headed toward had sat in water nearly fifty feet deep, but the lake had receded at a swift rate, leaving nothing but a sandy lowland. It seemed as if the lake had opened these holy sites to them.

The good news was that the receding waters had revealed new paths to ascend the mountains. In the past, pilgrims approaching from the west would be at the mercy of the Buduma tribe, who would wait in their canoes, ready to snatch travelers from the water. But now that the river had become a desert, both the sacrificial cave and the high peak of Hajer-el-Hamis itself were within easier reach. Mr. Talbot shielded his eyes to look at the cave again, which had all but disappeared as a result of their movement.

As they got closer, the soil became harsh and sandy. The only vegetation was a spiked grass that grew very tall, and the usual pale-gray asclepias, whose leaves had the consistency of human flesh. At the base of the hill they found boulders and tiny stones. Sharp pebbles carpeted the ground, and among them stood small antelopes that were so fearless that they did not move until one was close enough to touch them. Olive was able to look up into the three little hills. The rocks were exceedingly rugged, and gave the appearance of having been pushed, shard by shard, out of the earth itself. The entire surface was a shiny black.

Fluffy owls stared back at them from the lined crevices of the rock. The blank grayness of the sky was suddenly punctuated by a bursting cloud of blue pigeons that launched out of the hill and into the air. The flock wheeled back as a single curling shape and finally settled into the holes and crannies of the rock. Olive wondered if they were perhaps descendants of that first dove, who came with an olive branch to the ark.

Suddenly the chief raised his hand and pointed to the hill. The cave was once again visible behind a shoulder of jagged rock. They had reached the slope. Silently each member of the party chose his or her own way up, as there was no one path.

Olive scrambled up and was surprised to find it was not as steep as it looked, though it was very rough and dirty. She had little sense of the others as she grabbed handfuls of loose rock and slid over flat stone. She kept moving at whatever angle was presented to her. Her knees and lower arms were filthy, but she kept going up. Through a confluence of will and luck, she was the first to reach the cave.

Olive looked up to see a large rock outcropping blocking her way. When she got high enough, she stepped over it and into the opening, which yawned into a great hall. She had entered the cave. It was not a tiny, dank place of horrors but more of an open cathedral. The rock ceiling was very high. The atmosphere was light enough to see. Olive didn't test the echo but knew that it was there. An alcove stood opposite her, framed by a huge natural window. Olive knew this was a natural construction, but it felt like architecture.

Olive sensed a sacredness there, though it also felt very lonely. There was a narrow slit in the rock that let in a flat pane of light. There was no exit, only a small ledge followed by a sheer drop downward. Olive took a deep breath and looked at the floor. She expected to see bones and arcane symbols, but all she saw was rock and dust. She could find no evidence of humanity ever being there other than her own breathing.

Olive was finally alone. For all her months in Africa, she had always been escorted, guarded, or handled. But this cave was a place that demanded individual deliberation; it could not be avoided. Olive closed her eyes and felt the large room around her give way to the greater sky.

When the others finally joined her, covered in dust and scrapes, they praised their discovery. They examined the cave and made important sketches. Olive kept to herself, her mind filled with images of the past, both hers and not. Mr. Talbot examined the chamber and was fascinated, even though there was nothing living to hunt. When it was time to go, they all turned and left the cave, slowly retracing their steps until they were again in the little valley between the three smaller hills.

Olive wandered by herself among the strange heights of Hajer-el-Hamis. She found herself on the rise of a gorge, where a broad road led into the heart of one of the other hills. The way passed between two great balustrades, and through a vast archway supported by ancient columns of rock. A wall of stones, gathered in a way that indicated they had been placed there by human hands, barred the passage. Was this the sacrificial altar the guide had talked about? Olive could see no blood, neither old nor new. Beyond the stones the path bent inward, ending in an immense, roofless circular hall, walled by sheer cliffs. A high, tiered balcony ran halfway around the top. On the farther side, a shelf of rock jutted out, the canopy to some dead god's throne. Olive took some photos.

There was something about the desolation of the rocks, combined with the blank sky, that again reminded Olive of her favorite opera. She saw the Rhine maidens slowly rise from the waters of Lake Chad, their bodies twisting among the low clouds. She could hear the music, its forms taking shape in her mind. Olive remembered how it ended, when Siegfried, having slain the dragon and taken the ring, came upon a sleeping knight, he was surprised to learn it was really Brünnhilde, the leader of the Valkyries. When he saw her beautiful face, Siegfried knew fear for the first time. When she awoke, Siegfried gave her the ring and pledged himself to her. But the ring was still cursed, and he was cowardly murdered by the dwarf Alberich's son. As Siegfried's body was sent to the funeral pyre, a heartbroken Brünnhilde threw herself into the fire with him, leaving the ring for the Rhine maidens to take back to the deep waters below.

Olive looked out and saw the wondrous rainbow bridge before her, gleaming and vibrant, that pierced the gray sky and bridged the space between this world and another. She saw Brünnhilde and the Valkyries dismounting their winged horses, their broadswords gleaming in the sun. They then assembled with the heroes in the mighty hall before her, quaffing drink and singing songs of war and love. Though bare, this place was beautiful and triumphant in its ruin. Olive heard Mrs. Talbot cry out, shaking her from her reverie. Mrs. Talbot was beginning to climb one of the other hills. Olive made her way over to see Mrs. Talbot clutching her arm. Her friend raised her hand, her palm to her face. Olive saw smoke rise from her hand. She was screaming.

The rock where she was climbing was hot to the touch. As they bandaged her hand, Mr. Talbot said the strange effect was probably produced by dust from the burned grass. Olive looked back to the empty arena, now obscured to her. Mrs. Talbot felt fine, though she was tired. They agreed that she should go back to camp with some of the boys. Olive thought that Mr. Talbot might return with her, but he was already eyeing the tallest peak.

He was hunting Hajer-el-Hamis.

Sure enough, after Mrs. Talbot left, they began to plan their ascent.

Mr. Talbot knew he had a willing accomplice in Olive, and they headed toward the mountain.

THE CLOSER THEY GOT TO the actual hill of Hajer-el-Hamis, the more striking it became, black and sharp as it thrust into the sky. The summit looked nearly three hundred feet high. Their guides seemed discouraged. They said that no man, white or black, had ever been rash enough to attempt the peak, though French scientific expeditions had been in the area. The guides themselves admitted they had once tried and failed. Mr. Talbot said that Dixon Denham, another explorer, mentioned having seen the rocks, but not having climbed them.

Just as with the Mao Kabi Falls, Olive was not scared away by the inaction of some old explorer. She led their walk around the base hoping to spy a way up. Even the base was difficult going because of the tall, merciless burr grass that gripped them like tentacles. Olive wondered if it had been grown by the waters of the Flood to protect the sacred site. This hell grass, taller than any human, was yet another predator.

Just then the grass naturally split, and they spotted a point of entry that did not, in Olive's eyes, look wholly impassable.

Olive went first, looking up to see the faceted stones pushing upward like sharp jewels. She was about to step onto a pointed rock when she stopped to stare at her foot. She realized that her boot, which had been her bane for most of the trip, would never find good purchase on the black rock.

Olive bent down, and to the amazement of Mr. Talbot and the guides (and especially the French soldiers), took off her boots and started to climb.

When the others saw her success, they followed suit by discarding their own boots and climbing behind her. The ascent was surprisingly not as difficult as it had looked from the flat earth below. Olive was still ahead, until she got two-thirds up and stopped. She looked to her right, her left, above, and below. There were no more footholds to be had. She had been moving so fast that she didn't see that the rock ahead of her was smooth, hard stone. And it was much steeper.

Olive and the others reluctantly descended. Back on the ground, she slowly put her boots back on and continued her exploration around the base of the mountain, picking up an occasional porcupine quill as she went. Olive looked up to the summit in disgust. They had come so close.

At the south end of the hill, the base looked so rocky as to be impassable. Olive believed—and Mr. Talbot eventually agreed—that this might mean it would get easier at the top. They tried again, in the same manner. They slithered, slipped, scrambled, and struggled, and had to use their wits to guess where to poke and slide their hands over the rocks. It was movement by inches, as they had to use every part of their body to win their way up.

But Olive was wrong. Just as before, the texture of the rock became almost sheer when they got closer to the summit. Mr. Talbot didn't say anything, but Olive knew he was ready to turn back to camp. She knew that at any moment Mr. Talbot would try to persuade her to turn back.

Olive looked up instead of down and pushed herself ahead. Somehow her perseverance paid off, and she scrambled to the top. She smiled as the late afternoon warm sky stretched out before her on every side. The narrow summit was little more than a perched rock. In one of its corners Olive saw a pile of stones. As she walked closer, she realized it was not a natural formation. Could these rocks be the altar they had heard of? Olive had seen such a pile before. It was a cairn, a formation of stones meant as a memorial, or to mark an important place. She had seen them on Skye, near roads and on silent plains.

Once the others arrived, out of breath and with small cuts on their arms and legs, they were all equally surprised. The guides repeated that no man had ever climbed the peak.

No *man*, thought Olive.

In the book of Genesis, Jacob and Laban erected a cairn in commemoration of their covenant in Gilead. Maybe Noah and his sons had made one here in honor of their landing. Perhaps it was their thanks for a new start.

From the top of the peak Olive saw that the orange sun was setting over Lake Chad. The water pooled with the sky like a melting ingot, transformed in its appearance and properties. The lake itself was the only water left in the area, containing perhaps the only true drops of the Flood left in the world. Olive looked over its reddening waters. She could see a ridge of dark islands along its far shore. The rainbow bridge was gone. She thought of Boyd's words that "Every explorer looks upon the map of that part of the world which particularly calls him, and endeavors to find a spot that still affords opportunity for the special powers he may possess for finding out the secrets that it hides."

Time passed here, at the first steps of a second chance. These moments were not lost on Olive. But night was coming, and with it the fear of being overcome again. They scrambled down the back end of the rock, with some difficulty, having to hang from Mr. Talbot's coat in some spots. They finally reached the earth, knowing that their friends would be anxiously waiting for them.

Their descent was none too soon, for when they reached the ground, the sun had set and they were plunged again into darkness.

23

THE LAKE OF LONELINESS

*January 25, 1911: The Party Sets Out in Canoes onto
Lake Chad; a Storm Hits and They Drift for Days;
a Dreadful Truth Is Found on a Remote Island*

After Hajer-el-Hamis, the expedition bent their steps to a small town named Jimtilo, at the mouth of the Shari River. There, they would board canoes to finally take to the fullness of Lake Chad. The journey was dull, though they heard plenty of lions all through the night. The animals were far away, but their roaring made sleeping difficult. To add to the strangeness of the scene, there were mysterious heaps of ash everywhere, as if they were walking through the remnants of some forgotten world. The experience at Hajer-el-Hamis had left its mark on all of them.

When they reached Jimtilo, which was an Arab town, there was no sun, only gray painted over the sky. They were greeted by a very young man and were surprised to learn that he was the chief, having risen to the position based solely on the accolades of his father and grandfather, who had both lost their lives to Rabeh. The boy showed them some homes, including a strange, vast bed with black pillars meant to shield up to eight people from mosquitoes. They saw another bedroom with holes in the ground in which to light small fires to ward off insects at night.

Olive's method was less dangerous; She was still taking her five grains of quinine each day.

The next morning they boarded their lengthy new canoes and made their way up the river to Lake Chad.

THE BANKS OF THE SHARI were almost clifflike. The edge of the forest pushed directly to the edge until it fell into luxurious creepers that reached the water, choked with purple fruit and red flowers. Twenty-foot-tall papyrus trees towered over them. As the canoes slid closer to the lake itself, Olive saw a grim sentinel on the top of one of the trees. Sitting among large red flowers, a big gray baboon, his shoulders hunched, watched them float away.

As they started into the lake proper, they quickly came upon a tiny rise of dry land. They saw shapes slumped over in the sand. Olive thought they might be ancient statues, but one began to move. They were Buduma tribesmen, who seemed to be waiting for something. Mr. Talbot looked toward the lake and up to the sky. The dark clouds were the color of smoke. Olive didn't see a storm, but when Mr. Talbot saw the Buduma arranging their things against the growing wind, he knew that something was coming. Mr. Talbot made the signal to set camp. They would wait it out.

The Budumas' preparations were ingenious. Nets were hung on wooden posts, and against them shields were propped, behind which the men cowered for shelter from the biting wind. Oval wooden frames covered with matting stood beside them. These Buduma beds were protection against both storm and mosquitoes, for the matting could be turned in and sand heaped over it, after a man crawled inside and curled up tight.

The wind picked up and made the air cold. The misty effect of these gusts reminded Olive of the *haar*, the fog that came off the sea and billowed onto the Isle of Skye. In Africa they called this dry winter wind the harmattan and Olive felt that the words, and the worlds, were connected. The wind was like the banshee wail from Walter Scott's poem:

THE BANSHEE'S WILD VOICE SINGS THE DEATH-DIRGE BEFORE ME,

THE PALL OF THE DEAD FOR A MANTLE HANGS O'ER ME;

BUT MY HEART SHALL NOT FLAG, AND MY NERVES SHALL NOT SHIVER.

THOUGH DEVOTED I GO—TO RETURN AGAIN NEVER!

Once they were relatively settled, the *zakis* spilled out of their baskets. Olive gasped when they headed right for the Buduma, sniffing their fish and getting tangled in their nets. Luckily the tribesmen were amused, not only because of their innate friendliness but because of the invincible charms of the *zakoki*. As the natives laughed, Olive looked out into the water. Every so often she saw a hideous flat head peek out, with two bulbous eyes. She hoped her lions could not see it. That night the wind gathered itself into an even stronger gale and started to blow without ceasing. The tents were nearly knocked away; they had to keep the entrances open to let a current come through to keep them upright. Olive, under three blankets, shivered through the night.

The morning brought with it an impenetrable mist that seemed a ghostly extension of the lake itself. They couldn't tell if it was gathering them in or warning against further intrusion. The temperature had gotten even colder. Even the *zakis* were shaking as they looked for warmth in Olive's bed and bath. They eventually found shelter in a wicker basket of clothes, where they chewed up the blankets inside. They even went after Olive's pith helmet. She hung it high above them, but they eventually got it, leaving only fragments behind. Olive was sad at the untimely fate of her favorite hat, but Mrs. Talbot used the lining of her own tea gown, along with some cotton batting for stuffing birds, to make the helmet respectable again.

They were stormbound for forty-four hours. Olive could not walk more than a few feet in any direction without getting drenched. Hippos groaned and grunted in the mist without intermission. Each evening Mr. Talbot went out shooting, but he could barely see the end of his rifle. He had to climb anthills nearly eight feet in height just to catch a glimpse of prey. The mosquitoes were beyond all endurance; at dusk they rose in such clouds to cover them all with a black veil. Olive grimly pronounced them a large and hungry species, with all the tenacity of an English bulldog.

The first night, Mr. Talbot (with some luck) killed a waterbuck and doe but failed to find the latter's body in the thick reeds. Aji prophesied that the next day there would be a large gathering of her kind to mourn her, an idea Olive scoffed at. But the following afternoon they approached the spot and a herd of kob sprang away, startled.

As the hunting party trudged back to camp, wet and only half satisfied, they arrived in time to watch the Buduma raise their fishing nets. They had captured, merely by waiting, ten or so fish of nearly thirty pounds apiece. The Buduma said it was a poor haul because of the storm. Olive counted five different kinds of fish in the nets, photographing a specimen of each. Some of the scaled monstrosities had immense teeth, others had long, catlike whiskers. None were recommended as delicate eating, but two of the kingfish family were found to be excellent.

On the third day the wind finally abated and the air became quiet. Olive and the Talbots waved good-bye to their Buduma friends and set out in their two canoes. At last they floated into the true open waters of the lake. They felt a moment of quiet as they saw the waters spread out before them. But as if on cue, breakers swept in on them. The large canoes couldn't take on any great amounts of water, so the polers tied up to some rushes on another tiny sandbank.

By noon the wind died down again. The canoes set out, though the pitching was still considerable. At times, under the shadow of great waves, their destruction seemed imminent.

When things stilled, Olive sat up in the canoe. All she could see was a horizon of water. As they made speed under the wind, Olive looked back as the land became dim. Once the shore had completely disappeared, she realized there was nothing by which to measure their progress, except wide-spreading clumps of marea, papyrus, and rush. The Spirit of the Lake had laid her spell over them, and they paddled onward, still passengers in that quiet, lonely place. It was difficult, but Olive was able to write in her diary that night as Mrs. Talbot was getting dressed. Today was an important day, and she was not going to miss it.

> *Most dear Boyd*
>
> *Your birthday and I think of the happiness you have brought into the world and taken out of it again. Chad seems so closely connected with you that I am glad to spend this day so near it.*
>
> *Your ever loving,*
Olive:

OLIVE FOUND THAT EXPLORING Lake Chad meant a life lived on a canoe. Their great barge could hold twelve men, Olive and the Talbots, and the little *zakis*. At night the lions would be transferred to the other canoe to make things less dangerous. The second boat held drying skins and the boys' food, which mainly consisted of rotten fish, for which they had an inexplicable passion.

Mr. Talbot sat in the bow with his surveying instruments. They ate early suppers to avoid insects, usually tinned meats with colored bits of vegetable and jarred fruits. For breakfast they ate Mr. Talbot's favorite sardines with biscuits and sweet African honey. Their supply of English jam was long gone. When they ate, they pulled out a small folding table and three chairs. Cooku had a portable fireplace. He scooped water from the river, heated it for several minutes, and made their strong coffee. The only inconvenience was when the wind would shift and the smoke stung their eyes.

Olive found life on the canoe to be strangely agreeable. After supper the blankets were hung over the awning so that Olive and Mrs. Talbot could undress and wash. When they were done, the blankets were taken down, and a bed was made in the middle of the boxes to shield against the wind.

The only life they saw on the lake were floating clumps of moss. Olive couldn't remember the last time she heard a bird. At night they would tie up their canoes in the larger bunches of this grass to get shelter from the wind. On that first night, a hippo finally appeared and floated close, obviously wanting the brush for himself. Mr. Talbot stood for a long time with his rifle aimed, but the hippo would not come closer. The boys were terrified, for the Chad hippos had fierce reputations.

The hippo eventually floated off, content with the mischief it had caused. That night, water seeped in to lap at Mr. and Mrs. Talbot and Olive, lying three in a row. Mr. Talbot was drenched twice over, while Olive and Mrs. Talbot remained dry on their straw mat. But when they grabbed their day clothes in the morning, their garments were soaked through. All this while they saw no animal save the lone hippo. When the sun began to set, on the third day, they reached the island of Kumu.

THEY MADE CAMP BENEATH a tree on a shore of thick sand. But their pinions had trouble getting traction. Olive feared that if a wind of any significant caliber arose, their tents would fly away. Up past the slope of the beach lay the Buduma village, where lights flickered with the wind. Soon a group of headmen came down in the darkness to greet the party. They exchanged brief words and set a more formal visit for tomorrow. Olive could not get a good look at them. They seemed more like shadows than human beings.

The next day the sky was the color of bright slate. Olive and the Talbots walked through the early mist to the village. Their huts were low and scattered over the sand, surrounded by windscreens made of rush, accessible only by crawling through a small door. Their homes were mostly bare, except for exquisite grass pots that were so tightly woven that some held milk without losing a drop. A man told Mastaba that when a girl wished to propose, she would weave one of these pots and send it to the man she wanted. If he accepted it, they were regarded as engaged. In one house Olive saw a very tiny pot. She was told that it was a milk bottle for a *piccan*. It was the custom, she learned, for the child to live with its mother until it could feed itself; then they both returned to the father's house.

In the gray light Olive could see the Buduma more clearly. They were very tall and had a long reach that Olive thought remarkable. She found the women to be good-looking. The men were not. They had shaved heads and wore long robes that were ragged with age. Each man carried an amulet in a little leather case that hung on his breast. Some of them wore a single metal crescent in their left ear. The women had as many earrings as they could manage, hanging in clumps from both ears.

Olive and Mr. Talbot sat down with some of the tribesmen to learn more of their ways. Conscious of the importance of meeting this very remote tribe, she took notes. Through Mastaba, she found that the Buduma worshipped carved idol fetishes that they put in places of importance. But they were also part Mohammedan. The natives told Mastaba that they believed that the first people were born when they emerged from the earth in Chad.

Between the mist and the utter seclusion of the place, the small tribe seemed already removed from the map Mr. Talbot was trying so hard to fix them upon. The place had a dreamlike atmosphere that was very magical. Olive learned that when they slept, the Buduma were capable of a vivid second sight. They would wake, sometimes shaking, other times closing their eyes again and breathing slowly. Olive did not know what they saw, but she understood its power.

They also worshipped the *karraka* tree, a short, leafy bush. The tribe would neither cut nor burn it, as its leaves were used to make important medicines. When a man wanted wives, children, or cows, he got the medicine man to grind some corn into a bowl, to which he added milk. He then buried it in the ground under the sacred tree. These wishes would come true. The leaves' most powerful magic, however, was as a love potion. When Mastaba said this, he was smiling. Olive blushed.

Magic was not always used for positive outcomes. When the Buduma cut their hair or nails, they did so in secret and were very careful to hide the cuttings in the ground in case an enemy should find and use them to make dark magic against them. When a man died, he was washed in hot water and dressed in white garments. A hole was then dug, surrounded with boards, and he was laid in it on his side, with his hands between his knees. The Buduma believed that after death, all men went to the sky.

After a man's death, the elder son inherited the greater portion of his father's wealth, including his cows, biggest spears, and shields. The rest was divided among the younger children. The wives always went to the brother of the deceased, who also inherited part of the fortune. Divorce was a frequent occurrence on both sides. In a divorce all the deserted husband could expect was the value of what he had paid for his wife. The bridegroom gave the father of the bride, on average, two oxen and two cows, the mother five dollars, and the bride herself one cow in milk. When married, a bride received from her parents two robes, two trousers, and "two small women." Olive was sure that translation wasn't right; it was probably something about children. Indeed, the Buduma man explained that a man gave his wife a cow at the birth of each child, and at the birth of twins, prayers were offered and there was great rejoicing.

The law, however, was strict. Mastaba listened and slowly translated. If a child was born out of wedlock, it was taken onto the lake and drowned.

Olive gasped.

"The crops will not yield good harvest and the cattle will not bear young," the Buduma man explained.

Olive stopped writing. When the interview was over, Mr. Talbot thanked the tribesmen.

Later that day Olive walked along the shore. She thought of the lake they had been on for days. She had felt Boyd here, but the lake was windswept and cold, still and lonely.

She thought of those small babies, crying or laughing, dropped into the cold waters before sinking slowly into silence. As Olive looked out onto the lake, she felt her heart sinking with them.

THE NEXT DAY OLIVE SET out to explore the village alone. The farther Olive walked, the more she suspected that the Buduma tribe seemed to be made of at least three separate races. Olive stumbled onto this theory when she realized that different types of people worked on different tasks. Far out past the village, she found only Guria people. The fishermen who cast their wide nets on the other side of the island seemed to be from at least two different tribes. Olive could tell from their clothing and jewelry. When she told Mr. Talbot about her findings, he seemed puzzled. She then asked Mastaba, who inquired of one of the Buduma headmen.

All these races were still Buduma, the headman explained. They all had common ancestors, spoke the same language, and intermarried with one another. There were some of the usual tribal rules: A Buduma woman never married outside these tribes, but a man would often have a Kanembu wife on the mainland, though she would not accompany him back to the islands.

Olive was still curious as to one thing. She asked Mastaba why they had seen no one building houses or fishing on the boats. Mastaba repeated her question. The headmen listened, nodded, and took Olive and Mastaba to see a large hut on the edge of town. It was surrounded by people.

"They do all the work," the headman said, pointing.

"Who?" asked Olive. The people looked to be from all kinds of different tribes.

"Niggers," said the Buduma headman, using pidgin English.

The men and women looked to be kindly treated. The headman explained that they were workers. The average Buduma citizen owned two or three. Olive thought of the marriage agreement and the "two small women." "Sometimes a man will marry one of them," the headman said, adding that "Poor men didn't own any." He was talking about slaves.

The headman told them that the Buduma had a regular slave trade with the Kotoko. They held to some agreements: No Kotoko, Arab, or Fulani could be enslaved. The rest of Central Africa was fair game for the Buduma, who would regularly capture and sell natives of Ham, Niellim, Sara, and places even farther south down the Logone and Shari Rivers. Olive realized they had been to many of these places. The Buduma even raided mainland tribes on the northern Nigerian shore, escaping with goats, cattle, and people. They particularly preyed on the Kanuri, who dared not venture out onto the lake because of their fear of drowning. The Buduma took them all.

Later that day Olive found herself again looking out onto the lake. This was inescapable given the smallness of the island. She felt embedded, even trapped by the island. Olive looked out on the lake and saw a man and woman walking on top of the water. Once they dropped down again, Olive realized they were actually floating on pieces of buoyant ambatch wood, each about eight feet in length and thick as a man's leg. The curved end acted as a prow and cut through the water. Olive watched the woman propel it forward with an overarm motion, then jump, stand, and sit.

Olive had seen these corklike boards on the island but had not known their use. She now realized that the natives used them to "walk for water" to travel to adjoining islands at will. They didn't fear crocodiles, for there were not that many on the lake. But they greatly feared the djinns, some supposedly a hundred feet long. If a man should inadvertently set eyes on one, the djinn would slap him in the face and he would die. So they rode their boards of wood. Olive recalled Homer describing that Odysseus "bestrode a single beam, as one rideth on a courser, . . . and fell prone into the sea, outstretching his hands as one eager to swim."

THE NEXT PART OF THEIR JOURNEY on Lake Chad was spent mostly on the water, navigating and making measurements, though they stopped at a few destinations. Kika was an island four hours away. It was also populated by a Buduma tribe and was only three-quarters of a mile across and two miles long. Kika was a cowtown, and a place Olive very much wanted to visit. When they arrived, they found it flat and rocky. Goats and a few wizened little fowls toddled around on the principal islands, where they eked out a precarious existence.

When Olive first saw the cattle, her heart leaped. Large and humpless, they very much reminded her of the shaggy Highland cows that she saw on Skye. Mastaba was taken aback when she walked right up to one and began stroking its hairy head. She laughed. The Buduma loved their cattle so much that they dressed them up, frilling their ears and draping them with large papyrus necklaces and shiny pendants. The cows looked like squat Egyptian gods in some long-forgotten afterlife.

As Mr. Talbot and the boys pitched camp, Olive and Mrs. Talbot went out on a shell-collecting walk. They soon found fourteen different varieties on the beach, which was a vast and tiny armory. Olive found one odd little specimen that was as curly as a golden French horn. As she turned it over in her fingers, amazed at its natural proportions, a gray hare jumped out beneath her feet. As the animal bounded off, Olive regained her balance and noticed two sets of tracks: gazelle and leopard. Kika lay alone in the center of Lake Chad, miles from the mainland. It was one of the most remote places in Africa. As far as they had been told, there were only a few gazelles on another of the islands, but not here. This was a mystery.

Mrs. Talbot went to fetch her husband and his rifle. He had been head-down in his mapmaking, but they knew he could not resist a hunt. As they waited for him, Olive walked up the beach. She spied a spot of red in the brush. Olive became still. Out from behind a shrub, a tiny gazelle poked its head. In shape, color, and size, it looked like a red deer, though its horns were ringed and curved outward and up. Olive took a half step and the animal skittered off. Mr. Talbot arrived and made quick pursuit.

Olive crouched down behind some grass to watch. As Mr. Talbot stalked the other end of the beach, Olive watched in silence as the little red deer came back and lay down within fifty yards of her. Olive didn't say anything. She instead—slowly—crawled to within twenty yards of the deer. But instead of jumping off like a thunderbolt, the little red creature rose and looked full at Olive with its large black eyes. Then, with authority, the deer stamped, nodded, and walked slowly away. Olive lay there, hearing Mr. Talbot's loud pronouncements that he could not find the deer.

When Olive got back to camp, she read through the big-game book but could find no mention of the strange red deer, which made its escape exceedingly hard to bear. She thought of Boyd's okapi, and the falls, and how this could be her final major contribution to African knowledge. Mr. Talbot, who did not take defeat lightly, especially on an island at the hands of a small deer, organized a search for the next morning. Olive took her gun. But the beaters were untrained to the work, so that all the game escaped into a big swamp that flanked the northeast. Mr. Talbot got a kob, though it was not the red one. As Olive watched, Mastaba came up to her ear and murmured, *"Nama-nama."* Olive looked but could see nothing but hummocks of thick grass and scrub stretching away to a tangle of bush. Mastaba pointed eagerly to a tiny tree, and Olive saw the now-familiar patch of bright red beneath it. It was the mysterious red deer, staring at her once more. Olive raised her gun. She hesitated. Then she fired.

Had the deer remained motionless, Olive might have hit it, but it started running the moment she fired. When Mr. Talbot ran over, he was disappointed. He searched but could not find the animal. A steady gloom fell upon the party.

As they trudged back to camp, Olive thought of the red deer that lived on the Isle of Skye. They appeared in many fairy stories and were said to be the cattle of the Bright Folk. There were stories that no red deer could ever be found that had died of old age because their bodies had been hidden away by the fairies. Some said that fairy women could also assume their guise. Olive thought of the witch's prophecy of a red deer giving birth in the Fairy Tower, where she used to hear the stories from her sister.

She had hesitated—just for a moment—and was glad of it.

THEY PREPARED TO SET COURSE for the northern Nigeria village of Saiorum on the lakeshore. Lake Chad seemed like a dream, someplace out of step with the real world. Olive felt she needed to be on hard ground soon or be lost here like all the others.

Before they left, a native man told them a story. There was a man named Bulu, whose brother went on pilgrimage to Mecca. But before he left, he recommended his wife to Bulu's care, for his absence would be many years. As time passed and the brother did not return, Bulu assumed that his brother was dead and took his wife to himself, though he knew it was wrong. Finally the brother did return, and Bulu dared not remain and fled to the islands of Lake Chad. No man had ever ventured there, and there he led a solitary existence till one day a great wind blew from the west. Bulu saw an object that had been washed against the rushes. He waded out and found that it was a basketful of fine millet grain. It reminded him of farming and cultivation, and a life of peace and plenty, so he set out and landed on the shore. The chief welcomed him in friendship, and Bulu dwelt with him for a time. Now, the chief had a beautiful daughter named Saiorum, after whom the land is called, and she and Bulu loved each other. They had no hope of gaining her father's consent to their marriage, but Bulu could not force himself to leave her, so he remained to bring dishonor on the house that had harbored him. When the chief knew what had befallen his daughter, he would not allow her to remain with the people she had disgraced, and she and Bulu were together banished to the islands of Lake Chad. From them came the entire Buduma race.

For three days and two nights the party lived for water, in their canoes on the Lake of Loneliness. They ate ravenously and slept in the bracing air, and enjoyed the pure, cold, delicious water. On the afternoon of the third day, they hoped to near the shore.

The closer they got to Saiorum, the thicker the rushes became, almost as if the lake itself was trying to keep them there. But their boatmen found a secret track, and the canoes soon found open water. Mr. Talbot was, as always, sitting in the stern measuring out the route when he called that he had seen a flying fish! A few moments later, Olive saw one herself: a slender flash like a slippery arrow, buzzing over the top of the water. She watched it gather power, then leap.

The water again became a patchwork of colored water violets, lilies, and little yellow flowers—all growing out of huge green plants that floated on the surface. Olive liked the lilies best; these carpeted their way, standing high out of the water, and scented the air with a delicious perfume. There were five or six different varieties, some white, with shell-like pink tips, and others ranging from pale blue to a deep violet shade. Olive watched one of the polers drag one of the beautiful lilies out of the water. Very pleased, Olive put her hands out to receive it. The boy instead stuffed it into his mouth. Olive looked on with disappointment as the polers ate both the seed capsules and the long, snake-like stalks, a practice they repeated with the rushes, which again closed thick upon the waters.

Land was near, Nigeria was near, and through the gloaming Olive saw the forms of men alongside huge horned cattle. As they drew closer, they passed another fleet of papyrus canoes, some little more than eight feet long; others much bigger, enough to carry merchandise or even cattle. They soon arrived at Kaua Baga, the marketplace of Saiorum, where thousands of people had assembled for commerce.

As the canoe slid onto land and stopped, Olive slowly stepped onto solid ground. She felt heavier, but still in motion somehow.

24

THE PILGRIM TO THE STONE

February 7, 1911: After a Long and Arduous Journey,
Olive Finally Reaches Maifoni; a Medicine Man Refuses
Her; She Goes to the Graveyard

Olive stayed close to Mrs. Talbot as they navigated the crowded stalls and corridors of the busy outdoor market. After so many days on the Lake of Loneliness, walking through the bustling market full of moving, shouting people was almost overwhelming. More than one thousand people had arrived, for Kaua Baga was the only place that the mainlanders and the island natives could meet in peace to trade. It was the only place in the region where neutrality was observed.

The party made their camp in the center of the market along with the other visitors. Instead of single trees and seashells, Olive was met by loud shouts and smells. She saw salt, potash, and all types of cattle changing eager hands. Some of it was a welcome change, but they were tired and went to sleep. The next morning, when they were less crowd-sick, Olive wandered around with her camera. But Mr. Talbot could not walk three feet without the mob thrusting a medley of objects at him—spears, toe rings, pincers, shields, ambatch floats, and even canoes.

After a fair amount of buying, they left the bustle of the market to ride toward the town proper, taking a wide road through desert country.

Government regulations prohibited hunting, so Mr. Talbot could only gaze longingly upon the vast herds of hartebeest, antelopes, and gazelles. The animals looked at them from the side of the road, as if conscious of their own security. Olive heard there were elephants here, too, though they did not see any.

They passed a great caravan that was carrying potash from Kaua Baga to a farther market. As they passed, Olive looked up at the sliding, drooping sun. They had left at three o'clock in the afternoon and their trip was only supposed to last two hours. But it was already near sundown, and the city was nowhere in sight. The road was so thick with sand that it was becoming difficult for the horses. Olive then heard loud cries and feminine laughter from up ahead. The sound of women meant that the town must be near, she said, but Mastaba shook his head. She had heard a hyena.

When they finally rode into Kaua, everyone was famished and exhausted. Olive looked behind her. The chop box was still far behind them. Olive's stomach growled. She tried, as she always did when hungry, not to think of their dinners at Vinters, overflowing with roast meats, wine, and puddings. As she tried not to dwell on what was absent, a boy showed up with a package. They rejoiced: The local chief had sent them a gift of food! But when they opened it, they found only eggs and milk. Luckily, Washerman's wife had a bowl in which to boil the small eggs. She did her best, but the results were not appetizing, for thick skins formed on the milk, and the eggs were without salt. But they were hungry and devoured them eagerly. Olive felt fuller, if not full, when the carriers finally straggled in an hour before midnight.

The next day they began the march to Maifoni. Over the next days they passed through the towns of Mongonu, Dubala, and Massu, along the same gritty road. It was all more of the same, not because it wasn't full of minute differences, as Africa always was, but because it was dominated by Olive's thoughts as they got closer and closer to Boyd's grave. On the way, on February 18, Olive celebrated her thirty-first birthday. She was walking through the sand, far from Hobart Place in London, where she had been born to Reginald and Agnes MacLeod. She wondered if they would recognize her now. So much had changed, but as her parents often remarked, she had always had red hair, and the same penetrating blue eyes. That night, she wrote to Boyd:

Oh dear! To have to fight at Maifoni—Boyd, when I come to the place.

WHEN OLIVE MACLEOD ENTERED Maifoni at long last, no one was there to greet her. Everywhere she had been, from Forcados to now, there were residents, officials, soldiers, and chiefs, more than willing, regardless of their intent, to invite her into their personal corners of Africa.

But here, the place she had been striving for, step by step, thousands of miles from home, there was only a thin, sandy road through a small village in front of her. When they walked through the town of Maiduguri on the way to the fort, the natives regarded them with cool eyes. There were British soldiers there, but they did not salute. Mr. Talbot straightened his back. Mastaba was also disturbed by this lack of respect, though Olive was not sure if that was really the right word for it. She was surprised at how personally he took this. Mastaba asked Mr. Talbot that they ride in the center of the road to assert their dignity. He nodded, and they took the main road to the ancient fort of Maifoni.

The fort was smaller than Olive had imagined. On the end of a ridge rose five bungalows for the white men. Their complement, in total, consisted of a resident, an assistant, a doctor, and two officers, one of whom was away. Olive and the Talbots were supposed to stay at one of the assistant's houses, but there was confusion and they stayed in *zana* shelters instead, beneath a huge tree about a quarter of a mile away from the fort. Their rent for ten days was ten shillings, one-quarter of the purchase price of the hut itself. As they walked through the fort, Olive was physically sensitive to its history and was a little relieved they weren't staying in one of the houses.

After they settled in, Olive and the Talbots went to the Maiduguri market, which was surprisingly large. Walking through the stalls, all organized neatly by trade, Olive was mesmerized by the new types of items she found—everything from leatherwork and saddles to spears and knives. There were pots being painted, straw plates being plaited, and dolls of mud and honey being shaped and mounted on sticks. On one of the adjoining streets, there was a stall that sold old clothes and meat, though Olive found the juxtaposition unappetizing.

Olive purchased more than two hundred things, though most were exceedingly small, from carved miniatures to numerous bracelets. As the day wore on and she spent and spent, she knew it was only because she was postponing the inevitable. When she brought her treasures sheepishly back to camp, she almost tripped over an old man seated in the dirt. He wore so many different amulets—some small and heavy, others shiny and decrepit—that Olive could not even see his clothes. Then she saw that he wore a leopard skin on his head, its black claws dangling against his ears. Olive thought of the dancing man in the firelight.

This was a medicine man. Olive slowly put down her trinkets and took out her camera. She wanted nothing more than a photograph of him. When she asked, slowly, half with words and half with gestures, he declined. He said that he "lived for fear." She stared at him as he looked warily at her camera. Many of the natives feared the glass of the camera, even though they were familiar with them. There was something about the transaction of it, about taking something important away to a place they would never see but were keenly aware existed. The man was old and gaunt. Though sad and neglected in the dirt, he was still a person of powerful aspect. Olive regarded him and thought again of the Man-Leopard. She then stood up, and as he protested, took his picture anyway.

When she returned to the fort, Olive was surprised to see the soldiers at attention. It seemed that General Percival Spearman Wilkinson had arrived for a military inspection. She met up with the Talbots and went to see him. The general was delighted to see them as he praised the efficiency of the troops. Olive was surprised to see that her friend Major

Rose from Lokoja was there! She was very pleased to see him. He asked her if she was still a crack shot.

THERE WAS A VERY TALL TREE in the small graveyard. It was an acacia, the kind Olive had seen throughout their trip, and it bore white flowers.

Olive was still within sight of the fort, which stood atop a small slope. Great fields of grass surrounded its walls. A single sentry watched over the cemetery.

Olive considered the British. They had sent Boyd, but he had not been a soldier, not anymore. He was a birdman, an ornithologist. Why would a birdman want to go to the desert of Wadai? His previous trips had been to collect birds or survey waterways, never to negotiate peace treaties with dangerous warlords. But Boyd had experience in both Wadai and the Sudan. On his previous trip, which cost him his brother, he had made it all the way to Khartoum in rags. Was he sent just because he could get there?

Olive's eyes searched the headstones.

She was surprised to see Overweg, the great German explorer whom Chief Abbiga had traveled with. His body had apparently been found and moved from his unknown grave near Lake Chad. Then she saw Claud, Boyd's brother, whom she had never met. Olive knew that Boyd had chosen this exact site for his brother's final resting place. She wondered if he had known that he would join him. They died one thousand miles and four years apart, on the same continent, far away from home.

The sentry who was circling the spot sounded his bugle, as he did every hour.

And there was Boyd.

His stone was strong and fit, as Olive expected, every bit like him. He shared space with his brother, which she found appropriate. There were cracks here and there, but it was still sturdy.

As Olive stood over the grave of her beloved, she thought of the body beneath her. She tried not to think what it looked like, full of shot and torn by spears. She was tempted to get them to dig him up, just on the chance that he had falsified his death with José and had made the trip to see Ali Dinar after all. He could be in Khartoum right now, toasting his victory, just about to write her.

But there was another side to him that she had seen. She felt it now.

She thought of him, the man that her friends and family had considered her almost-husband, the man for whom she had worn black when he was reported dead.

The man she said no to.

Olive had been filled with guilt ever since that moment. She loved Boyd. But if she had said "yes," he might have stayed in England. He would be alive today.

She touched her locket, containing the heather and the hair.

She had read his diaries. She knew the many letters she had written and continued to write. She remembered the few letters he wrote her. She knew how much he loved Africa. And most of all, she remembered what she had expected to happen here. What she, in her lowest moments, had wished to happen to her.

She looked out onto the little river. This was, as she said, her "fight."

She was going to let him down.

She wrote to him that night, in very shaky handwriting, like a child's.

Very dearest Boyd

It is wonderful to be here near you in that I can understand your intensest feelings. So much comprehension of love and the mystery of Death: It did not seem like death, or parting, when I went to your grave—only intenser realization that your spirit lives and is with those who love more fully than in life—only. Only. Only lives so physically that there are long long periods when one needs the material. You know what I think I feel—I do—and I feel happier-much happier in your knowledge and sympathy and help—for I know I have all that. It is

terrible I think of the might have beens and life as it comes and to learn
the lessons you taught of trust in providence. What can one do? Don't
desert me, but guide me and help me—however wrong I may be and
however far I may stray. Dearest Boyd you give me strength for all.

Your intensely loving
Olive:

The next day they opened the wooden crate that they had brought
all the way from Liverpool. Olive supervised the boys as they lifted out a
massive stone Saint Andrew's cross that had been sculpted by Alexander
Fisher in London, just like the one for Claud. They placed it at Boyd's
grave and spoke and prayed and wept. Though Olive had not carried it
herself over the plains, jungles, and mountains, she felt as if she had.

Their party also became lighter as Kukaua and his little family left,
having finally arrived home. Mr. Talbot wished his former gun boy, one
of the best he ever had, good luck.

A few days later, on February 23, Olive wrote:

Most dear Boyd
Yesterday we passed a little knot of men digging a grave by the
wayside for an unfortunate Hausa trader who had been murdered for
the sake of his goods only 12 days before.

The entry stopped, with no postscript and no signature, the final one
written in Olive's secret diary.

The next day was blank.

25

THE ROAD

February 1911, Bornu, Nigeria: Olive Is Missing;
Mr. Talbot Receives a Disturbing Letter

As the party prepared to leave Maifoni, a horseman arrived with mail. Mr. Talbot took his share and stepped a few feet away for some privacy. Olive had some letters from London, but was nowhere to be found. This was uncanny because she was always quick to run to the mail. Mrs. Talbot called out, but there was no answer. The boys looked around, but no one had seen her. She had most likely wandered off for a walk. Perhaps she had not left her tent yet. The Talbots exchanged a worried glance. Then they heard a sound.

Olive was laughing. She had emerged from her tent to see Jimba-Giri, who was walking around triumphantly in an old coat that Mr. Talbot had lent him. It was a dirty old thing, but Jimba paraded about as if it were made of the finest sable. Olive smiled as Jimba-Giri strutted, confident that he would never have to give the coat back. Olive knew better. Relieved, Mr. Talbot resumed reading his mail as Mrs. Talbot gave Olive her letters. The sun was up, but not yet burning. It seemed like it would be a good day.

Olive began shuffling through her letters. She saw some from home, from Herbert, and other friends. She looked forward to reading them later. Olive took a smaller envelope and opened it. She took out a thin piece of paper that was folded. She read it very intently. She looked very confused. She took a long breath. She looked over at Mr. Talbot. He was reading his own letter with a look of concern. Mrs. Talbot noticed it too and walked over to her husband. She engaged him in low conversation. Her face looked surprised. As they made their way back, Olive pocketed her own small letter.

"Developments are very bad," said Mr. Talbot.

Mr. Talbot had been sending telegrams to the Nigerian office asking which square on the map he might survey next. Though the expedition had already gone well off the authorized path by leaving Yola and later going to Lake Chad, Mr. Talbot had reinstated correspondence with Governor Temple in hopes of negotiating not only a genial return, but a possible way forward, given their many discoveries and the unfinished mapwork left to do. Olive was hoping for leave to move toward Abechir and further answers. With Boyd's maps lost, their expedition provided an excellent opportunity to finish the job before conditions got even worse.

But Nigeria never answered. While at Fort Lamy, Mr. Talbot had wired again asking for further leave given that he had not received new orders. The answer finally came—in the letter that Mr. Talbot was holding—that the Colonial Office did not consider more mapping of enough importance. An extension could not be granted, and Mr. Talbot was expected to return to his post in Nigeria immediately.

Olive wrote Herbert: "It is *awful* and leaves Mr. Talbot in the double hole of failing to execute his commission and of course losing the renumeration for it which was vital to him—and worst of all we can't be back till a full month after his leave was up from Southern Nigeria, and, if the Governor can't be mollified he may be turned out of the service."

It seemed obvious that Mr. Talbot was being punished for leaving Yola, against orders, all those months ago.

"When?" asked Olive.

"All possible haste," Mr. Talbot said.

The worst part was there was no higher authority to appeal to; the letter was signed by Charles Lindsay Temple, the acting governor of northern Nigeria himself, their old friend from Lokoja. Olive looked forward to having strong words with him.

Like it or not, they were going home.

THE BORNU ROAD WAS THE safest and quickest way to travel from Maifoni to Zungeru, the seat of the Nigerian colonial government. They would have to double their marches to make the pace at which Mr. Talbot was being ordered to return. Major Rose very kindly lent Olive a pony, as hers had finally collapsed and refused to leave Maifoni. As the party said their good-byes and stepped onto the road, they were crestfallen and angry. At least the way was easier than the grasslands or the swamp. The bleak terrain was mostly sand and burr grass, anchored with thick-trunked baobab trees. Dull green fruit was often the only patch of color in the landscape.

For the first time on their journey they were not traveling alone. Caravans of livestock passed by at regular intervals, traveling to the next village for water. Much of the road was without shade, so Olive saw plenty of men (and their beasts) with sullen gazes and plodding feet. She felt the same way. The road was supposed to be civilized but it felt, in many ways, like a forced march. Even Mastaba found the pace to be grueling. At one point he rode up next to Olive and told her that Mr. Talbot said not to go so fast. Olive pulled back and slowed down, only to find that Mr. Talbot had said no such thing. Most people on the road would not even greet them. One man only dropped his gaze and said: *"Zaki, zaki."* Everyone on the road openly carried a knife or spear. There was no government security to be seen.

They made stops in some of the larger towns to replenish their stores. They tarried at Gabai, a walled city inhabited by the Ngassar, an Islamic tribe who traced their line all the way back to Constantinople. Gabai had a central palace of exquisite beauty, its walls decorated with diamond-shaped patterns and majestic pillars. The city itself was protected by three mud walls, all of which contained small holes. When Olive saw the many quivers of arrows hung near these openings, she realized their purpose. The arrows themselves were of exceptional craftsmanship. There were sharp arrows, long arrows, even coarse arrows, all designed to penetrate armors of varying thickness. Olive moved to touch one, but Mr. Talbot grabbed her hand.

"A scratch of the skin may be as effective as a deep wound, for all these arrows are poisoned," he said. The chief very generously gave them a careful selection of arrows for their collection, all of them unsullied by poison. The chief's armory was altogether very good, and numbered, besides long spears with four-bladed heads, some old pistols. The stock of one of them had a human head carved into the wooden handle. All these artifacts became Mr. Talbot's possessions for a fair offered price.

The road beyond Gabai was far more beautiful than anything they had yet seen in Africa. The Kerri-Kerri hills became visible to the north and the Bagi hills to the south; all the slopes and valleys were well and green wooded. Acacia and mimosa grew everywhere. Trees blossomed with clusters of mauve flowers and shiny leaves like laurels. Some had sweet-scented yellow flowers, while one big shrub showered down white petals that scented the air like syringa. Brilliant green and blue birds flitted from one tree to another, occasionally punctuated by the startling scream of a green parrot. Olive absorbed it all.

As part of their routine, Olive often let the *zakis* out to stretch their legs. One afternoon, when Mandara opened the basket, little Kusseri scrambled out, confused and dizzy. Apparently Lamy had decided to sleep on top of his brother's head. Kusseri was so out of sorts that they made a small stretcher for him out of a Buduma shield they had traded for. Mandara carried him as he whimpered. But now someone needed to carry Lamy. A boy was picked from the lot and was given the lion basket. He looked at it, very carefully set it down, and then ran away into the bush.

By the time Olive rode up, the boy was gone. Lamy had bitten his way through the basket and was wandering about by himself. Terrified, Olive dismounted her horse. Lamy immediately pounced on her from behind and flung his paws around her neck. Olive smiled at her fearsome little lion. They were such light burdens, despite their never-ending mischief.

WHEN THE PARTY FINALLY STEPPED off the Bornu Road, they were exhausted. They had ridden from Kaua Baga to near the walled city of Nafada, located on a high bank above the Gongola River. The city itself was large. They bought yet another replacement horse for Olive. This particular animal was recommended as being suitable for women, and at only five pounds was a bargain. When Olive began to ride it, she found the horse to be pleasant and comfortable. However, she soon found out it had no intermediate pace between a crawl and a gallop. As she continued to ride, now a bit unsure, Aji walked up to the horse and pointed to it sternly.

"I know this horse," he said. "I had care of it for five months. Look." Aji pulled up the sleeve of his robe and Olive saw the remnants of deep, punctuated teeth marks. Aji shook his head and walked away. Not looking forward to yet another murderous horse, Olive asked Mr. Talbot to ride the horse for a while, for he was a very good rider and might be able to tame it. He agreed to the challenge.

They finally reached the British post outside the city. The British were very sorry that Olive and the Talbots had just missed an event in the village by a few days. One of the officers tried his best to describe it: The young men of the village, all boys on the verge of manhood, first formed a circle. The other male members of the tribe swayed around them, chanting and moving. The eligible young women of the tribe stayed out of the circle but watched with great interest. Once the circle was formed, it began to move and swerve and slowly spin. The boys in the middle raised their hands in the air.

The men in the circle had long sticks. As the circle moved, one of the stick men would step inside and beat one of the braves with significant force. The officer said that the boys would carry the marks of those blows, the stripes, for the remainder of their lives. The violence could only be stopped when one of the women entered the circle with her own hands raised. Those braves who exhibited no outward signs of suffering were then considered men of the tribe, and from that point forward, eligible to take any of the ladies as his bride.

The British had seen this ceremony many times. Sometimes, though it was rare, a young man was already known for his courage and would not be beaten, even though he was in the middle of the circle with all the others; this was lest his demeanor should excite worship from too many girls.

Olive and the Talbots listened intently. They were not sorry to have missed this particular ceremony. Olive especially wanted no part of it. It seemed too familiar.

26

DECISIONS IN FIKA

March 1, 1911: The Party Travels through Nigeria;
They Encounter a Demon; Disaster Strikes
in Fika; Plans Change

Don't shoot!" yelled Olive.

Mr. Talbot turned his head ever so slightly and then lowered his rifle. On the road ahead, a dark shape scurried in the corner of the brush and disappeared into the shade of the borassus palms. The expedition was already close to Fika, where they would board the train back to Lagos. They were nearing the point of no return.

"It's a dog!" shouted Olive.

Mastaba became silent and proceeded to make a small, quaking sound. He was laughing. He said something in Hausa that made the boys laugh. Mr. Talbot closed his eyes.

"That is not a dog," said Mr. Talbot.

The animal peeked out from behind the trunk of a dum tree. The sheepish baboon had a gray, downturned face. As it turned and bounded away, it showed its red bottom to Olive. The boys laughed again, knowing full well Olive's long history with baboons. Olive did not share in their laughter. She was hot, hungry, and tired.

They continued in relative silence, marching up and down steep braes.

As they walked over a hill, they looked down to see a dull piece of water at the bottom of the road. Olive thought it looked dirty, more of a ditch than a pond.

The boys halted immediately. Olive knew to follow suit and did, her bracelets from the Maifoni market jingling as she stopped.

The boys turned to look at her in horror. Mastaba stopped her with a hand. Olive might have thought it a practical joke, until she saw his face. Then she understood. They believed an evil djinn lived here.

Throughout their travels Olive had watched as their route sometimes came to a halt because of a djinn-infested body of water or tree. These creatures, like the fairies, were magical. And like the fairies, their interactions with humans were dramatic. But their differences were great. Mastaba looked at Olive's bracelets. In addition to their many evil deeds, djinn coveted necklaces, bracelets, and rings; just the kind of things that she was jangling over the pool of water before them.

"They could pass as human," Mastaba said. "For there are amongst them chiefs and *mallamai*, rich men and poor, and women. They have fine sheep and cattle and slaves past what black men get, and their houses are like a white man's, with plenty plenty pans round the walls." Mastaba said that djinns had the power of turning black, red, or white at will. They could take on the appearance of human beings and come and live like good men.

"They are everywhere," he said. "If they dislike a man, they slap him on the face, and in four or five days he dies."

Olive watched Mr. Talbot. He was very well versed in stories of tribal magic and was in fact compiling a book on the subject. She watched as he led the party around the djinn hole. She thought of his many close calls with death and wondered if they were slaps of the djinn, of Africa itself, for his attempts to map its secret corners. Olive herself had little use for religion, but she did have faith in spiritual matters.

Mastaba told her that small boys could sometimes see djinns. Many chiefs kept such boys close to them because of this power. Olive saw their own up in front with Mr. Talbot. They had seen many boys this age throughout the expedition, both in kings' courts and on the road. These boys often looked a little defiant, though they retained their innocence. She wondered how long their second sight lasted.

As Mastaba moved up ahead, stepping gingerly around the still water, Mrs. Talbot came up behind Olive.

"A year or two ago," she said, pointing to Mastaba, "his wife was walking by the Maifoni River, and a djinn reached out his arms and pulled her in." She was never seen again.

Olive had not known this. Tears welled up as she watched Mastaba, good and strong, walk around a place that no doubt sparked memories of terrible loss. She had always liked the man—who was being paid to help them—but only then did she sympathize with him.

As Olive made her own way around, she had her eyes on the water and her wrists pulled close, holding her jewelry tightly in place.

WHEN THEY ARRIVED OUTSIDE FIKA, they found that the village chief was waiting to meet them. Maybe it was the wear of travel or the blazing sun, but Olive remarked to herself how something that had once seemed so novel—meeting an African chief—had become a dull routine. She didn't even catch his name.

They learned through Mastaba that this chief's greatest pride was that he had records of his line all the way back to the year 1538. He was a friendly man, but because of his station, he was bound by many ancient regulations. No one could watch him eat his meals, except for one boy, who waited on him with every morsel. This must have been a relic of the old, primitive fear that evil could enter an open mouth and reach a man's soul. In the old days this anxiety caused many African chiefs to always cover their mouths.

The next day Mr. and Mrs. Talbot visited the town. They had been spending more and more time together since their mutual illness outside Tchenka. Later that afternoon, at nearly five o'clock, Olive was reading in camp when two of the horse boys ran in, flushed and out of breath.

They went directly to Situ and started shouting. Their words came too fast for Olive to understand, but watching as the boys grabbed a hammock and ran off, she felt her stomach sink. Situ turned to Olive.

"Fall for horse," he said.

Olive nodded. Almost reflexively now, she grabbed the medical bag. But something in Situ's voice was different. He was collecting some other things. When they were ready they acknowledged each other and set off.

Olive ran as best she could on the soft sand, which threatened to swallow her feet with every step. Aji quickly outpaced her. When she finally reached the wall that marked the edge of town, she knew immediately that the news was bad. She didn't know who was hurt. Of course she thought it was Mr. Talbot, but then she thought—What if it was his wife? What if that was Africa's last vengeance upon them? Mrs. Talbot was not a very experienced rider and had been wobbly as of late. Olive's heart was sinking. When she got closer, she saw a small cluster of men, like flies, hovering over something, their faces ashen and serious.

Olive pushed through them. They looked at her with grief and sympathy. She shuddered, struggling to understand. She longed to hear arguments as to how the accident happened. She caught bits and pieces, with some help from Situ: "All was well . . . on way home . . . full gallop . . . cow . . . went down." That was all Olive could understand. She was sure Mr. Talbot was dead. They had come all this way to find about Boyd, and now Mr. Talbot was dead too, after all their work was done. And he was riding her horse.

Farther up the road, Olive saw a group of men slowly come into focus. She squinted and saw that they were carrying something on their heads, a makeshift gurney with a shape on it. She was right.

As Olive ran toward them, Mrs. Talbot appeared from behind them and embraced her, right there on the road. As Olive sobbed, she couldn't bear to look upon Mr. Talbot's body. She couldn't see him like this. Hausa was being spoken very quickly. Olive didn't even listen until she heard a word she knew—the one for "doctor."

Olive looked at Mr. Talbot. He was still alive.

Mrs. Talbot explained that they had already summoned the British doctor, Dr. Lobb. When he arrived, running down the road, they stopped the gurney and the doctor examined him, pressing his fingers on Mr. Talbot, who winced in great pain. The doctor opened Mr. Talbot's shirt and touched his hip.

His pelvis had not been broken, which was welcome news, but the doctor said that Mr. Talbot was still in serious peril from internal hemorrhage. The doctor said he couldn't examine him any further. They had to get him to camp, and then all they could do was wait.

At camp Olive tried to be cheerful. She watched as Mr. Talbot sensed his wife's presence, his eyes stealing glances in his obvious agony. He would sometimes nod or groan and mostly fall in and out of sleep. Mrs. Talbot would cry.

This limbo went on for a day or so. Every time Mr. Talbot fell asleep, they would silently watch his chest for movement. The doctor was always nearby.

When twenty-four hours had passed and Mr. Talbot was still alive, the doctor muttered, "Miracle," wished them luck, and left. Mr. Talbot had escaped the slap of the djinn once more.

THE NEXT DAY THEY SAT around a half-upright Mr. Talbot, who had again replaced the fire as the central focus of camp. Olive watched as Mrs. Talbot told the boys that because of Mr. Talbot's injuries, the march would be delayed anywhere from six days to three weeks. She said that they were free to seek other service. This was the end of the road.

Olive watched helplessly. She hated it too, but nothing could be done. They simply could not go on without Mr. Talbot. She watched the boys look at one another and speak in Hausa. Mastaba was leading the conversation. She worried that they might revolt, angry over the lost wages. Mastaba nodded very solemnly.

"They said," Mastaba told Mrs. Talbot, "that six days, three weeks, six months were all the same to them, and they would wait without pay till we were ready." He bowed his head.

Olive had never seen such a display of loyalty. She counted Mastaba among the best of men.

CAMP WAS NOT AN IDEAL SITE for recuperation, so they moved Mr. Talbot to a bed in a rest house in Fika, one of two reserved for white men. The other served as Mrs. Talbot's dressing room and Olive's bedroom, as well as a quiet room when either of them wanted to do any work. The other hut was big and round and had two main entrances. The roofs of both rooms were high and had two doors that could be opened for a breeze. Their thermometer registered 87 degrees Fahrenheit by night and 105 by day.

As Mr. Talbot convalesced, Olive explored Fika. The town lay on a river formed by two streams that came down from the hills. Both streams passed through valleys made brilliant by the blossoms of trees and shrubs in a tableau dominated by two peaks. One was sharp and rugged, with a point that looked to be unscalable; the other was a sheer white cliff. Now alone, Olive took out the small, folded piece of paper that she had received in the mail at Maifoni. She read it again quietly.

As the days passed, Olive grew bolder and ventured out along the stream to discover that it curled past slopes of broken ironstone. Sometimes there was a high bank of rock, and above it hung long golden clusters of cassia. Beneath the rock lay herds of goats, seeking shade from the constant sun. On the tops and slopes of the hills, circles of stones lay in ruin from ancient wars. From those aeries, leaders could command the approach of an enemy, and if necessary, escape to some other mountain. Olive saw greenswards on the deep cups that lay between the hills.

The local *mallam* told Olive, with Mastaba's help, that a strange race of tiny people lived there. They called them the rock dwellers, and they sounded like the African cousins of the fairies of Skye. According to the holy man, these little people were very hard to spot, though they often met together to play their guitars. On a still night, their music could be heard from miles away. Their tiny footprints could be be seen all over the hills, but only by those who looked closely enough. Some careful hunters even claimed to have found lizards transfixed by their tiny darts. Some were lucky enough to see the mannikins themselves, each with his ax or bow and arrows upon his back, dressed in bright-colored cloth, with skins hanging from his waist. Some were as high as a man's knee. These were the privileged class and wore a cowrie shell on the top of their heads. Olive then heard the story of a brave tracker named Baba the Hunter, who had been privileged to see the rock dwellers many times. But he was so fearful of their great powers that he got a medicine so that he could not see them anymore. Baba apparently said that the rock dwellers had big heads and big limbs. They were also very strong.

The *mallam* kept pointing to himself.

"Baba," translated Mastaba.

"He knew Baba?," asked Olive. Mastaba said no.

"He *is* Baba."

Olive knew from her walking that the rock dwellers were not the only inhabitants of this mountainous region, or the ones most commonly seen. Kobs lived there, and gazelles the size of hares, for there was good bush cover though the country was wild and rocky. Olive watched the Fikans hunt and was greatly impressed. They used dogs and rode down game on the plains. They snared and stalked. They attached a toucan's head made of wood, with a real bill, to their foreheads. As they crept close to their victim, the animal would stop to gaze at the strange bird that advanced, nodding its head as if in search of food.

One day the chief gave Mr. Talbot the skin of a lion shot the previous morning by a huntsman who had killed it with a single arrow. It was poisoned, and the hunter left it to do its slow, merciless work. Some hours later the hunter returned to the spot and found the lion dead. He gave an exhibition of his archery and showed that he could achieve fair accuracy at eighty yards. His arrows were unfeathered, as was invariably the case in that part of Africa.

The town had a character all its own. Date palms overshadowed it, and small boys climbed up them with glee to pick great clusters of the sweet golden fruit. Olive refused to eat them. The streets, both broad and narrow, wound through highly ornamented mud houses, whose entrances opened at unexpected angles. There were large numbers of mosques in the city, and in the principal one a sacred fire was kept burning, tended by young acolytes. Outside, old men fingered their beads in prayer, but they raised their eyes and gave a friendly greeting to the passersby—even when they happened to be unbelievers and women.

ONE AFTERNOON MRS. TALBOT worked on a sketch of a building as one of the *mallams* directed Olive to a house visit. Before long a crowd of people began to form around her. There were a lot of people in the city that day, and they all seemed to be coming out, following her in the streets. When she arrived at the house, the owner welcomed her with friendliness. As Olive moved to enter, the followers behind her pushed forward. The owner of the house moved to close the gate of his door, refusing them entrance. They would not fit, he motioned.

But the crowd kept pushing. They were also getting louder. The homeowner shoved the gate closed. The mass of people heaved forward anyway, pushing the gate open again. There were shouts of rejoicing. Elbows and knees pushed into Olive. She felt as if she were being drowned, except it was so loud. She twisted her shoulders and shouted at the top of her lungs:

"Let this noise cease!"

The crowd froze, then slowly backed off.

After the people dispersed, and at the owner's invitation, Olive finally entered the hut. Inside Olive saw a small boy crouched over one of the holes in the ground meant for fire. The boy was pointing to something in the ashes. Olive approached slowly, not knowing what to expect.

As she looked over his shoulder, the little boy showed her a small clay shape nestled in the dust of the dead fire. It was a figurine of a small horse, and the boy smiled as he pulled it up to show her. He also had a smaller shape that looked like a star. Olive realized this was the horse's rider, a figure borne as much of imagination as anything else. The boy next showed her—she guessed—a small saddle and a bag. The boy was proud of his soldier and steed. Olive also noticed some girls' toys, mostly simple dolls painted with thick white stripes. There were some with sticks in their noses, much like those of the children's mothers. Olive also saw something quite curious: a bird's beak bound up in cloth. The *mallam* explained that it was a toy for babies.

Growing up, Olive had few toys to speak of. A visitor once came to see their father and found the girls playing in their little garden. They had collected all the snails from the leaves and were plopping them, one by one, into a pail of saltwater. The man felt sorry that the girls had no toys; all they had was a handmade doll that barely had a face. When he next returned, the man brought them a wondrous new doll as a gift. She had shining curls and a dress made of pink satin. Her round eyes could open and close behind full, dark lashes.

After the man left, the girls took their new doll into the garden and threw her on the ground, and stomped on her wax face until it caved in.

They already had a doll they liked, they said fiercely.

After finishing her tour of the hut, Olive walked back onto the street. The people had all run away.

"They done fear," said Mastaba to the mystified Mrs. Talbot, who had come to see why her quiet sketching had been interrupted by a group of men who had fled right past her.

MEANWHILE, MR. TALBOT, THOUGH a prisoner in bed, spent his days talking with Baba the Hunter, the man who had somehow become the head *mallam* of Fika. According to Baba, the Bagirmi, Bornuese, and Fikans originally left Yemen, south of Mecca, and traveled together across Africa until they neared the mouth of the Shari River. There the Bagirmi split off and settled in the far country. The Bornuese and Fikans settled near Fort Lamy, where they lived a nomadic life. One day a Bornuese caught and ate a wounded kob shot by a Fikan. The Fikans, full of anger, left their dishonest neighbors and trekked farther west. The Bornuese also gradually journeyed westward, extending their kingdom wherever they passed.

The Fikans remained a very superstitious people. One afternoon when Olive was sitting with Mr. Talbot, Baba explained their use of potions. The Fikans had charms not only for medicinal purposes but also as protection against lions and similar dangers. They were most known, however, for their love spell, about which Mr. Talbot wanted to hear every detail.

"Call on the name of the woman," instructed Baba, "her mother's name, your own name, and her father's name. Put the prayer on a board, and then wash it with water—wash yourself in the same water. When the woman sees you, she will love you too much. Even if she does not see you, or live by you, she will come and follow you wherever you may be."

Olive listened. She had found pagan magic to be interesting from a certain standpoint, but the way Baba was telling it, as if reciting a recipe, it held a strange element of truth. Baba then explained that there was another version that involved a potion. It first required a prayer. He produced a vial of clear liquid from his robes and held it up.

"*Wa na Allaha!*" shouted Baba. "Thou who art everywhere. Thou who knowest everything. Thou who art greater than everything. Only Allah knows everything in the world. All people will come to Allah, but only few will see Him. Allah will make all come back to Him.

"First of all, nobody lived in the world, for Allah made everybody. Allah can take everybody from the world again. Allah is always near. Father and mother bear children that do not like one another. Allah can put sense in them, and then they will like one another. If one is stronger and flogs another, only Allah can touch him. If a man does evil, Allah can be sorry for him."

Baba explained that the potion could now be given to a woman.

"When a woman drinks, she will no longer hear her father or her mother. If the white man speaks to her, she will not hear him, but only her lover. She will never hear any other man, but only the one. *Ku n'Al-laha!* Allah can give man strength and then make him low. Allah sent a man to wake all people. When Allah wakes the world, it will be very soon—no one knows when.

"It will be noticed," said Baba, "that both these medicines subdue a woman to a man. The first he takes himself, the second he gives to her, and presumably it is he who writes the prayer on her board, and he who washes it and gives her the water to drink—perhaps without her knowledge."

"It seems hard," said Olive, "that a woman should have no opportunity of gaining a man's heart."

"If a man make this medicine, everybody will love him. The blood of his heart will change," he said. "It will become white."

This was not an answer. Olive watched as Baba finished the potion by putting in a little bit of hollowed maize stalk. He then gave it to Olive. Back in her tent, Olive placed it at arm's length. "As it is intended for the overthrow of my own sex, I shall not allow its efficacy to be tested," she said.

THE FIKANS WERE ALSO CAPABLE of second sight, which greatly intrigued Olive. Baba told them a story that dated from the end of the sixteenth century. A chief was seated with his brother, when the chief's child began to cry. When his uncle asked why, the chief said that he could understand him. But he said: "If I tell you what the child is saying, your heart will not be good." But the uncle wanted to know, for the child was just a child. The chief grudgingly agreed and listened intently to his son's cries.

"The child says that when I die, he will be chief, and you will be chief after him." The uncle was angry at this and ran off. The child's mother ran after him and pleaded with him. "Why are you vexed?" she asked. "If my *piccan* will be chief for plenty years, and you will be chief after him, you will live for many years, and that is good." But his uncle left the house in anger.

It came to pass that the chief died when his little son was seven years old. The child had spoken destiny, and the people chose him to be chief, and would have none of his uncle, though he forced his claim with a thousand warriors. Until then the child had worn no clothing, but when he became chief they put trousers on him, and that was the meaning of his name: *Dauwu* meant "trousers" and *Gan* meant "to cut or sew": *Gandauwu.*

He reigned for thirty years and had no children. As foretold, his uncle succeeded him as chief. Olive pondered the meaning of the story. Fatherhood and succession were apparently not only the means of securing the future, but they were also ways of telling it. Second sight, though powerful, could only be understood through the journey of experience.

Between the stories and the magic, the people of Fika accepted Olive and the Talbots into the life of the place. They would come and tell them little histories and bring contributions to Mr. Talbot's collection of animals, including monkeys, squirrels, rats, and a little duiker antelope. Mastaba even collected some scorpions from beneath the stones in the town. He brought them in his cap and overturned them on the table, where they scuttled about in a manner that greatly alarmed Olive. Mastaba picked them up one by one and placed them in the collecting bottle, assuring her that there was no need to fear, as he had a medicine that could counter their sting. Mr. Talbot, who still couldn't move much, examined them with great interest.

One afternoon the chief of the Fikans finally came to visit them. At the end of his long retinue was a native carrying a great old war drum, strapped together with hide, leather, and wood. Olive saw spots of something dark on its surface. The chief explained with great pride that this war drum had led the Fikans to victory in every battle they fought over the last sixty years. When they laid siege to a neighboring city and failed to capture it, they had only to throw the drum over the enemy's wall and no defense could keep their men from swarming in to claim it. The chief patted it as if it were some great dog. Since the white man had come and forbidden war, they wished the great Mr. Talbot to have it.

AS MR. TALBOT CONTINUED TO recover, they were invited to a wedding of the Fikan chief's second son. Mr. Talbot had to be carried via hammock, but he could not refuse after the chief's generous gift. Baba accompanied them. When they arrived at the great square, dancers were already beginning to assemble. Olive was excited. She had never seen an African wedding. But her hopes were soon dashed by the sheer monotony of the dance. A row of men, youths, and tiny boys slowly advanced, making two movements with each foot before they leaned their weight forward, and that was their dance. They were preceded by a man playing a small wooden calabash drum, who walked backward before them. It was, to Olive, a dull and tedious affair.

As she tried hard not to yawn, her attention was awoken when a strange figure in a costume of tin plates, animal claws, and teeth jumped into the square. He wore a funny quilted cap on his head, and his face was painted with red, yellow, and white stripes. As he danced about, a red streamer flowed from his back. He wore a full short skirt, and various animal skins hung over his person, between which flashed innumerable knives and daggers. In one hand he carried a large straw hat; in the other, a sword. A tomahawk dangled from his back.

Yet for all his accessories, he was not a dreadful character. He was young and fresh, his eyes sparkling with excitement. After posturing for two or three minutes, he did a series of jumps, after which he alternately thrust his stomach in and out. Olive found this provocative movement somehow childish. Suddenly the clown—for that is what she now thought him—stopped in front of Olive and flung his hat, sword, and cap from him, and ran quickly to a spot where horse dung had recently fallen. He gathered it into his hands, rolled it into a little ball, and stuffed it into his mouth.

Olive became nauseated. The clown next seized a dagger and grabbed a maize stalk that he cut clean in two. Having proved the sharpness of his blade, he raised his skirt, and before they could realize what he was doing, he cut into his leg again and again. Olive gasped. The clown then stopped and showed his leg to the crowd. Not a drop of blood flowed, and a scar showed white against his black skin.

Baba said this was due to the man wearing a special narrow leather bracelet, with magical properties that prevented any blood flowing from its wearer. All that he had done—the belly-dancing, the eating of dung—was done to awaken its powers. The clown next seized his tomahawk, swung it round and round, and struck his head with considerable violence. Olive stifled a scream.

The clown turned his head to the crowd in a lopsided way and slowly smiled. He had no visible injury.

Olive watched as the roaring natives threw cowrie shells and kola nuts at the performer. She tried to inspect him from afar as he was being congratulated. She could not believe there was no trickery about the weapons. Olive felt grateful for her incredulity, as it probably saved her from sickness. Thankfully the performance was brought to an end by the gathering of horsemen, in preparation for the wedding itself.

Just then a little boy gleefully ran out among the horses and received a hard kick on the shin. He crumpled to the ground, screaming in agony. A man walked out onto the central square and picked the little boy up, but his small leg dangled below him. It was destroyed, and so he was laid down again as the man ran off. Mr. Talbot hurriedly stood up, grabbed his walking stick, and went as fast as his injuries would permit to the boy, who had now become very quiet. Mr. Talbot broke his stick in two and improvised splints. Olive and Mrs. Talbot were not far behind and helped bind the leg with their handkerchiefs.

The boy struggled and began screaming again without interruption. Olive and Mrs. Talbot knelt beside him, holding him still and trying to soothe him, but the terror of the unaccustomed faces only added to his distress.

It was then Olive realized that they were the only ones in the square.

Olive looked to and fro. The boy's father was in the crowd, but he refused to come out to his little son. It was against the rules. His mother was off to the side with a group of other women. Her face was covered with tears, but she could do nothing because no woman could mix with men at a time of festivity. They all feared acting without the permission of their leader. Mr. Talbot sent a runner to tell the chief, who was waiting for his moment in the ceremony to appear. The ladies sat there with the boy in the middle of the great square, down in the dust.

The chief appeared and walked out at the head of his retinue. He reached the crumpled boy, knelt down, and spoke kindly to the little chap in a soft voice. He then directed some men to bear the boy away on a native bed, on which he had to be forcibly held, for he was still struggling and crying.

When she left that empty square, Olive's face wore an angry look. Mastaba told her that native surgery had the reputation of being very good, but Olive pretended not to hear it. She knew she could not leave without fear of offense, so she tried to watch the rest of the wedding. As the chief took his place on the stand, finely arrayed men in apricot-colored shirts pranced on their horses as women brought him endless gifts. The presents were carried back to the bride's house as music once again rose from the guitars.

Mastaba explained that in ordinary cases, a man selected his wife when she was still a child, by sending a dash of cloth and money to her mother. Half of this the mother gave to her relations. The wife received utensils. The father seemed to play very little part in his daughter's matrimonial affairs. When the wedding occurred, the prayer that was offered was: "May you stop long with this man in his house." Mastaba explained that men and women, even in their home, never ate together, and the law extended beyond this, for certain foods were also forbidden. No one could eat swine, monkeys, or dogs, and women were especially forbidden lions, leopards, or hyenas.

As they left the wedding, the party got word that the little boy was doing much better and was expected to heal well.

THE HEAVY INSTRUMENT SAT on its tripod in the sand, its spyglass pointed back toward the mud-decorated Fika houses. Mr. Talbot stood behind it, on his own two legs, making tiny clicks on a dial and notations in pencil in his small book. Olive was surprised that Mr. Talbot brought the theolodite out now when they were so close to their last destination. Mr. Talbot looked through the glass and made another small mark. Olive didn't know how it all worked, just that it used connecting points to make maps. One truth of Africa that the party had learned was that the true position of a town was often miles away from where it was marked on the published map. This happened so surprisingly often that it was no wonder that many placed credence in the tale that distances on these maps had been determined by firing pistols in the air and judging how far the sound carried.

Mr. Talbot surveyed Fika for two days to build up his strength. He proved that he could move under his own power, though not without considerable pain in his back. But his duties in Southern Nigeria called. When they said their good-byes to Baba and the chief, it was with real sadness. Olive knew they should have been home by now, and though she would do anything to take back Mr. Talbot's injuries, their time in Fika had been a gift.

When they were ready to depart, they sent most of the group ahead and ordered them to make camp halfway through the day's march. Due to Mr. Talbot's slowness, they were going to catch up to them there. Olive thought this a good idea, but also suspected that part of Mr. Talbot's intent was that he didn't want the boys to see him carried in a hammock.

27

POISONED ARROW

February 1911: On the Bornu Road in Nigeria, Olive
Gets Lost in the Dark; She Climbs a White Cliff; Tragedy
Strikes the Zakis; a Final Journey Is Taken

In single file they meandered up the narrow valley, along the gentle slopes of wooded hills, lit by brilliant sprays of golden-flowered cassias. Beyond the end of the mountain ridge, they journeyed past all visible settlement. Mr. Talbot's injury in Fika had added yet another deadline to their clock: Tornado season was coming. This meant they had to get to Kano before the rains washed out the train tracks. But even though they were pressed for time, the area they were traveling was woefully undocumented, so Mr. Talbot made it his business to map it as they went.

Eight Fikans carried Mr. Talbot on a hammock. They worked in turns, in shifts of four at a time. The carriers walked two abreast, never once sacrificing Mr. Talbot to any obstacle. Olive found it touching to hear them congratulate one another on a swampy patch navigated or a burr nest avoided. They carried him aloft in the sky.

Olive and Mrs. Talbot soon found themselves far ahead, so they stopped and sat on a fallen tree trunk to wait for Mr. Talbot, whose progress was as slow as expected. The light was waning when Mr. Talbot appeared over the rise. Even when carried, he was obviously exhausted.

Mrs. Talbot asked their guide how much farther the camp was, but he had no answer. Olive figured they must be close, and any minute she expected to hear the boys laughing and talking by the warm firelight ahead.

But the darkness increased, and no voices broke the silence. Their footsteps sank deep in the soft sand. The thick bushes that grew on either side of them made the way even darker. Gullies of loose stones slowed them down even further. Occasionally Olive would hear the cry of one of their own who had tripped and fallen in the darkness.

Olive looked up at the fixed stars. She hoisted her water bottle; it was nearly empty. They had had nothing except tea and biscuits since an early lunch, and it was now nine o'clock at night. They traveled for another hour, crossing a deserted plain without any sight or sound of a village. Their march raised clouds of sand, and thus made them even thirstier. Olive was so weary that tiny sparks of light floated before her eyes, and she thought she saw the campfire several times. But it was just a trick of her mind. Maybe the whole *thing* was a trick—all of it. It was past eleven when they reached two blocks of hills and heard voices echo along the valley.

Olive felt as if she was already asleep by the time they reached camp. She barely heard that the boys had misinterpreted their commands and had marched the whole leg. Olive and the Talbots had unknowingly done the same, even at their slowed pace. As they all collapsed into camp, Olive drank a great deal of water and retired. Bed that night was welcome indeed.

WHEN OLIVE WOKE THE NEXT DAY, she looked up and saw white cliffs towering over them. She had not seen any of this last night. Olive looked harder and saw short buildings on the cliff's crest, like tiny beehives. The village in the sky was called Lethe and had been visited by Mr. Talbot and Boyd's brother Claud almost ten years ago.

"We were met with hostility," recalled Mr. Talbot, as he shielded his eyes from the sun. "And poisoned arrows." Mr. Talbot pointed up the mountain. There, coming down from the village were two natives. They stopped halfway down and stood perfectly still. Mr. Talbot sent Mastaba to tell them they were peaceful travelers. Mastaba started to climb.

He had barely gotten a foothold when the two natives began making loud sounds of warning. One of them swiftly nocked an arrow into his bow.

Mastaba stopped, with one foot on the mountain. He slowly backed off. The natives remained still.

After a few tense moments, one tribesman put his bow away. Mr. Talbot nodded, and Mastaba took slow, tentative steps up the mountain. The natives let him come. When Mastaba finally reached them, they spoke briefly. Mastaba turned and beckoned to the group to come up.

These were fortress hills. As Olive approached the base of the cliff, she saw a trench concealed in the grass and leaves. Rising from it was three hundred feet of ever-increasing sheerness. But Mastaba shouted something, and the boys pointed to hidden blocks of wood that were laid into the white rock to be used as a kind of secret stair. Olive found this exciting, but there was no way that Mr. Talbot could attempt such a climb in his weak state. Turning to break the news to him, she saw him walking toward the stair instead, slowly and in pain.

When Olive reached the top, she was met by natives who were standing near some immense boulders. The men were thin and tall and had unpleasant expressions. Once Mr. Talbot arrived, after a very slow climb, the chief took them through the town. Though his subjects did not seem happy about this, they largely got out of the way. The village itself consisted of narrow domed huts, built in groups surrounded by walls of *zana* matting. There was also a large granary. The grain, grown on the plains below, was brought up and poured in. When grain was needed, a man climbed a rudely constructed ladder, leaped into the granary, and distributed its contents in big bowls.

All the unmarried boys lived together in undesirable huts. The doors to these sad places were so small that they reminded Olive of a kennel. Two of their Fikan carriers laughed so loudly at the sight of these small doors that they tried to see if they might fit. The first boy squeezed through. The second, laughing, went legs first, but the floor was lower than the doorway, and he got stuck. The only way to release him was to remove the roof, which might draw the villagers' ire. Mr. Talbot came to survey the situation. After unsuccessfully trying to get the boy out, it was decided to leave him to his fate. As they walked away, they heard him kicking and scratching for dear life.

THEY STAYED FOR A FEW DAYS as Mr. Talbot measured the horizons for his map. One night they had to make camp in the village because they had tarried too long, and it was already dark. The chief offered them accommodations. As the natives showed them their huts, Olive let her little lions roam in the inner courtyard. She set about making up her bed, but when she looked out again, Lamy was gone.

Olive ran outside and searched the vicinity. She feared the worst: It could have been an animal or one of the villagers themselves, hungry and sneaky. One of the boys sang out, *"Zaki!"* Olive ran toward his voice. The tall villagers regarded her strangely as she rushed by. Olive saw a group of their boys gathered around something. They were pointing downward.

It was a well.

Olive dashed to the edge, made of mud bricks, and looked down. There was only darkness and a slight scent of water. Mr. Talbot joined them, looked down, and ordered everyone quiet.

"Kai," he said.

There was silence, followed by a soft sound.

They called down again, and Lamy answered back every time. They heard splashing, too, but knew the water was not deep enough to drown the little lion. Still, his cry sounded weak and small.

They heard another, louder purr. Olive turned to see little Kusseri running straight for them. He began circling the well in terrible agitation. Olive feared he might go in after Lamy, so Mr. Talbot ordered him tied up, trying to think of a better plan.

Aji stepped forward and volunteered to go down. Mr. Talbot eyed him. There was no time to debate it. They attached the basket to the rope, and Aji climbed in. Mastaba and the others lowered him down. Before he finally disappeared, Olive saw a scared look in his eyes.

All went quiet as they tried to listen. The only sound was the creaking of the rope and of the basket swaying. It sounded as if they were at sea again. Finally, they heard a splash followed by an immediate scrambling sound that Olive recognized as her little lion's. Aji screamed.

Mastaba quickly started to pull up the rope, his muscles working against the weight at the end of it. When the basket finally emerged, Aji had a hollow look. Then Lamy appeared—he was soaking wet but alive. When Lamy jumped back onto solid ground, he rolled toward Kusseri and the two kissed each other all over. Olive was overjoyed. Aji said, through gritted teeth, that there had been just enough water to break Lamy's sixty-foot fall. As Aji stepped gingerly out of the basket, Olive noticed that his clothes had been cut to ribbons by Lamy's claws and were stained with blood.

Olive went over and thanked him.

THE KANO PROVINCE LENT a welcome variety that was refreshing after the drabs and browns of the plains. They passed over ridges that were beautiful in their rocky bareness. Once or twice they passed still pools, the drinking places of birds and beasts, surrounded by brilliant green grass. They even passed through a forest of borassus palms, with an undergrowth of sweet-scented flowers. Africa was awakening as they got closer to home.

They finally arrived at the bustling city of Kano on April 8. The number of people was overwhelming. Olive was so tired, she simply walked through the stares and bodies as if they were rain. The march had thoroughly exhausted Mr. Talbot. He took refuge in a white rest house as the rest made up their tents. The next afternoon they went to the town market, excited to see what treasures this famous place would offer them. The emir of the city had sent a guide to meet them at the village gates. The man was tall and paid them many compliments, especially Olive. When they got to the market, Olive was surprised to find that civilization had made Kano uninteresting. Many of the articles for sale were either imported or made in imitation of white men's goods, and they were all excessively expensive. It was a great contrast to what they had seen in the interior. Olive debated taking some photographs but everything seemed dull.

After they returned from the market, Olive was changing clothes in her tent when she saw their tall guide peeking at her through an opening in the door. She covered herself up as he ran away. When confronted by Mr. Talbot, the false man simply lied his way out of it. Olive covered every open corner of her tent with boots or cushions, but the *zakis* romped and made it airy again. She caught him again later, trying to watch her. Mr. Talbot told the man he must leave. The tall man put on the most wretched faces and became excited; he knew the emir would not forgive him. He left their presence, stripped off all his fine garments, and returned in a rag. He cast himself upon the ground before them, bowed his head, and repeated, *"Zaki, zaki."* They had heard this before. It seemed that Olive was gaining a reputation not only for her hair, but for her strange mastery of the two lions. As the tall man lay before them in the dust, Mastaba good-naturedly begged Mr. Talbot to have pity on him. Olive agreed. They allowed him to accompany them while in Kano, and he was thus saved from public humiliation. When they finally left the tall man behind, Olive turned her head to make sure he didn't follow them.

The train they were waiting for, a construction line to Zungeru, was scheduled for the next day. When they boarded, it was with thankful steps. Even though the tornado season had already begun, there had not yet been a heavy rain to wash out the tracks. Africa had spared them a long, final march. They were not looking forward to the end of their journey, but at least they would not have to make it on foot.

They traveled in a luggage car, where they set up a bed for Mr. Talbot and chairs for everyone else. The little lions ran loose about the floor. Olive watched as the poor little fellows, frightened at the noise and constant shaking, rushed ceaselessly from end to end of the car, jumping up and trying to get out. Every now and again they would give up and seek consolation in her arms. There were no windows, and the doors had to stay shut for the cubs, so it was stifling. The sun baked through the wooden roof till the van became an oven, and for ten hours they sat and suffered. Olive actually wished they were back on the march, not in the belly of this mechanical monster.

The trip gave Olive time to think. Their next stop would be the command post of Zungeru, where they would make a last-ditch effort not only to explain their actions to Governor Temple and hopefully spare Mr. Talbot's career, but possibly to extend their journey. And there were still questions about Boyd.

Olive hoped she would find answers. So much had changed, but she had not forgotten what had brought her to Africa.

28

MR. CHARLES TEMPLE

April 1911, Zungeru, Nigeria: Olive Confronts Governor
Charles Temple and Has an Awkward Dinner; Secrets Are
Disclosed and Terrible News Arrives

Before they reached Zungeru, the train made a brief stop. Olive stepped outside and saw a massive sandstorm billowing out over the horizon. Africa, it seemed, was not done with them yet. This was the first sandstorm Olive had seen. Watching as the rolling orange cloud enveloped everything in its path, she craned her neck to see if it would hit the tracks ahead of them, but it looked unlikely. The air felt heavy. Olive watched the whirlwind until it was time to board the train again.

Olive didn't know what to expect in Zungeru. Instead of facing a mad hippo or an angry tribe, they were going to confront something far more unpredictable: the face of the British Protectorate in Nigeria. Olive wasn't exactly sure why Mr. Talbot had been called back. He had exhausted his leave, but that seemed a thin excuse, especially given the ways that Acting Governor Temple had been limiting their movements since those first days in Lokoja. Olive remembered his thoughts on white men's wives in Africa, and how he had later shut them off from Yola. But their expedition had pushed on anyway—to Fort Lamy, to Lake Chad—in defiance of his wishes.

In calling them back, Temple had shut down any hope they had of going even farther, possibly to Abechir. Or, Olive thought, to el-Fachir itself to ask Ali Dinar about what had happened to Boyd Alexander. Olive hoped they would be able to appeal Temple's decision and return east, but given Mr. Talbot's condition, she had no confidence in such a possibility. She wondered if she could go on her own, but without the Talbots, this was even more unlikely. And they were all so very tired. Instead of hope, the only emotion Olive could muster was anger. Why would the British approve their trip, only to attempt to stop it?

When they finally arrived in Zungeru, it was eight thirty at night. The sandstorm had given way to a deluge. Dark rain seemed to ricochet from every open surface except the ground, where it formed deep, large pools. The earth itself seemed full. Olive and what was left of their party splashed through the rain until they found a small encampment near the railroad. They slept there under tarps, the loud rain trying its best to beat them into the ground.

The sun was out the following morning, the eventual victor against all African weather. Olive and the Talbots left the others to walk toward the middle of town. Zungeru was a wide settlement with rounded sand walls and huts. When they reached the British section, the houses were made of brick and whiteboard and rose a story higher. Government House, their destination, was the best house on the street—a comfortable, superior bungalow.

A soldier showed them in. They passed beautiful furniture and clean rooms. Olive felt her own unkempt state for the first time in many days. The shelves were filled with figurines, instruments, and masks from tribes Olive could not identify. At last she and the Talbots were shown through a door. Olive took a breath: This would be the last uncertain corner of their adventure together.

The soldier opened the door. Light filled the room, which appeared to be a study.

Olive saw Governor Temple, who was turning from the window. He regarded them, for a moment, with a look much like surprise. As Olive shook his limp hand, she was glad she had survived long enough to prove him wrong about women in Africa. Mr. Temple smiled a welcome and moved toward his chair. His clothes were rumpled, and when he sat down, he seemed to breathe a sigh of relief, though he tried very hard to hide it.

After they were seated, Mr. Talbot briefed Temple about their adventures. He told him of Mount Patti, the Lamido, and of Olive's discovery of the McLeod Falls. Governor Temple looked directly at Olive during this part, but she looked away. Mr. Talbot told him about the Germans, the French, the swamps, and even the Man-Leopard. The governor looked out the window, listening. Olive watched him closely. She stood ready to jump in and fight for their reasoning in going to Fort Lamy, but when Mr. Talbot got to the subject, Governor Temple only nodded.

Once Mr. Talbot broached the topic of Lake Chad, the governor shifted in his seat. When Mr. Talbot told him of Hajer-el-Hamis, Temple seemed mildly astounded. He glanced at Olive again. Of course Mr. Talbot then told him of Maifoni and their business there.

Olive began to get agitated.

"Why did you call us back?"

All was quiet, and though the sun had now returned after yesterday's rain, the room still retained a piece of darkness. Mr. Talbot spoke up to silence Olive, something about it being his duty to return to his post, but Governor Temple answered for himself. He asked Mr. Talbot if he had completed his commission. Mr. Talbot said yes, he had for the most part, but there was still more to do. "Have you completed your commission?" the governor asked again. Yes, said Mr. Talbot. "For whom?" asked Temple.

"The War Department," replied Mr. Talbot.

The governor then asked to see Mr. Talbot privately, inviting the rest of them to stay as his guests and adding that he looked forward to seeing them at dinner. He bowed his head.

As Olive left, the door closed.

OLIVE WAS SHOWN TO HER ROOM upstairs, where she bathed and made an honest attempt at appearances. She stood for a moment in the large furnished room, almost forgetful of what it felt like. There was so much space, so many things.

When they ate dinner with the governor that evening, Olive found herself enjoying the moment more than she had expected, or perhaps even wished. The well-furnished rooms, the butter on the table, even the conversation with men who knew what had been happening at home was immensely invigorating. Mr. Talbot was going to keep his post, so that was good news indeed.

At the table Olive found out more about the elusive Mr. Charles L. Temple. He was a company man, born in India to a baronet and educated at Trinity College, Cambridge. He had been in Africa for several years since coming from a post in Brazil. He believed in the practice of indirect rule—that is, letting native tribes rule themselves—and was known for his skill in defusing violent situations among the natives without resorting to violence. Given the man's quiet demeanor, Olive could understand this. He had made peace with the pagan tribes and had driven the slave trade in Boautshi to extinction. Olive was appreciative when he turned to ask her directly about her adventures on Hajer-el-Hamis. Olive tried to put her experience into words, but she was not at all pleased with the results.

That night in bed, there were many questions in the air. Not from a diary or a phantom, but from something increasingly corporeal. If Mr. Talbot had a directive from the War Office, why would the acting governor of Nigeria be working against those very orders? Was the War Office requesting maps because the British were going to move on Wadai and Dar Fur? Why else would everyone be so interested in Boyd's missing maps?

Olive wondered, then, in the steamy dark, what her own unwitting role in this had been. Had her coming here been a coincidence? Had it been her idea to come to Maifoni or Mr. Talbot's? She couldn't remember much from that time, but the question that took shape was the same one she had started with:

What was an ornithologist doing in Abechir?

Boyd's diaries had intimated that he thought Ali Dinar might be a way forward for peace in the region. Had this been Boyd's own idea? Or had the War Department been funding his trip, too? The thought occurred to her that they were all doing the same work, either contracted like Mr. Talbot, or as part of a larger, invisible machinery.

Or was Boyd, for all his enthusiasm, just a pawn in a great game being played over the last open square of Africa? Olive couldn't answer that. But she knew that the Boyd she had known at home, however briefly, seemed very different from the voice in his diaries. Perhaps that was normal for a writer, though she couldn't be sure.

The rooms were very quiet, and Olive searched for answers with her mind.

No one came to give them.

WHEN THEY LEFT GOVERNOR TEMPLE the next day, Olive knew that she would not be going to Abechir. Perhaps it had been a foolish thought. There was construction on the railroad, so they traveled on an open truck car with an awning over it. The *zakis* were a very popular attraction along the line. They were eventually switched to a parlor car, where the little lions first encountered a new experience for them: carpet. After licking and scratching it to test if it had any practical recommendations, they conceived an immense contempt for it and dove in with their claws.

By the time they reached Southern Nigeria, natives and officials alike stood on boxes and climbed up telegraph poles to see the lions. Lamy and Kusseri became quite animated before the crowds, and often boxed each other or posed in some bewitching way for the benefit of their admirers.

Once it was time to board the train again, the crowd lifted the chant of "*Zakis! Zakis!*" Olive found out later that only a few of the natives from that part had ever seen a lion. Many of them asked if they were "dawgs."

Though much reduced at the end, the party held within its remaining core a deep and lasting bond. Olive knew she would never see some, if not all, of them ever again. Cooku, Washerman, and the gun boys and horse boys were already gone, having sought employment elsewhere. Small Boy and Mastaba remained; they were going to continue with the Talbots. Olive heard the word "elephant" and became worried for them. As she watched her friend Mastaba walk away, Olive felt it was she who was really disappearing from things. Jimba-Giri had also just left. He had heard the unfortunate news of his mother's death and was running to his home village so that he might get a share of her worldly possessions.

Olive found the whole end of things to be very grievous. She knew Mr. Talbot had his work to do as a district commissioner in Southern Nigeria, and his wife would stay with him. The three had spent close to nine months together in complete intimacy, and it was hard to part, but the time for good-byes had come. She would see them someday, she was sure, in London.

Olive and the Talbots would spend one last night together in Nigeria. The *Dakar* was going to call the next day. Olive had every intention of boarding it. She had every intention of going home.

A LOVER'S PILGRIMAGE.

Rumored Murder of Miss MacLeod

Passengers, who arrived at Plymouth yesterday from the West Coast of Africa stated that when the mail steamer Dakar left Forcados a rumour was current there that Miss Olive MacLeod, who had gone on a pilgrimage to the interior of Africa to the grave of her lover, Lieutenant Boyd Alexander, had been murdered with her companions, Mr. and Mrs. Talbot. There was no means of obtaining confirmation of the story as Miss MacLeod's destination was in a wild and savage country, which had never before been penetrated by a white woman. The journey inland from Forcados was expected to occupy three months.

29

THE FATE OF
OLIVE MACLEOD

May 11, 1911, Plymouth, England: A Crowd Gathers

Sir Reginald MacLeod pressed the front of his dark coat down as flat as it would go, but not nearly as flat as he wished it would. No matter. He looked out at the small crowd before him, gathered in front of the low brick buildings. At his back was the cold water of the English port of Plymouth. Sir Reginald found it easy to avoid their eyes because they were looking at the boat behind him. He could put it off no longer. Wiping his eyes and face with his handkerchief, he cleared his throat. He was here to say a few words.

"My daughter, Olive MacLeod," he said, his voice getting teary, "of whom I am so proud . . ."

He took a moment to collect himself. They had all read the papers, but he still wanted to say it:

"She traveled 3,700 miles in Africa, through British, French, and German territories. For four months she passed in territory unknown to British travelers. For six months, she passed in country never visited by white women. She visited the unseen falls at Mao Kabi, which are to be named MacLeod Falls. She ascended the highest peaks of Hajer-el-

Hamis, venerated as the spot where Noah's Ark rested. This was the first such ascent ever made."

And, here he paused again, but this time because he was so proud.

"She crossed Lake Chad in canoes."

He paused again, that Old Waxworks. He added, almost mumbling, that "A full and detailed account of her journey will very likely be published in the near future." The last few words barely made it out.

The people in the crowd were dressed for the drafty May wind. They stared up. The boat behind Sir Reginald creaked. He looked up again.

"And she is finally home."

From the gangplank behind him came the passengers of the SS *Dakar*, the weathered vessel that had journeyed to, and returned from, the coast of Africa. People saw loved ones and embraced. Sir Reginald craned his neck and saw a clearing in the surge of passengers, up near the top of the plank, past all the other people. Shouts went up through the crowd.

He saw a flash of red.

"Olive!" he said.

There, walking down the plank in a khaki dress was Olive MacLeod. As she smiled, the *zakis,* carried aloft in their wooden cages, were at her sides, glowering at the crowd and pacing in protection of their mistress. When the papers printed that Olive's reported "death" was false, they also printed her arrival date, resulting in dozens of people crowding the docks to welcome her home. Sir Reginald thought it fitting to say a few words of welcome.

Olive's helpers and carriers brought down bags and trunks and baskets, many with odd wooden instruments and feathers sticking out of of them. The children on the docks looked on, wide-eyed. There were no native carriers or any Talbots; just Olive, come home at last, walking down upon English ground.

At the end of the walkway, she embraced and kissed her father, whose face was scarlet again.

FROM HER FATHER'S OFFICE AT 10 Downing Street, Violet Asquith wrote in her diary on May 10, 1911. "Olive is back—though I haven't seen her—placards are covered with 'Lady explorer's return.'"

Details of her trip were indeed being inked all over the newspapers from London to Dublin, and even in the United States. Olive had agreed to talk with a reporter from Reuters at her home. He asked about the natives first. "From start to finish, we never experienced the slightest difficulty with them," Olive told the reporter, "although many of the tribes we visited were wild . . . and certainly had never seen a white woman. At first they ran away, but afterwards returned and their chief excitement seemed to be caused by the appearance of our hair."

There were many questions about Boyd and her journey to place a cross at his grave. She answered them. When she later saw the articles, some of them had wide illustrations of her on the march with a gigantic cross. The reporter then asked how the lions fared at sea.

Olive explained that they had constructed big wooden cages for the *zakis* to travel in. They did not care for their first real imprisonment, and howled accordingly, but they placed the cages opposite each other on board so that at least they could see each other. Olive said that the ship's butcher was particularly good to the lions, smuggling them beef, chicken, liver, and mutton. When they finally docked, the butcher gave Olive a large bag of bones so that they might have breakfast on the train.

The lions were so big now that Olive could not even hold them in her arms. Before she left Nigeria, Olive and the Talbots had debated about what to do with the *zakis*. The little lions could not survive in the wild. Someone suggested the London Zoological Gardens. They would be well cared for and would be seen by many visitors as part of the King's African Collection. They all agreed. After they arrived in

Plymouth, the lions were taken off in a cart for a period of quarantine before they would go on display at the zoo.

"They are rather dangerous pets for Maidstone," Olive said.

When she said good-bye to the lions, Olive felt her heart breaking. "They will be fine," she said. "They will be fine."

"Olive is, I am glad to say, in excellent health," Sir Reginald told the reporter, "and, beyond the rough cooking and the difficulty of beating a way through the dense bush inseparable from such expeditions, has suffered few hardships." When the article came out the next day, the reporter noted that Olive thought "that humanity is very much the same beneath the surface all over the world." The title of the story was striking: "All the World Is Kin."

After the initial surge of attention, Olive was looking forward to seeing her mother and her friends, but also her bed so that she might rest. At Vinters that night, she lay down and tried to sleep. Whenever she saw a stray flit of down, all she could think of were birds—Boyd's in his little outhouse, still and glassy eyed yet somehow alive—and Mr. Talbot's, that bled even after they were dead.

One of the reporters showed her an article that claimed she had been killed by natives. It was all rubbish, of course, and they could not determine where it originated. Olive revealed that someone had sent her a copy of this announcement—of her death at the hands of savages—when she was still in Africa, just outside Maifoni. It was quite alarming to read an official notice of one's own death while still breathing. It was like seeing a future that wasn't real. Olive did notice a retraction that surprised her:

> News has been received by the Colonial Office from the Governor of Northern Nigeria that the rumors circulated last week as to a disaster to the expedition of Mr. and Mrs. Talbot and Miss Olive MacLeod are devoid of any foundation.

Olive read the article again. The governor of Nigeria had been the one to write in and correct the falsehood of her death? She was a little surprised. Mr. Charles Temple must have changed his mind about women in Africa after all.

OLIVE LOOKED OUT UPON THE very small, and very inaccurate, replica of Lake Chad on the pasturelands near Swifts Place. The sun was out, and it was a beautiful day. But the water was murky and shallow. After seeing the real Lake Chad, the little pond, though precious, now looked like a sad toy.

Olive had talked to Boyd's parents, his brothers Herbert and Robin, and everyone else.

They had Boyd's diaries now. Herbert especially was looking forward to reading them. They had hoped to recover his signet ring, but it was lost. Only his words were left, and a chestnut lock of hair. Though Olive had made peace with Boyd, there was still the question of his death. Its circumstances had never been resolved for her.

José was Boyd's most faithful companion. But his account differed from the French version, so one of them had to be lying. If it was José, what role had he played? Had he sold Boyd out to Ali Dinar or had he just turned coward and abandoned his true friend? An equal argument could be made that it was the French themselves who were complicit in Boyd's death. By sending him out to the frontier, they knew it would cause an incident that might, in turn, allow them to retaliate. Then they could make inroads into British territory without seeming like they were invading.

On the other side of things, Ali Dinar could easily have ordered Boyd's death. The fact that his note missed Boyd by mere days seemed suspicious. If Dinar could draw the French and British into a battle, it might benefit him, especially if he had connections to the Germans, as was rumored.

There were so many questions. The biggest mystery still was why Boyd was there in the first place. Why would a soft-spoken naturalist go to Dar Fur to negotiate a slavery treaty with a bloodthirsty sultan? At Wilsley, in the room covered with dark paintings of dogs hunting amid strange biblical scenes, Herbert, who had always made himself close to Olive, lowered his voice and told her that Boyd had confided in him about his reasons for meeting with Ali Dinar.

"He spoke to me on several occasions of the possibility of a peaceful mission," said Herbert, "adding that it would be a grand thing to do, to get through to el-Fachir, the capital, and win the confidence of the great Sultan, Ali Dinar, and try to make him see that a wholehearted acknowledgment of Britain's suzerainty, with active co-operation in the suppression of the slave trade, was the wisest course for his own welfare.

"This I think was Boyd's chief object," Herbert continued, "but as far as I know he did not speak of it to another soul for fear of official interference. Besides, it was extremely likely that he would be obliged to turn back." Herbert explained that Boyd had portioned off his trip into three phases: hunting for birds in San Thomé, ascending a Kamerun mountain, and visiting Claud's grave. Then, "if the fates proved propitious, to fit out a caravan of camels and make the journey through Wadai to Dar Fur and thence to Khartoum." His expedition was a distraction.

The French had thought Boyd a spy—was he? His maps had disappeared. Perhaps they were the precious treasure of his journey that the French wanted—or had already taken. Or had the British used Boyd's idealism just to get maps from him? Perhaps that is why the War Department sent Mr. Talbot. Not only to recover Boyd's maps, but perhaps to make new ones. Olive's journey was the perfect cover story. Maybe they were all spies for the protectorate and just didn't know it. Or maybe Boyd had really been a man who just loved birds and believed he could change the world through grand acts. The only thing Olive kept coming back to—because she had proof of it—was that José Lopez had changed his story. Or the French had changed it for him.

Herbert told Olive that while she was looking for José in Africa, he was actually in England, where he met with Boyd's father. José told Colonel Alexander that before his son's death, Boyd had wished to change his will but was too weak with blackwater fever to do so. Boyd dictated his wishes to José, but sadly the signed paper was lost somewhere near Abechir. José said that the only two things he could remember were that Boyd wanted the entirety of his bird collection to be gifted to the British Museum, and he wanted his bequest to José to be increased to £700. The colonel looked him up and down. He paid him what he asked, but told José Lopez that he was no longer welcome at Wilsley.

Herbert later received one final letter from José, postmarked Kano:

Dear Sir,

Just a few lines to let you know that I am quite well and hope you are and mrs alexander. I am leaving her for Maifoni sun I am going to be manager of a trading Company in Catagum. You will see Capt. Brocklebank when he gets back then you will fin out that I have been rongly driven from Wilsley by my enemies but I fel that I have don my dute as I don car I know that som day I shal win up and down in this I know that I shol in the next for cert. I am going to be out there for 12 months before I go on lefe to England. My enemies ar afid to put tinges in the newspapers but wen I get back I shol writ what I can prufe and put Ladies and Gentlemans in them. Sir I hop you will forgiven me for writ lick this. I will close with my hart best wishes.

From your servant
José Lopez

Having written this letter, José walked back into the African jungle and disappeared.

After her visit, Boyd was on Olive's mind. She wrote to Herbert on June 13, 1911:

I am going to try and write an account of my journey. . . . I want to write it for two reasons—first that the public may realize it was a sen-

sible journey, for the papers have made it appear that Boyd was engaged to a sentimental ass—secondly to repay Father the additional money that the lengthened journey cost. An article comes out in London . . . *they have however written a foreword, most of which I have had to excise. I wish there had been more time to consult you about it, for I steadily refuse to have my private affairs mentioned, but your father sent them Boyd's photograph which rather forced my hand—and as it stands at least it isn't vulgar. They had printed José's account in the* Morning Post, *but I could not allow this to stand and have written a brief narrative that did not require mention of his name. It exposes nothing. . . .*

Olive was determined to write a story that focused on the merits of the journey, not on personal details, or even the conspiratorial threads of Boyd's death. She had gone to Africa to perhaps write a book about Boyd; she had returned to write one about her own adventure.

THE DARK, TWO-STORY ROOM was filled with tables and had large faded maps hung on the walls. The room smelled of wood and tobacco and men. And if the men looked puzzled—it was hard to tell under all their mustaches—it was because of who was sitting at the main table in front of them. This was the January 11, 1912, meeting of the Royal Geographical Society in London, though it wasn't an altogether normal one. Finishing at the lectern was Mrs. Fanny Bullock Workman, an American. She wore a squat wool suit and vest, and a tall hat with flowers. She was speaking of her trip to the Himalayas. At the table next to her sat Miss Olive MacLeod, the recently returned African explorer. Her red hair was pinned up, and she had notes in her hands.

As Olive was introduced, she was aware of the importance of the crowd below her. Here were famous explorers and authors. Here were adventurers and great men. Boyd had spoken here, been a member, and had received their highest honor. But he was not here. When it was Olive's turn to speak, she did so in a way that was more storytelling than scientific, with a bloom of fable laid upon the fact. Whether this was a choice or just the instincts of someone who grew up on fairy tales made no difference, because it was largely the way many of these explorers wrote, full of hyperbole and lyric, but never at the expense of a carefully articulated skeleton of truth.

Olive told her captive audience everything she had time for. She told them of the falls and of Gauaronga and his many wives. When she said the great chief's name, she knew he was far away. But his name still carried an echo of power and fear there in that dark room. She showed them artifacts, like a flute and a bird catcher. The society men were utterly astounded at her findings. They knew her story from the papers, but they were moved by this side of it, and by what she had brought back. She said nothing of Boyd, as always.

When Olive was done, they clapped and shouted. She stood there for a moment. No one asked about her hair.

"Amazingly interesting," wrote Alec Jameson, a reviewer in the *London Standard*. "It was difficult to realize that this slender, dark-eyed girl had accomplished such feats of exploration unharmed. Recital of the marriage customs and the treatment of women has caused a sensation of horror amongst the ranks of advancing womankind in London." Jameson found unmistakable parallels "between the City men who let ladies strap-hang in the Tubes and the Bagarimi natives who make their women stand whilst the men sit!" Gauaronga was, unsurprisingly, the character who stayed with people the most. "The Sultan is a most astonishing man! He believes in the subjugation of womankind, but the two Princesses, his daughters, whose husbands he chose for them, are very exalted personages." Whenever Olive spoke of Gauaronga, she shared the results of the report she received when she sent the dates she had saved to a chemical expert. The scientist's reply was simple.

November 21, 1911.

Dear Miss MacLeod,—There is no doubt that there is some poisonous substance in the dates, but I cannot identify this as any poison with which I am familiar.

I am, yours sincerely,
W. H. Willcox.

Jameson also pointed out something about the Royal Geographic Society itself: "The society welcomes these notable women travelers as lecturers but appears to decline to admit them into the Fellowship. Is this logical?" The question remained hanging in the air, like so many others, unanswered but undeniable in its asking.

In 1912 Herbert published his brother's diaries in a volume titled *Boyd Alexander's Last Journey*, including an extensive biography by himself, along with many of Boyd's photographs. Herbert painted a rosy portrait of his beloved brother:

It was only natural, seeing the shuffling that was going on upon the border, that the French should regard him as a spy at first, or even worse, a fate-sent accuser, for his arrival at Abechir was nothing less than a marvelous historical coincidence. But as we read on we can see how his transparent honesty was steadily breaking down all prejudice . . . believing in the power of his name as an Englishman, he presses forward unarmed to interpose himself between the Furians and the French and persuade Ali Dinar to refrain from joining in the war against the white man.

Herbert did not credit Olive for finding and copying the diary he reprinted in his book. He mentioned her only a few times.

Later that year the parish church of Cranbrook unveiled a splendid marble relief honoring the dead Alexander brothers, Claud and Boyd. The sculpture was funded by subscriptions from local citizens and admirers around the world.

THE SKY WAS BLUE AND THE AIR COOL as Olive walked up to the front gate of the Zoological Gardens at Regent's Park. A crowd was lining up, as always. There were excited children tugging their parents' hands. There were mothers in skirts and men in dark suits. Almost everyone wore a hat. There were couples as well, holding hands as they all waited in front of a two-story house in the Tudor style, with bricks and white-trimmed windows. All the children were looking up, trying, however impossible, to see over the gates.

Once inside, Olive walked the familiar paths. Before heading to her appointment in the main zoo, she walked over to the other side of Public Drive to take a quick peek at some of the other animals. She walked past the outside yard, with the still, blinking deer, to get to the Hippopotamus House. Situated on the back end of the Giraffe House, it was mostly made of smooth bare cement girded by thin iron bars. There had been many hippos here over the past decades, including one named Guy Fawkes. In the murky artificial pond in the middle of the cage was a pygmy hippo. As Olive watched, it meekly wandered up to the plain cement, where it stood on its little feet, whiskers on its bell-shaped mouth. All the children squealed. Its ears were very tiny, and it did not seem scary at all. Olive kept her distance.

As she walked around the back, Olive saw the tall giraffes, yellow and brown in the sun. The giraffes came out of actual houses, complete with tall gabled doorways. Olive couldn't catch their eyes. She wondered how tall Josephine was now. She tried to limit her imagination there.

Olive made her way back, seeing the elephants on the way. They were slowly circling their well-trodden track. She saw one of the massive beasts at the far end of the circle, with its fluffy headdress and a riding platform for the lucky children. The elephant moved but didn't seem to. The place had a smell to it. But not like Africa.

Olive crossed back to the other side of the zoo (there was a pedestrian underpass) and entered the main area. People with parasols bounced around her as she glanced at the birds.

She made her way through a familiar route down to the Lion House.

Olive walked up to the iron bars slowly. She could sense their footfalls as they padded toward her. As they came out of the darkness, she saw the black patches on their ears and the dark tips on their tails. They were getting so big. Even their paws were larger and heavier. Olive saw that they still wore their leather collars and a piece of rope.

There was a moment, just a moment, but it didn't last as Olive reached in and shook Lamy's, then Kusseri's white paws through the cage bars. She could see their curved claws. A worker showed up to sweep out their cage, but the *zakis* were so energized by the sight of Olive that they began chasing the poor man, and finally seized his broom.

"They are delightful," said the zookeeper, who always met Olive whenever she wanted. She looked at the concrete floor and straw of their cage.

"They are a great contrast," he said, "to the two young lionesses next door from the Sebakwe River, in Southern Rhodesia." He took Olive over to the adjoining cage. It was even sparer. She saw two young female lions that were nearly white in color. "They are of an extremely savage disposition," said the zookeeper, "They growl in a very provocative manner at the slightest attention shown them; one of them even goes so far as to refuse to be seen, but sits in the corner in a box turned on its side." The keeper walked Olive back to her own lions' cage. They were fighting over the broomstick, which had already splintered.

"The present intention is to bring them all up together, but that, of course, will not be possible for some time yet."

OLIVE LOOKED AT THE MASSIVE flat surface of the gray stone. The slab was chipped at the edges, and a large part had been cracked off, revealing the obsidian beneath. A cascade of small, blurry white markings ran down the entire face of it. Olive looked even closer, peering at the Rosetta Stone. She knew there were three languages there, all meant to come together in a single meaning.

While Olive was writing her book, she took time to visit the British Museum. When she finally got admittance to the African curators, they were delighted to meet the person who was part of the Talbot expedition. They knew who Olive was from the romantic stories in the newspapers, but they were more interested in talking about the great P. A. Talbot. They were very disappointed he was not with her.

Olive didn't have Mr. Talbot, but she instead showed them some things she had brought back from Africa, including a bracelet and a small musical instrument. The curators were spellbound. When Olive said she had more, they agreed to see them. When she returned with not one bag, but a trunk, then another, and several more, all stuffed to the seams with previously unknown artifacts, the esteemed experts of the museum were speechless. Olive MacLeod personally donated more than 180 items—from drums to throwing knives; figurines to clay pots—that are still in the museum's collection today. She is currently officially identified by the museum as "Miss Olive Macleod (collector; Female)."

In addition to her physical discoveries and geographical claims, Olive made other contributions to African knowledge, though not all of them came at the Royal Geographical Society or in the British Museum. Mr. Percy Waldram analyzed some of her photographs of native huts and included them in his book *Structural Mechanics* about how tribal architecture echoed the perfect forms of the natural world. The least expected thing to happen—though she found it quite funny—was that a new species of African rat they had sent back from the bush was going to be named for her. Olive suspected Mr. Talbot's influence in pushing for this. So much was changing for her. She thought of her life before Africa, and it seemed almost unrecognizable.

As Olive wrote her book, she was still speaking before explorer groups and working with the British Museum in the cataloging of some of the treasures she had brought back. All of these activities helped her remember things. She went through her photos, her diaries, and consulted new friends to best re-create her trip. She didn't remember everything, and sometimes even her own accounts differed, but she had enough facts—and enough imagination—to tell the story she needed to. After all, she had been there.

As Olive went through all of her diaries, she read over hundreds of pages that described the events of each particular day she spent preparing for and traveling in Africa. The squid in the sea, the Black Magira, all the way to dear Josephine—all had their place in her words. But for all the wonderful variety of the details of her trip, each diary entry had one thing in common: They were all—every single one—addressed as a letter to Boyd, who was dead. They were filled with other words that Olive read once more. Some of the entries brought her right back to when she wrote them.

June 30, 1910

Best beloved
    The last day of June, but to me it seems as if all life had stopped still when I heard that yours had on the 24th of May.
    It is Spring that is unfulfilled.—The measurelessness of Time gives one a slight foreknowledge of Eternity, for to live it has seemed longer than my longest time gauge and yet Time has not moved.
    Oh Boyd I feel you with me again tonight—first distant across the room—now wrapt in your arms. Beloved—I love you. I love you.
                                Yours through Eternity
                                      Olive:

July 26, 1910

Boyd darling

Gradually I become sentient again, for I had gone back to the old stage of numbness. It saves a lot of pain, but the glory of your love goes too—Shall I find you—or is it not to be for a while yet? It would be cowardly to seek it, but I long for our reunion—all the same I am a physical coward and you must come to meet me and help me at the hour of death.

Goodnight.

July 29, 1910

Most beloved Boyd

I am so utterly tired that I must just shut my eyes and be in the dark—be with me.

August 7, 1910

Dearest Boyd

I feel that you are welcoming me to Africa with a smile—for there we shall be alone together, you and I.

I am coming.

August 29, 1910

Dearest Boyd

It is so soothing being in the country which meant so much to you, but oh do I so long for you to be here to show it to me. I hear a

*voice saying you are here—I know it Boyd, but my faith is weak—
help me—*

⸺⸺⸺✦⸺⸺⸺

September 12, 1910

My best Beloved
    *When shall we be together again? I am getting everything I can out
of life because to do otherwise would prove me unworthy of your love,
but it seems so empty all the time—and life is only a journey to me, I
long to reach the destination where you await me.*

⸺⸺⸺✦⸺⸺⸺

October 3, 1910

Dearest beloved Boyd
    *It gave me such joy yesterday when you came to me though somehow
you seemed pained to me—am I doing anything you dislike which delays our reunion?*

Yours eternally
Olive:

After Olive returned, a story was syndicated to American newspapers
recounting her journey. Titled "Come Bid Me Farewell in My Lonely
Grave," the full-page story was illustrated with an eerie drawing of Olive
reaching into the jungle to touch the spectre of Boyd Alexander. In the
article, "It seemed as though the spirit hand of her murdered betrothed
was leading her, directing her progress through streams and jungles." The
writer claimed that Olive, who was "betrothed" to Boyd, had a dream just
before his death where he seemed to call her to Africa.

In all of her diaries, Olive insisted that only one of these things was true.

When her diary finally ended—in the middle of her second African notebook, just after visiting his grave site—Boyd had become more of a listener in Olive's work, as she recounted her amazing adventures each day. He seemed, slowly, to finally disappear.

Olive's book, *Chiefs and Cities of Central Africa: Across Lake Chad by Way of British, French, and German Territories* (1912), was largely an extension of her diaries. Rich with excellent detail, fascinating description, and a full-size map in the back, the book was very well received. She was as good as her word about not mentioning her private affairs. In her personal account of her incredible African journey, she mentioned Boyd Alexander only three times, all of them professional references to his work only.

Olive did not mention his death, or why she was there, or what he meant to her, even once.

One day, as Olive worked, writing and transcribing and bringing things to life, she stopped to look at the mail. She saw an envelope. Her breath caught in her throat.

In the pile of mail was a letter, and a name, that she never expected to see again.

30

THE LIGHTHOUSE

April 1923, Granada, Spain:
A Famous Author Visits Olive

The little black dog was growling quite viciously at Virginia Woolf. The author laughed, recrossed her legs on the deep chair, and made a face at the little monarch whose domain she was obviously impinging on. The dog immediately bolted away on tiny feet that knew a perfect path through the towers of books and other odd treasures that were stacked on the Oriental rug.

Virginia sat back with her tea and looked around her. The sitting room was a panopticon of Arab and primitive delights. It was unkempt—a disaster, really—but in a way that was rather comforting. Shawls were thrown over chairs, books were piled everywhere, and a strange instrument that looked like a guitar leaned against a wall. Interesting curios filled every available space; there was a bronze bust up on the top shelf. Virginia saw beads, and even a giant drum with some photos scattered across it. There were small dark splotches on the drum itself that were probably paint. In the corner, propped up like a mop, was a rifle.

She looked around for her book.

Virginia missed her own dog terribly. She and her husband, Leonard, were in Spain for a month on holiday. After Madrid, they had come to Granada to meet a man who was a friend of a friend. This man had read Leonard's book on Africa—which of course was quite good—and wanted to meet its author. In the back-and-forth of arranging the trip, they realized that the man's wife—whose name was Olive—was a distant cousin of Virginia's! With all these connections at play, the Woolfs decided to stay two days before their next stop in the Sierra Nevada.

The home itself was a most quaint but-and-ben—a two-roomed brick cottage in the Scottish style located in a beautifully rustic stretch of country. When they first arrived, Virginia found the whole area to be remarkably picturesque. The Spanish climate was intoxicating, which helped the whole affair a great deal. Situated in the hills above Granada proper, the house overlooked the most beautiful irrigated fields and had a wild garden out back. Given the altitude, the air seemed to sway about them. It felt as if they were on some mysterious island.

In the next room Leonard was quarreling with Olive's husband. Olive explained that though her husband had a lingering illness from Africa, he certainly loved to talk about the place. Virginia overheard the phrase "balance of power" and decided to leave them to it. There was a small corridor connecting the two rooms, and the dog went in to investigate.

Olive came in with more tea, and Virginia regarded her in sharper focus. She was Scottish, and a gentlewoman: clean, discreet, and shabby. Virginia was struck by her blue eyes, which were like those of their shared cousin, Mary Margaret Vaughn. Olive seemed like a woman of character. Virginia dubbed her, much to her host's chagrin, "lord of the Scottish Isles."

Olive left again to check on her husband. It was then that Virginia noticed an artist's easel in the opposite corner of the room, almost as if it were hiding. She walked over to it. On the white canvas, a landscape was starting to take shape, with green and blue. Virginia wondered who had made it.

She turned to see Olive walk back in. The men were with her, obviously having reached a friendly stalemate. Virginia smiled.

"Who's the artist?" she asked.

"My husband," replied Olive. "Charlie."

WHILE WRITING HER BOOK in 1911, Olive heard from a friend that Charles Temple was on leave in London. She found out where he was staying and wrote him a short letter asking him to dinner at Vinters.

He never replied.

Olive sat down and wrote him again immediately. She had never been one to go unanswered or let things be. Still, she never expected him to write back. Not him.

But this time he did respond. He felt that he couldn't say no to the woman who had walked across Africa. "It was kismet," he said. They had dinner together. A few days later they were engaged. And in three weeks' time they were quietly married at Boxley near Maidstone.

Once Olive finished her book, Charlie proofread it, though she didn't always follow his suggestions—they moved to Nigeria and she stayed with him at Government House. Olive became an active part of the government. They traveled all over western, northern, and southern Africa, exploring new lands, tribes, and animals. They collaborated on the book *Notes on the Tribes, Provinces, Emirates and States of the Northern Provinces of Nigeria* (1919), which was written by Olive and edited by him. They continued to send artifacts to the British Museum. They even procured important wax cylinder recordings of native African music. Olive's photographs, many from her first expedition, were reprinted widely before finding a home in the Bodleian Library in Oxford. Charlie began to paint.

They had many adventures together. They were in Marrakech during World War I and in Monaco for the end of it. Sometimes they were together, sometimes Olive would come back alone to London to see her friends and family. Olive didn't think of it as a second chance, but more like the most unexpected corner of all.

Then Charlie got sick, and they had to leave his job in Nigeria. They moved back to England, but the climate was too damp for him. So they went to Spain. Sir Reginald visited once, but was, in Olive's words, "horrified" at their choice of residence.

They bought a vineyard and tended a garden. They helped the local poor, some of whom lived in caves. Flora and the family came to visit once a year. Olive said this time "was the heaven of our lives." Soon after the Woolfs left, Virginia wrote a novel, *To the Lighthouse,* set on the Isle of Skye that had two characters by the names of Lily Briscoe and Charles Tansley.

Six years later Charlie died of angina. The city of Granada was so grateful to him that it provided the plot for his grave. Many of the poor people the Temples had helped came to the service to honor him, saying that their father was gone. Olive stayed in Spain. She would not let others pity her.

Olive had taken to writing short stories. Some took place in Africa, some in Spain, and at least one in a magical version of Nigeria. One story involves a Colonel C who unfortunately has gout and walks with a cane. He complains a great deal to his wife, who can't understand many of his very particular habits. While traveling, they come across a Mr. B, who has married an old friend of Mrs. C. He is described in the story as the owner of a considerable ostrich. There is also a German professor, a female doctor, and a bishop, but they are ancillary to the plot, which involves taking Colonel C to a hotel with a rejuvenating hot spring in hopes of healing him. Mrs. C spends most of the story trying to do so, with Mr. B fading into the background with his own wife and children.

After Charlie's death, Olive took over guardianship of a four-year-old girl, blond-haired Mary Northcote, a relative on her mother's side. They traveled the world together to London, Gibraltar, Australia, India, and New Zealand. They even summered a few times at Swifts Place, enjoying sunny afternoons around the little replica of Lake Chad.

THE TALBOTS LIVED IN Nigeria and both wrote books, separately and together. In 1923 P. A. Talbot's *Life in Southern Nigeria* revealed much of his life as an administrator before he traveled with Olive. In 1897 the British sent an expedition to Udung-Uko, a small settlement of natives. A crime had taken place: The second son of Chief Osung Atanang Oron had killed one of his father's wives after accusing her of being a wizard. The wife was pregnant. The man cut the baby out of her belly and sliced off its head. Mr. Talbot was sent in and arrested the man, who was then sentenced to death by hanging.

When the chief heard this news, he said that if the white man was going to hang his son, he would take measures to prevent it. All his people stood with him. Everything was in place for a very ugly uprising.

But Mr. Talbot had a plan. He invited Chief Oron and his followers to the nearby village of Oro, where he fed them, entertained them, and engaged them in conversation. It was a pleasant time and the chiefs were well satisfied.

As they ate and drank, Chief Oron had no idea that at that same time Mr. Talbot had arranged for the chief's son to be hanged until he was dead.

Afterward, when the body had been buried, Mr. Talbot told the chief to his face what had happened.

"You shall see what will happen in consequence of this!" spat Chief Oron. He was so incensed that he immediately ordered that Mr. Talbot be killed and then skinned.

The next several days were ones of great tension and tragedy. The appointed assistant clerk of courts for the area, a native named Etetim Ene Okom, was killed and his body cut up and distributed to all the neighboring villages as a warning. The chief's followers also marched upon the courthouse and burned it down.

Mr. Talbot and another sixty soldiers arrived to establish peace. He tried to persuade the guilty villagers to surrender. When that failed, Mr. Talbot looked around, trying to think of a way to quell the uprising without making it worse. He tried a surprise tactic: He rounded up the neighboring chiefs, except Chief Oron, and had them executed on the spot. He then appointed a new agent to be stationed there. Chief Oron and his followers made no trouble after that.

As a young officer, Mr. Talbot specialized in being called into any situation that needed a swift, if sometimes merciless, hand. When medicine men were accused of attacking British forces with thunder and lightning, Mr. Talbot stepped in to stop them with his own knowledge of tribal magical rituals. He also dealt with secret societies, such as the *Ogboni,* which he found stretched across even the most diverse and hostile tribes. According to Mr. Talbot, Africa, in spots, was far more united than anyone had guessed.

Mr. Talbot had been threatened so many times by local chiefs that he said it would be too tedious to tell of the many attempts to poison him. Calabashes meant for him were found filled with deathly toxins; one chief even poisoned a chicken that he presented to Mr. Talbot as a dash. In Nigeria he was a marked man.

P. A. Talbot died in 1945. His wife established The Amaury Talbot Prize for African Anthropology, still being given annually to esteemed works on Africa with a prize of £750. In 2007 the winner was David Pratten's *The Man-Leopard Murders: History and Society in Colonial Nigeria,* published by Edinburgh University Press.

When Olive published her book about her journey, she included a photo of her dear companions the Talbots, smiling, sitting side by side atop a slain elephant that looked like a pile of gray mud.

SIR REGINALD MACLEOD, the chief of Clan MacLeod, died in Dunvegan Castle in 1935, at the age of eighty-eight. When his wife, Agnes, died earlier in 1921, the papers said he was heartbroken: "Theirs was a true lovers' romance, without a quarrel, and without a hard word." The papers claimed that she would watch him come up the long drive to Vinters from the front porch, a half mile away.

On May 14, 1936, Flora was at Dunvegan when she received an unwelcome telegram: Her sister Olive was very ill. Flora wired back: "Shall

I come?" but the answer was reassuring: It was not urgent. Nonetheless Flora flew the next day from Glen Brittle to London to Madrid. When she arrived at the airport, the first thing she did was call Granada, where Olive was now living in a little boardinghouse. The person on the line had good news: There was an improvement in Olive's condition, and coming by train would be fine. There was no urgency.

When the train arrived at Granada, Flora was met by the manager of the boardinghouse. He said that Olive died twenty minutes ago.

Flora was told that her sister died peacefully and without pain. Olive had known her sister was coming and had given orders to light a fire in the guest bedroom. When they tried to give Olive some supper overnight, she said: "Oh, don't bother."

At her funeral, which was held the next day, flowers covered her coffin. Olive had always loved their variety in bloom and their strength when not. Flora wept bitterly, not only for the loss of her sister but because she remembered all the times she thought she had been cruel to her. As she gathered up Olive's papers, which included piles of correspondence, stories, and two little notebooks, Flora found letters that she had given Olive some time ago. They were from Boyd. After the time of their first meeting, after Olive said no to him, Flora took it upon herself to write to Boyd. Flora explained some things about her sister and urged Boyd to have faith in her. Though Flora believed she was doing the right thing, when Olive found out about the secret letter, she was livid. Flora wasn't sure if she ever forgave her. Flora gave her the letters much later, including Boyd's reply.

December 5 & 10, 1908

My dear Mrs. Flora Walter,

    Your kind & welcome letter has given me much comfort. I had a letter from Olive a few days ago. A postscript to it upset all the other part of the letter, clearly skewing her state of mind.—I think you will agree with me that time is the only thing which will make her decide as to where her own happiness lies. I admire her immensely for her great sense of duty (truly a Scotch characteristic) but it pains me when I hear her talk of self-sacrifice.

As regards the expedition itself, there was a time when I could have drawn back, but now it is too late. The game must be played out.

The expedition is a dangerous one and I somehow feel that it is only fair I should tell you so. Anyway, you may be sure I shall do my best to come back safe & sound for Olive's sake. I feel very depressed . . . home does not improve my state of mind.

My collector leaves tomorrow & I on the 12th. I shall write to Olive before I go. Would it be too much to ask you to write to me at San Thomé?—to tell me how she is going on. I shall probably be there till the end of February and then I shall leave directions for letters to follow me.

You ask me how long I shall be away? That is a difficult question to answer just now. . . . I shall make it as short as possible.

Olive will never leave my mind—I shall always see her close to me.

Your friend,
Boyd Alexander

Olive was laid to rest next to her husband in perfect concord. Her diaries ended up in Dunvegan Castle on the Isle of Skye, locked away for decades. Letters to the dead have nowhere to go.

Mary Northcote and Olive's dog watched as the Moorish treasures were packed up or discarded. The painting she loved was packed off to be hung in the library at Dunvegan. With a civil war looming in Spain, Flora tried to imitate her sister and gave money to all of Olive's servants and friends in the area. The dog was then given his little taste of poison. Then Flora went home to Scotland, taking Mary with her.

Flora MacLeod became the first woman chief of Clan MacLeod in 1937. There was opposition to this, of course. She campaigned that "it was better to have a woman who knew Dunvegan, lived there and was a dedicated servant of the community, than an absentee Australian whose nearest link with the castle stretched back 300 years." She had an unprecedented and beloved rule, uniting clan members through goodwill trips all over the world, many of them with Mary. Flora was made a Dame Commander of the British Empire in 1953. She remained chief until her death in 1976. A full-size portrait of her draped majestically in the clan yellow-and-black tartan greets visitors at Castle Dunvegan, along with the motto, "Hold Fast."

ON NOVEMBER 29, 1938, Flora MacLeod was only one year into her tenure as clan chief when she was driving very fast in the dead of night on the Isle of Skye. As she got closer to Dunvegan, she saw smoke looming over the darkness.

Her castle was on fire.

Flora pushed her foot down and went even faster. She was in Aberdeenshire when she got the telegram that a fire had started in the south wing and was burning unabated. No one had been injured. She instead thought of the castle, the ancient symbol of her people. She thought of all the things it held: the records, relics, and artwork, all priceless in one way or another.

She thought of the Fairy Flag.

She pulled up near the castle. There were reporters outside, so she killed the headlights and made her way to the back entrance. As clan chief, Flora always had time to tell a story to the public. But not tonight. She went to a back entrance and gave a single, tiny knock. The signal was heard, and the door opened. She was quickly pulled inside.

Flora MacLeod walked among the embers. The new addition was destroyed, but damage to the Fairy Tower was limited. Flora walked through the room where she had told stories to Olive by the firelight. She could almost see her there. Only one painting had been destroyed.

Flora was told how the people of the island, including two hundred men and some nurses, had formed bucket brigades to put out the blaze. Some even risked their lives to run into the castle and save its treasures.

"And the flag?" she asked.

It was safe. When the man who rescued it carried it over the burning threshold, people said the fires receded.

None of this surprised Flora.

When she finally confronted the press, Flora said: "I have not made any plans on purpose because the experience of a long life [tells me] it is a great mistake to try and act too quickly. Poor castle, I have to say, though I hate saying it, that it will be a very long time before it is habitable again."

She paused, her heart in her throat.

"I shall never forget what we owe the people of Skye," Flora said.

The press was most concerned about the flag. There were as many versions of the Fairy Flag story as there were members of Clan MacLeod, but no one seemed to care which one was right—only that it survived.

A few years later, during World War II, Dame Flora wrote Prime Minister Churchill and said she was willing to wave the flag off the White Cliffs of Dover if a German victory looked likely. She never had to, but she was true to her promise to the people of Skye. She cut off small pieces of the flag to send to Scottish soldiers as they fired on German bombers or zigzagged over the skies of London. They kept the pieces in their wallets. The cut-out squares seen in the flag today, as it hangs in Dunvegan Castle, are proof of that.

In the 1920s, Sir Reginald took the Fairy Flag to the Department of Textiles in the Victoria and Albert Museum in London to have it mounted in its current frame. The noted archaeologist Alan B. Wace, who worked on the Tutankhamen treasures, took great interest in the relic and gave it a thorough examination. When Sir Reginald returned, Wace told him that he believed the flag to have once belonged to King Harald III of Norway, who had taken it from the Middle East—a theory he proved via the composition of the silk, which had probably been woven in Syria.

"Mr. Wace, you may believe that," Sir Reginald replied, "but I know that it was given to my ancestor by the fairies."

"Sir Reginald," said Mr. Wace, "I bow to your superior knowledge."

THE LAST KING
OF DAR FUR

*May 1916: The British Army Prepares to Wage War on
the Stronghold of Ali Dinar in el-Fachir, Dar Fur*

Ali Dinar's power had grown in the East. Though he had stayed out of the Great War, he had stopped paying his annual tribute to the British. There were hints that he was pledging support to the Ottoman Empire, and perhaps even to the Germans. There was great fear—real or imagined—that he was going to invade the Sudan. In the early hours of May 15, 1916, the British, under Lt. Col. Philip Kelly, mounted a force of some two thousand troops, including sixty mounted scouts, heavy machine guns, and the usual manner of support, including members of the vaunted Camel Corps, riding high on their dromedary steeds, loaded with water, supplies, and rifles. The corps' scarves were wrapped over their shoulders, neck, and heads so that only their eyes could be seen. The big guns were loaded on mule carts. Everyone else rode and marched through the blazing emptiness of the Sudan.

For days the force moved forward, capturing outlying villages with little or no resistance. Kelly had to send a small force to secure the local water source, but it was not difficult. All that was left was el-Fachir, sitting flat on the desert with a small peak at its back. There were some palm trecs, but the sprawling conglomerate of low buildings seemed at first uninspiring. Kelly was conscious that he was one of the first white men to see the city. He wondered where Ali Dinar was—in the shimmering buildings preparing his plans or out with his troops on his rumored white camel? Where was the infidel monster, and what plans had he made for them?

When the British advanced on the city, the Furians had dug themselves into trenches. British Intelligence had told Kelly that the Fur Army could put eight hundred regular cavalry, three thousand regular infantry with rifles, and perhaps up to two thousand irregular spearmen into the field. "But," concluded the report, these natives were "very badly trained and ill-equipped with ammunition."

The British moved slowly, expecting a trench war. They started to prepare their firing orders for a by-the-books, methodical operation when the Furians, screaming at the top of their lungs, sprang out of their trenches and attacked the invading British. Some of the natives had long rifles and some were stripped to the waist and held swords. Kelly watched the wave of brown men, their voices rushing to a swelling wave, pour out toward him.

He gave the order to fire.

The machine gun was placed on a slight rise and required four men to operate. As it whirred to life, its operators did not have to crank or even aim. They merely pushed it in one direction or another. One man held up the rolling strap of ammunition—long and flat—that was being fed into the water-cooled machine. The spent cartridges hissed and popped out onto the sand below. The gun could fire upward of six hundred rounds per minute. This was the famed Maxim gun. Kelly's forces had twelve of them.

The British had used the Maxim throughout Africa mostly as a persuasive agent of peacekeeping. One burst of it across the tops of some huts would scare an entire tribe into submission. There was never a real reason to actually fire it.

The guns were spitting and sparking. No one could see the bullets, just the Furian men, in turbans and belts, being bent in sudden, unnatural ways as they stood apparently suspended in the air, shaking, before falling down to the blood-striped sand in a matter of seconds. The machine guns kept firing and sounded a steady mechanical drone. The Furians did not stop. They kept coming. When the guns finally stopped, smoking and searingly hot to the touch, the Furians had been annihilated. Colonel Kelly surveyed the field. Most of the dead were piled close to the trenches they had burst from, but a few had gotten to within ten or fifteen yards of the guns before they were bowled over. Kelly thought this impressive.

The British casualties were three officers wounded and five others killed. The Camel Corps was dispatched to investigate the trenches. Many Furians had retreated amid the smoke back to el-Fachir, presumably to Ali Dinar, who had not yet been seen on the battlefield. The British moved closer and prepared for another attack. At three o'clock the next morning, a fresh surge of Fur horsemen and infantry pushed out of the city. The British fired star flare shells into the sky, illuminating their enemies in an eerie glow. The Maxims took advantage of the light, and ten minutes later the attack dissolved. Both sides seemed to be preparing for a fresh assault when a high, whistling sound was heard in the air.

As dawn broke, an explosion burst out of the back of the city. The Furian cavalry, some two thousand strong, had been waiting there undetected. They had just been hit by a bomb.

Some of them pointed to the sky.

Out of the smoke of the explosion soared a B.E.2c biplane, its lone machine gun chattering, piloted by a nineteen-year-old British lieutenant named John Slessor. The clunky aircraft pulled up as Slessor dropped another twenty-pound bomb to devastating, fiery effect. The Furians were scrambling: There was a devil in the sky.

Slessor zoomed over the horsemen, releasing a third bomb that bowled over clumps of riders and horses like they were toy soldiers. The ground below imploded with holes in the sand. From the edge of the chaos, Slessor could see a large man on horseback directing the others. He was on a white camel. When Slessor saw the glint of his sword, he knew who he was looking at.

Slessor pulled the plane slowly over as it gave a buzzing drone. He saw Ali Dinar dismounting his camel to get onto a mule. Slessor dropped his bomb. Its blast tore the camel to pieces, hurling the sultan to the ground and sending his army fleeing. As Slessor pulled his plane back, he saw that Dinar had turned and shouldered a rifle.

Slessor heard a zing and felt a sharp, slicing pain in his leg. The plane lurched; the rudder controls had also been hit. Slessor saw Dinar ride off, but he was out of bombs and knew he had to turn back immediately. He gritted his teeth and flew the plane to Abiad, six hours away, for eighty miles, with a Remington bullet in his leg.

At ten o'clock in the morning, Kelly and his men walked into el-Fachir. All that were left were women, children, and old men. Ali Dinar himself had escaped. With approximately fifteen hundred men, he stole across the desert for almost two days to get to the foothills of Jebel Marra.

Meanwhile the British were exploring the mysterious el-Fachir. The sultan's two-story palace was a work of art, with fish grottos, beautiful gardens, and remarkable ebony trellises. The quarters for his harem had silver sand dusted over the floors. The air was perfumed with spices.

The palace records were meticulous and revealed that Ali Dinar had 120 sons. His number of daughters was less clear. He had also collected quite a few amazing relics, including the latest musical records and modern photographs. He had a luxury motorcar and a full-size steamroller with a comfortable armchair mounted at the top. Some of the palace men told the British that Ali Dinar was furious when he bought the car because there was nowhere to drive it. The steamroller he could drive anywhere.

A week or so later Kelly received a letter from Ali Dinar himself, who was in the countryside with his troops. Dinar renounced his sultanate and requested that he be allowed to live with his family quietly on his lands. Kelly accepted his surrender but insisted that Dinar and his family be sent into safe exile. Dinar agreed but requested that it be after the rains. When Dinar wrote again, explaining that he was having a hard time convincing all of his men, the British thought he was playing for time.

After escaping el-Fachir, Ali Dinar and his men went to Deriba Lake to consult the oracle there. But when the prediction there was most unwelcome, they rode out to Kulme, a narrow pass that would provide some cover in case the plane returned. With a few of his sons, Dinar made plans, drank coffee, and said his daily prayers. He sent letters to el-Fachir but wasn't sure how long he could keep it up. By the time the British finally caught up to him, most of Dinar's army had become refugees. His last remaining warriors engaged the small British scouting force over a series of ridges, exchanging shots only when the other side was visible. When the shooting stopped, the British found Ali Dinar, strong and dignified, with a bullet drilled into his forehead, lying on the ground. His sons surrendered and laid their father, the last sultan of Dar Fur, on a rug in the sand. The ranking British officer called for a photograph to be taken.

On April 18, 1910, Ali Dinar had written to his frequent correspondent, the Austrian Rudolf Carl von Slatin. Known as Slatin Pasha, the famous spy was then inspector general of the Sudan in the British colonial administration. In the letter Dinar explained his version of the Boyd Alexander affair. He said that Sultan Assil of Abechir had written to him, saying that an English traveler had arrived in Wadai and desired passage to Dar Fur. Dinar replied that unless the Englishman carried a pass from the governor general, he would have to go another route. But before this letter reached Abechir, Boyd set out on the road to Dar Tama. Dinar believed very strongly that the French had done this on purpose to induce the inhabitants, who were friendly to Dar Wadai, to kill the traveler on his arrival in their country, which they eventually did. He thought the French knew what would happen—and let him go anyway. On July 27 Ali Dinar added:

> My men were there when this murder took place, and they seized two men, and brought them here. I at once crucified them in the marketplace as an exemplary punishment for others. I hung on their necks a short statement of their crimes for the information of the public.

After the French again attacked, Ali Dinar called for a jihad against them. "God will recompense you," he said, "and grant you the pleasures of Paradise. . . . Be sure of victory and stand fast in fighting the infidels."

On December 18, 1919, a small package was delivered to the Alexander family home at Wilsley. Enclosed was Boyd Alexander's signet ring, which had been missing since his disappearance and death. It was returned by the Sudan government in Khartoum.

IN TRYING TO SOLVE THE MYSTERY of who killed Boyd Alexander, I was able to locate a single official file titled "Boyd Alexander" from the days of the Anglo-Egyptian rule in the Sudan. I had no idea what was in it, but its very existence was mysterious, and thus full of possibility. The file is located—after many moves over the years—in the National Archives at Khartoum. The archives do not have an email address, a phone number, or even a fully working website. For help, I contacted many people, including Dr. Ali B. Ali-Dinar, senior lecturer at the Department of Africana Studies at the University of Pennsylvania and a highly respected voice in modern Sudanese scholarship and outreach. In addition to teaching and publishing, he has spoken out on several contemporary issues affecting Africa, including the revelation that African refugees continue to be auctioned off as slaves in Libya today.

He is also the grandson of Ali Dinar of el-Fachir. When I asked him if he had any advice for getting into the archives at Khartoum, Dr. Dinar told me that he had not been to the National Archives for decades. "Unfortunately," he said, "I don't have contacts there, nor a reliable person whom I could recommend now." But he volunteered that his niece, a student, was going to go back to the Sudan soon to resume her studies and could check for me.

At the time we were corresponding, a massive sit-in in support of a democratic Sudan camped in Khartoum around the army headquarters, which is next to the archives. On June 3, 2019, the Rapid Support Forces, a government paramilitary group, dispersed the protesters by killing thirty-five of them, dumping their bodies into the Nile, and raping at least seventy women.

Dr. Dinar wrote me again a few weeks later. He said, "My niece has arrived, away from the 'inferno' in Sudan." He promised that "when she makes it back (we don't know when)" she would check on the archives for me.

"Don't bother," I said.

I knew at that moment that this story was over because it was about to repeat itself. Not exactly in the same way, but more like the faint indentations on a page from the writing ahead of it. As Dr. Dinar's words reminded me, it is that part of the story—the echoing traumatic one, of the Sudan, of Africa—that persists like some unappeasable ghost in part because of the endless line of men who continue to seek power over their kin.

Notes

The main sources for this story are Olive MacLeod's *Chiefs and Cities of Central Africa: Across Lake Chad by Way of British, French, and German Territories* (Edinburgh: W. Blackwood and Sons, 1912); the Olive Macleod collection of papers and letters at Dunvegan Castle on the Isle of Skye; NRAS 2950/4/2119/1–6; Boyd Alexander's diary as reprinted in *Boyd Alexander's Last Journey* (London: Edward Arnold, 1912); Anne Wolridge Gordon, *Dame Flora* (London: Hodder and Stoughton, 1974); Olive MacLeod, "A Romantic Quest," *London Magazine*, August, 1911, 849–860, and the various newspaper accounts, books, and correspondence surrounding not only Olive's journey but African context in 1911.

The MacLeod papers, especially Olive's diaries, are the primary source for a few chapters of this story. The overall collection encompasses a wide variety of documents including letters, diaries, telegrams, short stories, and even sheet music. They comprise hundreds of documents. Because they are grouped according to the National Register of Archives for Scotland (NRAS) records, I will cite them as such so that anyone who wants to may locate them as easily as possible. They are cited as MacLeod Papers at the beginning of each section of notes, followed by their specific number. They are identified in the text by date. The papers are unnumbered, so are cited only by group. These papers are all located in Dunvegan Castle on the Isle of Skye.

Since this story is meant to be understood from Olive's point of view, to preserve her voice as much as possible, I have at times used her language directly from her diaries and book. These instances are sourced in the notes but not in the text itself because I want the reader—as much as possible—to *hear* her tell her own story rather than *see* her words as some sort of evidence. This is Olive's story. The emotions she expresses come directly from her diaries as much as possible.

Notes are used mostly for dialogue or for sources other than Olive. All dialogue is sourced. At times I have transferred the dialogue from what Olive remembers a person saying to the person actually saying it—if only to keep the narrative moving and so as not to subject the reader to an entire book about a young woman in Africa reading and writing by lamplight. If there is a large block of dialogue, the note will be at the end and will be assumed to include everything before it. There are a (very) few spots where I have added short dialogue to keep a conversation going, but the words are never factual or emotional, only transitional and limited to a few. This is a story; it is not a transcript.

To re-create Africa, I have consulted Olive's writings first to be as close as possible to her own experience. To fill out more general gaps I have studied photographs and diaries of other explorers. For turns of phrase and language, I have referenced (and in some cases used) works contemporary to the times.

Abbreviations:

Olive MacLeod, *Chiefs and Cities of Central Africa* = *Chiefs*

MacLeod of MacLeod Papers, National Register of Archives for Scotland = MacLeod Papers, NRAS

PROLOGUE

The material in this chapter is from the MacLeod Papers, NRAS 2950/4/2117/1–24.

1. THE FAIRY FLAG

There are numerous versions of the legend of the Fairy Flag. For this particular version I consulted, in order of relevance: A. H. Malan, "Dunvegan Castle," *Pall Mall* 24 (May–Aug. 1901), 5–19; Gordon, *Dame Flora* 206–207; Brenda MacLeod, *Tales of Dunvegan* (Stirling, Scotland: Eneas Mackay, 1950), 2–17; "The Fairy Flag of the MacLeods," *Dundee Evening Telegraph*, August 21, 1935, 10. The details of the castle are from the *Pall Mall* article. The background of their relationship is from *Dame Flora*. The witch's prophecy is detailed in "Extraordinary Fulfillment of a Highland Prophecy," *Rutland Echo and Leicestershire Advertiser,* June 7, 1878, 10, and reprinted widely elsewhere. This chapter is not meant to portray a historical moment but rather the story itself as it was shared and understood by the sisters—"more or less."

2 *a* Bean Sith*:* Donald Alexander Mackenzie, *Wonder Tales from Scottish Myth and*

Legend (London: Blackie and Son, 1917), 193–194. This is the origin of the word "banshee."

3 *Dauntless thy following:* "The Cradle Spell of Dunvegan." Alasdair Irvine, "The Fairy Flag of Dunvegan 'Isle of Skye,'" scotlandinmyheartsite.wordpress.com, February 25, 2016. (Thanks to bethsnotesplus.com for the transcription.)

6 *the west turret:* Alexander Mackenzie, *The Prophecies of the Brahan Seer (Coinneach Odhar Fiosaiche),* (Inverness: A. & W. Mackenzie, 1882), 47–49. Bruce Munro, "Brahan Seer: The Scot Who Could See the Future," bbc.co.uk, July 7, 2011. The Brahan Seer does not seem to have been a real person, though there is an earlier historical candidate named Coinneach Odhar who was suspected of witchcraft. More likely, the figure and his prophecies are the opportune product of Scotland's longstanding fear of witchcraft.

2. THE PARTY GIRL AND THE NATURALIST

The details of the London Zoo are from Isobel Charman, *The Zoo: The Wild and Wonderful Tale of the Founding of London Zoo* (New York: Viking, 2016). Olive's visit to the zoo is from the MacLeod Papers, NRAS 2950/4/2116/1–15. The details of Olive's social life are taken from Violet Bonham Carter, *Lantern Slides,* ed. Mark Bonham Carter and Mark Pottle (London: Weidenfeld & Nicolson, 1996), 43, 58; Lawrence Evelyn Jones, *An Edwardian Youth* (London: Macmillan, 1956), 217; and Gordon, *Dame Flora*, 61, 76. Olive's visit to Swifts Place and facts about Boyd's life are taken largely from the introduction by his brother Herbert in *Boyd Alexander's Last Journey,* ed. Herbert Alexander (New York: Longmans, Green, 1912), 40–60. Details also from Joan Alexander, *Whom the Gods Love* (London: W&J Mackay Limited, 1977), 198–203; "Mr. Boyd Alexander's Birds," *Clifton Society,* December 29, 1910, 11; W. R. Ogilvie-Grant, "Boyd Alexander and His Ornithological Work," *Ibis*, October 1910, 716–719; "Across Africa," *Belfast Telegraph*, February 9, 1907, 6.

9 *"only bits of paper":* MacLeod Papers, NRAS 2950/4/2116/1–15.

9 *held a knighthood:* "Sir Reginald MacLeod Dead," *Dundee Courier*, August 21, 1935, 5.

11 *"embodiment of repose":* Gordon, *Dame Flora*, 62.

13 Leaves of Grass: Alexander, *Whom the Gods Love,* 18.

14 *been used as a chapel:* Christopher Hussey, "Wilsley House, Cranbrook, Kent, the Residence of Mr. Herbert Alexander," *Country Life,* August 21, 1920, 240–246.

16 *"the interval of silence":* Boyd Alexander, *From the Niger to the Nile* (London: Edward Arnold, 1907), 253. Boyd's museum is no longer in existence, though some of the birds may still be at the British Museum. Mike Huxley of the Cranbrook Museum and Archives said that he heard that Ianthe Alexander, a relative, inherited the house, sold it, and put things into storage. The book collection was also sold.

16 Olive's birthday: Marquis of Ruvigny and Raineval, *The Jacobite Peerage* (Edinburgh: T. C. & E. C. Jack, 1804), 107. An alternate date of January is given sometimes.

17 *"splendid grit"*: Alexander, *Whom the Gods Love*, 201–202. She writes this to her husband.

18 *in the head:* Ibid., 49–51. I do not know if Boyd told this story at this exact moment, but he did tell (and write) about it.

18–19 *the South Pole:* Ibid., 1.

19 *with enemy soldiers:* Ibid., 13.

20 *"secrets that it hides":* Ibid., 19.

20 *servants at Swifts:* Alexander, *Whom the Gods Love*, 15, 29.

20 *"expects it of me":* Boyd Alexander's Last Journey, 46.

20 *"my bones in Africa":* Ibid.

22 *"African Explorer Murdered":* Dublin Daily Express, May 25, 1910, 5.

3. LEVIATHAN

The facts of Olive's departure and sea voyage are taken from *Chiefs* and the MacLeod Papers, NRAS 2950/4/2118/1–2 and NRAS 2950/4/2119/6. The story of the sea battle is from the same sources. Maps of the time do show both sperm whales and giant squid to have been sighted near the coast of West Africa, directly in the *Dakar*'s path. But actually witnessing a sperm whale fight a giant squid was extremely rare, and there is no corroborating evidence in newspaper accounts or ship records. In one diary Olive refers to it as a "cuttlefish," but changes it in her book. A giant cuttlefish, though native to the African coast, is too small to battle a sperm whale. In reading nearly all her written work, I have found her a very trustworthy source, so I have no reason to believe she is fabricating; at the same time, it makes a terrific beginning to her tale. Information about Forcados is from Binebai Princewill, "Forcados: The Untold Story of Where Nigeria Began," *Gbaramatu Voice*, August 17, 2016, as well as contemporaneous photographs and newspaper articles.

29 *"or the man":* Charles Henry Robinson, *Hausa Grammar with Exercises* (London: Kegan Paul, 1905), 7–8.

30 *grieving young fiancée:* "Fiancee of Famous Explorer," *Dundee Courier*, August 13, 1910, 5.

4. THE ARRIVAL

The primary sources for this chapter are *Chiefs* and MacLeod Papers, NRAS 2950/4/2119/6. The descriptions of Lokoja are from Abdulrazaq Oyeabnji Hamzat, "The Importance of Lokoja in Nigerian History," *Nigerian Voice*, May 18, 2013, nigerianvoice.com; Constance Belcher Larymore, *A Resident's Wife in Nigeria* (New York: E. P. Dutton, 1908), 6–14; and Ifor L. Evans, *The British in Tropical Africa* (New York: Cambridge University Press, 1929), 134–145. The material about Agnes MacLeod is from Gordon, *Dame Flora*, 29–30.

34   *"the boys":* Throughout this book, I have chosen to use the words familiar to Olive and the colonial British in Africa to tell the story from their point of view.

37   *"determined Britannic fashion": Chiefs,* 5.

37   *eye clinic:* Gordon, *Dame Flora*, 29.

37   *paralysis:* Her mother's illness (blindness leading to paralysis) remains unnamed.

38   *collected grasses: Chiefs,* 5.

39   *"Help me":* MacLeod Papers, NRAS 2950/4/2116/1–15.

5. THE PROTECTORATE

The primary information for this chapter is from *Chiefs* and the MacLeod Papers, NRAS 2950/4/2119/6.

41   *"at your disposal":* Ibid., 7.

43   *"fall upon him":* Ibid., 8.

44   *Lee-Enfield:* Bob Campbell, "British Lee Enfield .303 Rifle: The Legendary Smelly," *Gunworld*, March 6, 2018, gunworld.com; Terence Evans, *A Guide to the Lee-Enfield .303* (Amazon Digital, 2017), 694–720. The Lee-Enfield Rifle Association was also helpful (lee-enfield.org). Thanks also to Sean Mulder and Dean Valore for further details about firing this weapon.

45   *"climate affects the eye": Chiefs,* 10.

45   *"in this search":* Ibid., 10.

46   *Sir Frederick Lugard:* M. F. Perham, *Lugard: The Years of Authority, 1898–1945* (New York: Collins, 1960), 23–26, 77.

46   *a small bungalow:* Itodo Daniel Sule, "Mount Patti: The Spot from Where Nigeria Was Named," *Daily Trust*, September 2, 2018, dailytrust.com.ng; Nutase, "Mount Patti—Home to Lord Lugard," *Nairaland*, August, 26, 2014, nairaland.com; Chidi Nkwopara, "A Visit to Lord Lugard's Rest House," *Vanguard*, September 2, 2017; photos on nigeriagalleria.com.

47   *"Niger-area":* This was incorrect; the word "Nigeria" was in use at least forty years previously, but this is the version Olive probably heard. C. C. Ifemesia, "The Country of the Niger River," *Studies in Southern Nigeria History* (London: Frank Cass, 1982), 22.

48   *"for daily choice": Chiefs,* 9.

48   *"Call me Dorry":* I do not know exactly when Olive was granted this luxury, only that it happened sometime in this first part of the trip, so this is an educated guess.

50 *Abbiga:* Steve Kemper, *A Labyrinth of Kingdoms: 10,000 Miles through Islamic Africa* (New York: W. W. Norton & Co., 2012), 218–223; Heinrich Barth, *Travels and Discoveries in North and Central Africa: Timbuktu, Sokoto, and the Niger Basin* (London: Ward, Lock, and Co., 1890), xiii, 386-400; Sulieman, "'A Piece of Black Mahogany,'" 37–51.

50 *"deep-deep":* Chiefs, 9.

51 *"of black mahogany":* M. D. Sulieman, "'A Piece of Black Mahogany' in the Niger-Benue Confluence: The Life of Abubakar Abiga, c.1850 to 1916," *Faculty of Arts and Islamic Studies,* Vol. 1, 1998, 39.

51 *"Should emergencies arise":* Ibid., 11.

52 *first reached England:* "Explorer's Fate," *London Daily News,* May 25, 1910, 4.

52 *and became secluded:* Alexander, *Whom the Gods Love,* 180.

53 *"more than interest":* MacLeod Papers, NRAS 2950/4/2116/1–15.

6. A CORRESPONDENCE, PART 1

The material in this chapter is from the MacLeod Papers, NRAS 2950/4/2117/1–24. Bracketing material is mine using details from the letters.

55 *Mr. Hardy:* Olive never names her suitor other than "GGH" and that he is a "Hardy" and a barrister. Given her location at Eaton Place, there are some extant clues (that I have reproduced), but nothing that I could fully corroborate. By not naming him outright or going into more detail about his family, I also wanted to make a point about how little information Olive gives us sometimes.

7. ON THE HUNT

66 *Like tiddlywinks:* MacLeod Papers, NRAS 2950/4/2119/6.

68 *"someone read it!":* MacLeod Papers, NRAS 2950/4/2119/1–6.

68 *"the insect tribes:"* Ibid.

69 *end of her rifle:* See previous chapter notes on the Lee-Enfield.

70 garri: William R. Bascom, "Yoruba Food," *Africa: Journal of the International African Institute* 21, no. 1 (Jan. 1951): 41–53.

70 The lion hunt: Most of this is cobbled together from Olive's account; William K. Storey, "Big Cats and Imperialism: Lion and Tiger Hunting in Kenya and Northern India, 1898–1930," *Journal of World History,* Fall 1991, 135–173; Kalman Kittenberger, *Big Game Hunting and Collecting in East Africa, 1903–1926* (New York: St. Martin's Press, 1989), 1–24.

72 *desolate landscape:* I have relied mostly on Olive's localized accounts, but when necessary I have consulted photographs of these areas to best re-create 1911 Africa. For

weather conditions, The World Bank's Climate Change Knowledge Portal has deep tools for assessing past climate patterns; I also used local Nigerian newspapers and military records, when available.

73 *"than to the knife": Chiefs*, 29.

74 *Ali Dinar:* L. B. Jureidini, "The Miracles of Ali Dinar," *The Moslem World Vol. XI*, January 1916, 409–414. Dinar's alleged cruelty and his magical power were well-known tropes. Also note that this account was published by the Christian Literature Society for India.

76 *"characteristics of a mule":* Ibid., 38.

77 *called in pidgin English:* Ibid., 41.

78 "Coloured convolvulus": *Chiefs*, 32.

78 *brilliant sapphire:* Ibid., 41.

8. THE GREAT LAMIDO

The main events of this chapter are taken from *Chiefs* and the MacLeod Papers, NRAS 2950/4/2119/6.

83 *"utmost expectations": Chiefs*, 45–46.

84 *"moments of rest":* Ibid., 47.

87 *"hundred and fifty":* Ibid., 50. This dialogue has been adapted from the text.

89 *a small fiery star:* MacLeod Papers, NRAS 2950/4/2119/16.

9. DEVIL IN THE FOREST

The sources for the discovery of the falls are numerous. In addition to *Chiefs* and the MacLeod Papers, NRAS 2950/4/2116/1–15, there is also Olive MacLeod, "Lake Léré and the Discovery of the MacLeod Falls on the Mao Kabi," *Blackwood's Magazine*, July 1911, 35–41.

91 *burning-hot canoe: Chiefs*, 53.

93 *"All is settled":* Ibid., 63.

94 *"have been carried off":* Ibid., 64.

96 *"not very heroic":* Ibid., 69.

97 Violet and the cliff: "Miss Asquith Lost," *Central Somerset Gazette*, September 25, 1908, 6; "Miss Asquith's Adventure," *Manchester Courier*, September 25, 1908, 18; Michael Shelden, "PM's daughter 'jumped off a cliff' after being ditched by Churchill," *Daily Mail*, November 23, 2012, dailymail.co.uk; Michael Selden, *Young Titan* (New York: Simon & Schuster, 2013), 188–191; Violet Bonham Carter, "Winston Churchill As I Knew Him," in *Winston Spencer Churchill: Servant of*

Crown and Commonwealth, ed. James Marchant (London: Eyre and Spottiswoode, 1965), 218–220.

98 *"end was already near": Chiefs*, 70.

99 *"have done me": Chiefs*, 71.

99 *"It was fun":* MacLeod Papers, NRAS 2950/4/2119/16.

10. A CORRESPONDENCE, PART 2

The material in this chapter is from the MacLeod Papers, NRAS 2950/4/2117/1–24, and NRAS 2950/4/2116/1–15. Framing material is mine using details from the letters. The letters in this chapter may not seem to be chronological if you look at the dates, but that is because sometimes Boyd's letters took a month (or more) to reach Olive. I have tried to place the letters in the order of Olive's receipt based on context and reaction.

102 *Savage-Landor:* Arnold Savage Landor was a writer, painter, and explorer who wrote a dozen popular books about his adventures, most notably in Asia.

104 *Baden Powell:* Lt. Gen. Robert Stephenson Baden-Powell wrote *Scouting for Boys* (1908), which led to the formation of independent Scouting groups that would later become the Boy Scouts. In 1910, along with his sister Agnes Baden-Powell, he formed the Girl Guides for girls who were already part of those early Scouting troops.

11. INTO THE SWAMP

110 *unfolded it three times:* This is a guess, since the map that accompanies Olive's book is also folded in thirds, as are most maps this size.

111 *"equal to the long walk": Chiefs*, 72.

113 *"small, small* nama*":* Ibid., 73.

114 *"get down and walk":* Ibid.

117 *"Hippo!":* To get an accurate description of hippos, I observed them at the Cleveland Zoo, looked at African hippo-attack videos, and consulted wildlife photographer Dr. Kevin Kerwin, who has observed them in the wild.

118 *"Two hours:" Chiefs*, 75. This dialogue is adapted from the text.

12. THE TWO LAKES

123 *"an unclothed man carry me": Chiefs*, 80.

123 *"I am Master":* Ibid., 57. I moved this scene up in time, just for ease of narration. Based on comparisons between the diaries and her book, Olive does this herself at times, making it difficult to construct a single timeline.

124 *"that is so":* Robinson and Burdon, *Hausa Grammar with Exercises, Readings, and Vocabularies,* 11, 13.

125 *"will treat you accordingly":* Chiefs, 83.

126 *"within sight of camp":* Ibid., 84.

128 *"his medicines strong":* Ibid., 90.

130 *"he is still alive":* Ibid., 92.

13. THE MAN-LEOPARD

133 *Compagnie française de l'Ouhame et de la Nana:* Adolf Friedrich, *From the Congo to the Niger and the Nile* (Philadelphia: John Winston, 1914), 25.

133 *between four children:* MacLeod Papers, NRAS 2950/4/2119/16.

134 *Curse of Ham:* Gen. 9:20–27; "At the Cape," *Bradford Daily Telegraph,* March 3, 1908; Felicia R. Lee, "From Noah's Curse to Slavery's Rationale," *New York Times,* November 1, 2003, newyorktimes.com.

134 *"Sardines":* Chiefs, 99.

134 *medical manual:* I am reasonably sure that the book Olive refers to is Charles Heaton, *Medical Hints for Hot Climates* (London: W. Thacker, 1897).

136 *"a great medicine":* Chiefs, 100.

136 *"one big man":* MacLeod Papers, NRAS 2950/4/2119/16.

137 *"your while to come":* Ibid.

139 *she used to play: Chiefs,* 102.

140 *"to keep the ladies":* Ibid., 103. There is a chance that what Olive encountered was the infamous secret society known as the "Man-Leopard" cult. See David Pratten, *The Man-Leopard Murders: History and Society in Colonial Nigeria* (Bloomington: Indiana University Press, 2007).

14. A CORRESPONDENCE, PART 3

The material in this chapter is from the MacLeod Papers, NRAS 2950/4/2117/1–24 and NRAS 2950/4/2116/1–15. Framing material is mine using details from the letters.

15. A PAINTING ON A WALL

155 *"party as yours":* Chiefs, 104.

155 *"one big man":* Ibid.

156 *"is expected of me":* Ibid., 107.

157 *"Chorus slower":* Ibid., 119.

159 *"late to go back":* Ibid., 109.

160 *half wheels of skin:* Ibid., 116.

160 *"passes all bearing":* MacLeod Papers, NRAS 2950/4/2119/16.

161 *"victim to a crocodile": Chiefs,* 117. This whole paragraph is unaltered from Olive's words in *Chiefs.*

162 *the fresco:* Ibid., The painting is reproduced, presumably from Mrs. Talbot's sketches, on the cover of Olive's book.

162 *crocodile began pulling the girl:* Ibid.

164 *"you are coming": Chiefs,* 120. This dialogue is adapted from the text.

165 *"all the rest":* Ibid., 126.

166 *"must go home":* Gordon, *Dame Flora,* 44.

16. FORT LAMY

168 *"from Wadai": Chiefs,* 129.

169 *"Colonel Moll":* Ibid.

170 *he was not:* I don't know the exact moment of this realization but hearing it from an official must have been hard to disregard.

171 *Ali Dinar:* Much, if not all, of the French and British thinking about Dinar seemed to be born of religious, racial, and territorial xenophobia. This characterization is portrayed as is in order to preserve Olive's narrative so that we can best understand and question it. See A. B. Theobald, *Alī Dīnār: Last Sultan of Darfur, 1898–1916* (London: Longmans, 1965); J. E. H. Boustead, "The Youth & Last Days of Sultan Ali Dinar: 'A Fur View,'" *Sudan Notes and Records* 22, no. 1 (1939): 149–153; Ali Dinar, "A Fragment from Ali Dinar," *Sudan Notes and Records* 34, no. 1 (June 1953): 114–116; Jacob Slight, "British Perceptions and Responses to Sultan Ali Dinar of Darfur, 1915–16," *Journal of Imperial and Commonwealth History* 38, no. 2 (May 2010): 237–260; L. B. Juredini, "The Miracles of Ali Dinar of Darfur," *Muslim World,* October 1916, 337–447.

171 *account of Boyd's death:* Alexander, *Whom the Gods Love,* 272–276. Alexander quotes from the original French reports. *"The Murder of Boyd Alexander," Northern Whig,* July 27, 1910, 12. "The French have recovered the remains, diary, and papers of the dead officer."

172 *giving the diaries:* The framework for this scene is from *Chiefs,* MacLeod Papers, NRAS 2950/4/2119/1–6, and Alexander, *Whom the Gods Love.* Some of the dialogue has been adapted from the text. Olive writes that the French tell her what happened, give her the diaries, and that she later hears the official report.

172 *the falls:* MacLeod Papers, NRAS 2950/4/2119/16.

174 "La première victoire!" *Chiefs,* 137.

17. A CORRESPONDENCE, PART 4

The material in this chapter is from the MacLeod Papers, NRAS 2950/4/2119/16. Framing material is mine using details from the letters.

180 *little Schipperke puppy:* Alexander, *Whom the Gods Love,* 202. I have placed this story here, as told by Miranda, as an aside to the reader, where it makes the most sense both narratively and chronologically.

18. THE WANDERER

The entirety of this chapter is adapted from Boyd's diary, reprinted in *Boyd Alexander's Last Journey.* I have focused on only the last part of it as I think that would have been of most interest to Olive since it led up to his disappearance. *Boyd Alexander's Last Journey* reproduces most of his diary and is well worth reading in its entirety as a companion to this book. More enterprising readers may seek out the original.

195 *going to Abechir: Boyd Alexander's Last Journey,* 184–185.

196 *"before their time":* Ibid., 216.

198 *"reduced to eight":* Ibid., 248.

198 *captain Fiegenschuh:* "A Grave Military Disaster," *The Scotsman,* December 10, 1910, 8.

200 *"a secret agent": Boyd Alexander's Last Journey,* 270.

202 *"Dear, oh dears!":* Ibid., 286.

202 *"never say die!":* Ibid., 58.

19. THE GREAT GAUARONGA, PART 1

205 *to lower white prestige: Chiefs,* 159.

205 *Rabeh:* Michael M. Horowitz, "Ba Karim: An Account of Rabeh's Wars," *African Historical Studies* 3, no. 2 (1970): 391–402; Kyari Mohammed, "Bornu under Rabih Fadl Allah, 1893–1900: The Emergence of a Predatory State," *Paideuma* 43 (1997): 281–300; "Bloodshed and Rapine in the Central Soudan," *London Daily News,* April 21, 1896, 7; "England and France," *London Evening Standard,* March 31, 1899, 5; "The Death of Rabeh," *Sheffield Daily Telegraph,* May 8, 1912, 6; "In Unknown Lands and Waters," *Northern Whig,* February 17, 1908, 10; "From Private Correspondence," *The Scotsman,* June 2, 1915, 9.

207 *left long alone: Chiefs,* 148. This dialogue is adapted from the text.

208 *"served under Rabeh":* Ibid., 32–33.

209 *"The Magira!":* Ibid., 160. For more on the Magira figure, see Augustin F. C. Holl,

Ethnoarchaeology of Shuwa-Arab Settlements (Lanham, MD: Lexington Books, 2003), 20–23; Annie M. D. Lebeuf, "Women in Political Organization," *Women of Tropical Africa*, ed. Denise Paulme (New York: Routledge, 1963), 105; Barth, *Travels*, 90.

210 *"the Great Chief himself"*: *Chiefs*, 160.

211 *to get let off:* Ibid., 162.

212 Mbang Ngoolo: Ibid., 246.

213 *eunuchs:* See Heidi J. Nast, *Concubines and Power: Five Hundred Years in a Northern Nigerian Palace* (Minneapolis: University of Minnesota Press, 2004), 276; Shaun Marmon, *Eunuchs and Sacred Boundaries in Islamic Society* (Oxford: Oxford University Press, 1995), 33–39, 100; Piotr O. Schotz, *Eunuchs and Castrati: A Cultural History* (Princeton, NJ: Markus Wiener, 2001), 67–77; Murray Gordon, *Slavery in the Arab World* (New York: New Amsterdam Books, 1989), 92-101; Edwin M. Yamauchi, *Africa and the Bible* (Grand Rapids, MI: Baker Academic, 2004), 161–177. The relationship of eunuchs, small boys, and slaves to men of power is a frustrating part of understanding Africa.

214 *Olive stood up:* See Druann Maria Heckert and Amy Best, "Ugly Duckling to Swan: Labeling Theory and the Stigmatization of Red Hair," *Symbolic Interaction* 20, no. 4 (1997): 365–384; Jacky Colliss Harvey, *Red: A History of the Redhead* (New York: Black Dog & Leventhal, 2015).

217 Bata Kuji: *Chiefs*, 170.

217 *the queen mother:* Ibid., 260.

219 *the* Ring: Gordon, *Dame Flora*, 37. Also "The Ring at Bayreuth," *Pall Mall*, August 20, 1896, 1.

220 *"Don't go to Abechir"*: MacLeod Papers, NRAS2950/4/2119/16.

221 "Mais, Madame, elle exagère": *Chiefs*, 179.

221 *"Run away"*: Ibid., 181.

221 *cobra:* Olive identifies it as *Naia nigricollis*.

20. THE GREAT GAUARONGA, PART 2

224 *"almost uncanny"*: *Chiefs*, 182. This dialogue is adapted from the text.

225 *"That's absurd"*: Ibid., 182. Adapted.

226 *something about rest:* Ibid., 185. Adapted.

226 *"feeling very ill"*: Ibid. Adapted.

227 *"bidding of the Sultan"*: Ibid., 186.

227 *"be a mirage"*: Ibid., 187.

227 *sacred ibis*: Ibid., 187.

228 *"those of dysentery"*: Ibid., 188. See Tom Gale, "Hygeia and Empire: The Impact of Disease on the Coming of Colonial Rule in British West Africa," *Transafrican Journal of History* 11 (1982): 80–91.

229 *"what is wrong?"*: MacLeod Papers, NRAS 2950/4/2119/16.

230 *illness seemed very grave: Chiefs*, 189.

230 *dates:* Poisoning dates was apparently a common tactic of assassins. See David Henry Slavin, *Colonial Cinema and Imperial France, 1919–1939: White Blind Spots, Male Fantasies, Settler Myths* (Baltimore: Johns Hopkins University Press, 2001), 42; "The Massacre of the Flatters Expedition," *Dundee Evening Telegraph,* April 18, 1881, 3; "Poisoned Dates for a Woman," *Pall Mall Gazette*, March 17, 1913, 2. This practice is also, of course, fictionalized in the film *Raiders of the Lost Ark* (1982).

230 *"have you been?"*: Ibid., 189.

231 *"is very difficult"*: MacLeod Papers, NRAS 2950/4/2119/16.

21. THE FRENCH REPORT

236 The murder of Boyd Alexander: Alexander, *Whom the Gods Love,* 269–276.

239 *little lords: Chiefs*, 192.

239 "Kai!": Ibid., 244.

240 *a spear:* Ibid., 202. This dialogue has been adapted from the text.

241 *Ali Dinar:* Olive does not mention that she thinks of him at this very moment, but given his strong presence in Boyd's diaries and his possible role in his death, I think she must have quite often. He is not mentioned once in her book, a fact that also invites inquiry.

241 *magic sword:* One of Ali Dinar's swords was auctioned at Sotheby's for £31,250 in 2011. See N. D. Khalili, *Collection of Islamic Art*, vol. 21, D. Alexander, *The Art of War* (London: 1992), cat. no.144, and Howard Ricketts and Philippe Missillier, *Splendeur des Armes Orientales* (Paris, ACTE-EXPO1988), cat. nos. 256 and 257, 317.

242 *"allegiance to her sway": Chiefs*, 204.

242 *"know what that means"*: MacLeod Papers, NRAS 2950/4/2119/16.

22. VALKYRIE

244 *"land of Noah": Chiefs*, 206.

244 *"of human sacrifice"*: Ibid., 206.

245 *the ark:* See "Looking for Eden and the Arks," *Britannia and Eve,* November 1, 1949, 16; A. J. N. Tremearne, *Ban of the Bo Demons and Demon-Dancing in West and North Africa* (New York: Routledge, 1914), 431; P. A. Talbot, "Lake Chad," *Geographical Journal* 38, no. 3 (September 1911): 269–278.

247 the ring: Gordon, *Dame Flora,* 37.

248 *French scientific expeditions:* J. Tilho, "The French Mission to Lake Chad," *Geographical Journal* 36, no. 3 (September 1910): 271–286.

250 *honor of their landing:* Gen. 31:44–36.

250 *into darkness: Chiefs,* 211.

23. THE LAKE OF LONELINESS

251–252 *ward off mosquitoes:* For a good sense of this ongoing battle in historical context, see Arthur E. Horn, "The Control of Disease in Tropical Africa, Part II," *Journal of the Royal African Society* 32, no. 127 (April 1933): 123–134; Gordon Harrison, *Mosquitoes, Malaria, and Man: A History of the Hostilities Since 1880* (New York: Dutton, 1978), 1–20, 220–240.

252 *curled up tight: Chiefs,* 215.

253 *"To return again never":* Sir Walter Scott, "Mackrimmon's Lament," *The Complete Poetical and Dramatic Works of Sir Walter Scott* (London: George Routledge and Sons, 1883), 546. The first two lines read: "MacLeod's wizard flag from the grey castle / sallies."

253 *helmet respectable again: Chiefs,* 217.

254 *of an English bulldog:* Ibid., 218.

254 *were found to be excellent:* Ibid., 219.

255 *"so near it":* MacLeod Papers, NRAS 2950/4/2119/16.

257 *to the father's house: Chiefs,* 226.

258 *"will not bear young":* Ibid., 229.

259 *"didn't own any":* Ibid., 227.

260 *"walk for water":* Ibid., 231.

260 *"one eager to swim":* Homer, *The Odyssey,* trans. S. H. Butcher and A. Lang (New York: Collier, 1909), 81.

263 *came the entire Buduma race: Chiefs,* 235–236.

24. THE PILGRIM TO THE STONE

266 *heard a hyena: Chiefs,* 241.

267 *whom was away:* Ibid., 245.

268 *"lived for fear":* Ibid., 246.

269 Boyd's grave: *Boyd Alexander's Last Journey,* 53; Alexander, *Whom the Gods Love,* 119, 231–233, 283–284; MacLeod Papers, NRAS 2950/4/2119/16. Olive makes no mention in her book—none—of visiting Boyd's grave.

270 *might have stayed:* Gordon, *Dame Flora,* 76.

271 *"me strength for all":* MacLeod Papers, NRAS 2950/4/2119/16.

271 *"12 days before":* MacLeod Papers, NRAS 2950/4/2119/16.

25. THE ROAD

273 *"out of the service":* Alexander, *Whom the Gods Love,* 284.

273 *"all possible haste":* Ibid.; *Chiefs,* 248.

275 *"arrows are poisoned":* Ibid., 252. This dialogue has been adapted from the text.

275 *air like syringa:* Ibid., 255.

276 *light burdens:* Ibid., 243.

276 *"for five months":* Ibid., 261.

26. DECISIONS IN FIKA

278 *"Don't shoot!":* *Chiefs,* 259. This dialogue has been adapted from the text.

279 *"five days he dies":* Ibid., 260.

279 *small boys:* See Stephen O. Murray, ed., *Boy-Wives and Female-Husbands: Studies in African Homosexualities* (London: Macmillan, 2001).

280 *"pulled her in":* *Chiefs,* 259.

280 *an open mouth:* Ibid., 261.

281 *"Fall for horse":* Ibid., 261.

282 *could do was wait:* Ibid., 263.

282 *luck, and left:* Ibid., 263.

283 *"till we were ready":* Ibid., 263–264.

283 *105 by day:* Ibid., 264.

284 *top of their heads:* Ibid., 265–266.

285 *"Let this noise cease!":* Ibid., 269.

286 *"They done fear":* Ibid.

288 *"its efficacy to be tested":* Ibid., 273–275.

289 *"and that is good":* Ibid., 275–276.

292 *"this man in his house":* Ibid., 281.

27. POISONED ARROW

294 *golden-flowered cassias: Chiefs*, 285.

295 *"and poisoned arrows"*: Ibid., 287. This dialogue has been adapted from the text.

28. MR. CHARLES TEMPLE

304 *immensely invigorating: Chiefs*, 298. Of all the scenes in the book, this is the one about which I had the least information, which is why it is posed largely as a series of questions for the reader. They visited Temple, stayed with him, then moved on. I have attempted to re-create their meeting using more physical facts and Olive's mentions in her diary, but this is for the most part just an impression of what might have happened.

306 *"dawgs"*: Ibid., 301.

29. THE FATE OF OLIVE MACLEOD

310 *"Lady explorer's return"*: Violet Bonham Carter, *Lantern Slides*, 272.

310 *"appearance of our hair"*: "Come Bid Me Farewell in My Lonely Grave," *St. Louis Star*, June 4, 1911, 26.

311 *"suffered few hardships"*: "Girl Makes 3,700 Mile African Trip," *The Inter Ocean*, 24.

311 *"All the World Is Kin"*: *News Journal*, March 29, 1912, 4.

312 *question of his death: Boyd Alexander's Last Journey*, 287–289.

314 *welcome at Wilsley*: Ibid., 59.

314 *"your servant José Lopez"*: Ibid., 288–289.

314 *jungle and disappeared*: Alexander, *Whom the Gods Love*, 292. Alexander finds "no trace of him." I searched death records, criminal records, colonial records, and African newspapers, but found no trace of him, either.

315 *"It exposes nothing"*: Ibid., 286.

317 *"Is this logical"*: Alec E. Jameson, *London Standard*, January 13, 1912.

318 *Zoological Gardens*: See chap. 1 notes.

318 *named Guy Fawkes*: This famous hippo was named after the chief mastermind behind the 1605 Gunpowder Plot and now iconic symbol of resistance. See James Sharpe, "The Explosive History of Guy Fawkes," *National Geographic*, November 3, 2018, nationalgeographic.com.

321 *her diaries*: MacLeod Papers, NRAS 2950/4/2119/5 and NRAS 2950/4/2119/6.

323 *her to Africa*: "Come Bid Me Farewell in My Lonely Grave," *San Francisco Examiner*, June 11, 1911, 63.

323 *"delays our reunion:"* MacLeod Papers, NRAS 2950/4/2119/1-6.

323 *"where you await me":* MacLeod Papers, NRAS 2950/4/2119/6.

30. THE LIGHTHOUSE

326 Virginia Woolf's visit: Virginia Woolf, *The Letters of Virginia Woolf, Volume Three, 1923–1928*, New York: Houghton Mifflin, 1980, 27–28. The interior of the home is from Gordon, *Dame Flora*, 97, 108–109.

326 *"balance of power":* These terms are from Leonard Woolf's book, *Empire & Commerce in Africa* (Westminster, UK: The Labour Research Department, 1919), 57, which they were said to have discussed.

326 *her blue eyes: The Letters of Virginia Woolf, Volume III, 1923–1928*, 26.

327 *"My husband":* This is invented dialogue, though it is probably a good bet that Olive said it many times.

327 *began to paint:* The only archive of their work together is *Photographs and Paintings by Olive and Charles L. Temple,* Reference GB 161 MSS. Afr. s. 2000 and Afr. t. 37, Bodleian Library, University of Oxford, [c.1910–1918]. Their book is Olive Temple, Ed. Charles L. Temple, *Notes on the Tribes, Provinces, Emirates and States of the Northern Provinces of Nigeria* (Cape Town: Argus, 1919).

328 *P. A. Talbot's:* Percy Amaury Talbot, *Life in Southern Nigeria* (London: Macmillan, 1923), 324–236.

328 Olive's later life: Gordon, *Dame Flora*, 108–110; MacLeod Papers NRAS 2950/4/1811/1–9 and 4/1831/1–13.

331 *"Oh, don't bother":* Ibid., 108.

333 *castle was on fire:* Gordon, *Dame Flora*, 111–117.

334 *"your superior knowledge":* Ibid., 105.

EPILOGUE: THE LAST KING OF DAR FUR

335–338 Battle of the Desert: "Battle of the Desert," *The Scotsman*, October 26, 1916, 7; "Flight of the Sultan," *The Scotsman*, May 30, 1917, 6.

339 *"information of the public":* Alexander, *Whom the Gods Love*, 289.

340 *"fighting the infidels":* Theobald, *'Alī Dīnār: Last Sultan of Darfur*, 95.

340 *Boyd's signet ring:* Alexander, *Whom the Gods Love*, 276.

340 *Dr. Ali Ali-Dinar:* For more information on Dr. Dinar see his faculty website: https://africana.sas.upenn.edu/people/ali-dinar.

340 *slaves in Libya:* Ryanne Persinger, "Revelation of Libyan Slave Auction Shocks

the World," *Philadelphia Tribune,* December 2, 2017, phillytrib.com; Nima Elbagir, Raja Razek, Alex Platt and Bryony Jones, "People for Sale," cnn.com, November 14, 2017.

340 *"I don't have contacts":* Email to author, May 19, 2019.

341 *least seventy women:* Zeinab Mohammed Salih and Jason Burke, "Sudanese Doctors Say Dozens of People Raped During Sit-in Attack," *Guardian,* June 11, 2019, guardian.com.

341 *"My niece has arrived":* Email to author, June 12, 2019.

Bibliography

This story is built largely from Olive's book, followed by archival sources in the form of diaries and journals. Minor works are given in the notes.

Boyd Alexander's Last Journey, ed. Herbert Alexander. New York: Longmans, Green, 1912.

Alexander, Boyd. *From the Niger to the Nile*. London: Edward Arnold, 1907.

Alexander, Joan. *Whom the Gods Love*. London: W&J Mackay Limited, 1977.

Carter, Violet Bonham. *Lantern Slides*. Edited by Mark Bonham Carter and Mark Pottle. London: Weidenfeld & Nicolson, 1996.

Galton, Francis, ed. *Hints to Travellers*. London: Edward Stanford, 1878.

Gordon, Anne Wolridge. *Dame Flora*. London: Hodder and Stoughton, 1974.

"Lady Explorer's Return." *London Daily Graphic*, April 11, 1912.

MacLeod, Olive. *Chiefs and Cities of Central Africa*. Edinburgh: W. Blackwood and Sons, 1912.

MacLeod of MacLeod Papers, NRAS 2950, Castle Dunvegan, Isle of Skye, Scotland. Private collection.

Malan, A. H. "Dunvegan Castle," *Pall Mall* 24 (May-Aug. 1901): 5–19.

Robinson, Charles Henry, and John Alder Burdon. *Hausa Grammar with Exercises, Readings, and Vocabularies*. Boston: Harvard University Press, 1905.

Slight, Jacob. "British Perceptions and Responses to Sultan Ali Dinar of Darfur, 1915–16," *Journal of Imperial and Commonwealth History* 38, no. 2 (May 2010): 237–260.

Acknowledgments

My thanks, first and foremost, to Jeroen Roskam, the official castle custodian of the MacLeod Estate at Dunvegan Castle. His retrieval and sharing of the archival manuscripts that make up parts of this story was selfless and heroic, in the unique way that dusty archival work can sometimes be. It took me a long time to locate the lost diaries of Olive MacLeod, but it was he who physically rescued them and literally brought them to light. We read her story together, corresponding over a distance of three thousand miles, which now seems very appropriate. I can think of no better guardian of her work. Thank you, my good friend.

Thanks as well to Josephine Dixon, assistant registrar of the National Register of Archives for Scotland, who was a helpful and persuasive ally in this search. Also to Clan MacLeod itself, all over the world; proud and legendary and eternal, now headed by Hugh Magnus MacLeod. I hope you enjoy this story of one of your own.

Thanks to Francis Grotto, the archivist of the Library and Heritage Collections at Durham University, for his help in navigating the Sudan collection. Also to Mike Huxley of the Cranbrook Museum in Kent, Dr. Steve Howard, and Dr. Ahmad Sikainga. Thanks as well to Dr. Ali-Dinar of the University of Pennsylvania for his kind help. Much gratitude to the Mystery Writers of America, who changed my professional life, the Ohioana Library, the Cleveland Public Library system, Rosa Ransom, and Suzanne DeGaetano for her warm words at the Cleveland Arts Prize.

Cheers to the following for words of wisdom, inspiration, or just general support when it was needed: Andi Cumbo-Floyd, my neighbor Bill, Lance Parkin, Claudia Rankine, Bryan Dyer, Kyle Korver, Pete Brown, Mary and Susan Grimm, Charles Cassady, David Giffels, Dave Lucas, Lee Chilcote, the SAGES Fellows, Tim Beal, Robert Spadoni, Christopher Flint, Kristine Kelly, Peter Whiting, and Gary Lee Stonum. Also to Jessica Johnson and my friend who visited me at the Hudson Library. Thanks also to Dr. Elaine Arvan Andrews for helping me to finally understand *Jane Eyre*.

Thank you to the Music Settlement Early Childhood School for doing the real work of teaching my kids, especially to Kim Tate, Libby Steiner, Barbara Krivanka, and Muriel Robinson for teaching James and his friends to make art and write books. Thanks also to all the parents I met and became friends with. Thanks to the Coffee House at University Circle for providing a haven during preschool to write near the fireplace tiles of Africa.

Also thanks, though I wish I didn't have to, to my friends and acquaintances who all experienced profound personal losses during the writing of this book and wrote about them publically in heartbreaking and beautiful ways that helped inform my understanding.

Thank you to my new family, the Clockblockers, who showed me what real fans are capable of. You are all unstoppable. Thanks as well to the great Jeff Trexler, who is a superhero in the best sense of the word. And to Noelle Pangle, for making other dreams come true.

To everyone in my St. Martin's Press family, including Hector DeJean, Cassidy Graham, and John Morrone. Also thanks to Lauren Jablonski and Sue Llewellyn. Most of all, to Michael Homler, my editor and friend, who gave excellent advice on this book that I should have followed when he first told me. Michael is always pushing me to try something different and better, and supports the unconventional things I want to do. Having an editor who is on my side—while still vocal and helpful—has been a great gift. This is our third book together, for which I am very glad and very grateful. See you at Comic-Con.

I am very appreciative of my agent, Scott Mendel. As nearly everyone close to me has said of him: "You'd be nowhere without him." As appreciative as I am of such words about my skills as a writer, I completely agree. I am very grateful for his guidance, tenacity, and utter fearlessness. He is the big brother I always wished I could walk out with onto the playground. He also came up (once again) with the perfect title. Onward!

To my extended family and friends for their support: Richard, Theresa, Bobby, and Alexa; and also Janet, Irene, Mary, Donna, and Liz. Also to Shirley Hoecker, Scott Rudge, Karen Pace, and Beryl Burkle for being the best readers. To Steve and Elaine Ricca and the rest of the family. Same to Karen Hoecker, who I always thought of when writing about red hair. Thanks to the doctors and nurses at University Hospitals Ahuja

Medical Center, Katherine Bissett, and Phil Metres for their help when I got a concussion. I should have listened to you a little more.

Most of all, to Caroline, who inspired this book and me, in so many ways, especially when she went to Africa and came back changed. To James, Brandon, and Alexander, who are the most awesome people I have ever met. And to Chris, Stephanie (and Sally), at all points on the timeline. And to my mom, Nancy, who took me as a kid to meet Ezra Jack Keats, which made me want to become an author. Love to you and Dad, and all.

Author's Note

August 22, 1910

I love my connection with you to be known by all the world for it makes me so proud, though I should have preferred it not to have a mass publicity.

This was the line in Olive's diary that haunted me as I wrote this book. At times, I felt like I was trespassing. But Olive also said that she could never write a book—"think of the humiliation!"—and she did anyway, so that made it easier. Sometimes.

More important was what I thought Olive's story could do. In nearly every written account of Olive's journey, she is portrayed as a lovestruck, heroic young woman of superhuman ability. But her own accounts add other depths to this—of sadness, grief, and wishful thoughts of her own death—that (I think) make her story far more realistic and poignant than just hippos or colonists. This is the part of the story that spoke to me and made me wonder about those letters in the castle. Maybe there was somewhere they could go. Maybe there was someone they could reach.

I don't know how Olive got through this perilous part of her life, nor do I wish to speculate, and above all, I don't want to present the theory that going to Africa can be a cure for the grief of great loss, or the heavy labor of mental illness. All I can hope is that if you need it, you can find something in Olive's story that is helpful to you. Olive is neither a savior nor a victim, but she is courageous. In that interior land of whispers and shadows, she finds help where she can, even if she has to make it up. If you need it, do the same. Sometimes seeking out help *can* feel as colossal an act as getting on a boat and going somewhere impossible. Call or message someone. You can do it. You know where to look. Or get in touch with me. I've been there, in that place. You are not alone. Think of tomorrow—it will be better.

RESOURCES

National Suicide Prevention Lifeline
suicidepreventionlifeline.org
1-800-273-8255

National Alliance on Mental Illness
www.nami.org

South Sudan Hunger Crisis
help.rescue.org

Help Children in Sudan
donate.unicefusa.org

The Malala Fund
malala.org

The Agnes MacLeod Memorial Fund
www.agnesmacleod.org

The Amy Biehl Foundation
www.amybiehl.org

Index

Christopher M. Ricca

BRAD RICCA is the author of the Edgar Award–nominated *Mrs. Sherlock Holmes*, and *Super Boys*, winner of the Ohioana Book Award for nonfiction. He won the St. Lawrence Book Award for *American Mastodon*. Ricca lives in Cleveland.